Traditional
WOODWORKING
TECHNIQUES

also by
Graham Blackburn

FICTION

For Love or Money?

The Castilian Suite

The Stanford Solution

Tango Slim

NON-FICTION

Illustrated Housebuilding

*The Illustrated Encyclopedia of
Woodworking Handtools, Instruments, & Devices*

Illustrated Basic Carpentry

The Postage Stamp Gazetteer

Illustrated Furniture Making

Illustrated Interior Carpentry

*The Illustrated Encyclopedia of Ships, Boats,
Vessels, & other Water-borne Craft*

The Illustrated Dictionary of Nautical Terms

The Parts of a House

An Illustrated Calendar of Home Repair

Quick & Easy Home Repair

Floors, Walls, & Ceilings

Creative Ideas for Household Storage

Year-round House Care

Furniture by Design

Traditional Woodworking Handtools

Traditional Jigs & Fixtures for Handtools

Furniture Design & Construction

Andante: a memoir

for

Paul Potash

& Marc Adams

Joiner working in his shop
a 19th century engraving of a miniature from the end of the 15th century

Traditional

WOODWORKING TECHNIQUES

Fundamentals of Furnituremaking

written & illustrated
by

GRAHAM BLACKBURN

CEDAR LANE PRESS

Published by
CEDAR LANE PRESS
PO BOX 5424
LANCASTER, PA 17606-5424
WWW.CEDARLANEPRESS.COM

Library of Congress Card Number: 2021931065
Paperback International Standard Book Number: 978-1-950934-78-2
ePub International Standard Book Number: 978-1-950934-79-9

Designed by Graham Blackburn
Set in 11 point Caslon

First Edition
0 9 8 7 6 5 4 3 2 1

Printed in the United States of America

wood will do what wood wants to do...

ACKNOWLEDGEMENTS

People are drawn to woodworking for many reasons. For some it may be the pleasure of using certain handtools, for others the sense of control that power-tools may offer. Some people are primarily interested in the techniques of construction, others chiefly in the end product, large or small. Still others are attracted simply by the endless variety of the material itself: its color, grain, and varying aromas. But for many, as for myself, the attraction is more usually a combination of various factors, chief among which is a sense of accomplishment, and the peculiar satisfaction that comes only with the right attitude towards the material and the craft. Construction techniques and methods of work may be gleaned from books, but the right attitude, which can transform a mechanical task into an uplifting experience, may be obtained only through contact with someone who already possesses the awareness. For endowing me with this right awareness I would like to express my gratitude to my father, John Blackburn; Hugh Harris and David Boyle, two fine craftsmen; and R. J. Puttick, my art teacher. It was these people's beliefs and enthusiasms which made possible for me the rewards that come from trying to make things as well and as beautifully as possible.

In addition, I would like to recognize the enthusiasm of all those countless woodworkers whom I have had the privilege of meeting through my books and classes, and who have continually fed my own appreciation for this timeless and age-old craft.

Grateful acknowledgements are also due to the following magazines: *Fine Woodworking, Popular Woodworking,* and *Woodwork,* in whose pages much of the material (sometimes under different titles) contained in the following chapters first appeared:

PART ONE: Chapter 7: DINING TABLE
Popular Woodworker, 1989
PART TWO: Chapters 11 & 12: MORTISE & TENON JOINTS
Woodwork, 1989
PART TWO: Chapter 13: DOVETAILS
Woodwork, 1990
PART TWO: Chapter 14: SPLAYED JOINTS
Fine Woodworking, 1989
PART TWO: Chapter 15: MOULDING
Fine Woodworking, 1989
PART TWO: Chapter 16: RUNNING CARVING
Woodwork, 1990
PART TWO: Chapter 17: FRAME & PANELING
Fine Woodworking, 1987, 1998
PART TWO: Chapter 18: DRAWERMAKING
Woodwork, 1991
PART TWO: Chapter 19: FURNITURE STYLES
Fine Woodworking, 2000

CONTENTS

PART TWO

JOINTS & TECHNIQUES
A close look at furnituremaking details

CONTENTS   ❧ x ❧

PLATES

The following plates are all from *Industrie du Meuble: Principes de Construction,
Éléments Généraux* (Furnituremaking: Principles of Construction, General
Elements), by J. Boison, 1922:

PREFACE

MOST OF PART ONE OF THIS BOOK WAS ORIGINALLY PUBLISHED IN NINETEEN SEVENTY-SEVEN UNDER THE TITLE: **ILLUSTRATED FURNITURE MAKING**. MY ORIGINAL intention was to present a progressive course in the fundamentals of furnituremaking; consequently, the book was designed to be read from beginning to end rather than in a haphazard fashion, since each chapter was written on the assumption that previous chapters had already been absorbed. Indeed, frequent references were made to material covered in earlier chapters; unless this material had been understood, subsequent details might have appeared difficult.

SUFFICIENT UNTO THE DAY...

WITH THE ADDITION OF MUCH NEW MATERIAL, ESPECIALLY PART TWO, such a rigorous progression is no longer absolutely necessary. Many topics and techniques listed as the subtitles of the projects described in PART ONE are amplified in greater detail in PART TWO, and may be referred to at will, thereby enabling the reader to skip projects without jeopardizing his or her understanding of the subject.

These projects are designed to introduce the beginning woodworker to fundamental woodworking concepts and techniques. Each of these nine pieces might no doubt be built in a more sophisticated fashion, but the point is to gain some immediate experience so that you will be able to proceed with confidence towards more complicated pieces.

In any event, there is more reason to be proud of a simple but well-made nailed box than a poorly made dovetailed affair with sloppy joints. The former will produce justifiable satisfaction and confidence, whereas the latter will only result in disappointment and frustration. Moreover, once having successfully produced a few relatively straightforward pieces, rather than having attempted something too complicated and failed, you will be better able to appreciate the finer points of the craft as explained in PART TWO. Subsequently revisiting any of the projects in PART ONE will result in a greater understanding of the virtually endless choices that make woodworking so rewarding.

PREREQUISITES

FOR THE BOOK AS A WHOLE, TWO BASIC ASSUMPTIONS HAVE been made: that the requisite tools are available, and that their use is understood. If, indeed, you cannot tell a chisel from a screwdriver you should first refer to *The Illustrated Encyclopedia of Woodworking Handtools, Instruments, & Devices, Third Edition* (Blackburn Books, 2000), and if you have never actually held a tool, and have little or no understanding of its correct use, refer to *Traditional Woodworking Handtools: A Manual for the Woodworker* (Blackburn Books, 1998).

Actual techniques indicated in this book call almost exclusively for handtools. This is not because powertools will not do the job, but because I believe the respect necessary to use and work wood well and beautifully is developed more readily through the close contact obtained by the use of handtools than through the more impersonal sense of omnipotence imparted by the use of powertools. To sit on a piece of wood and work a moulding with a handplane is to come to know that piece of wood almost as if it were a person. To thrust it through a noisy machine in fear for your fingers, your senses insulated by safety glasses, earplugs, and dust masks, is to be at an unfortunate remove from its knots and its grain, its feel, smell, and texture.

This is not to decry, far less to prohibit, the use of powertools, because for many jobs we are lucky to have them, but merely to point out that by learning to use handtools first, an understanding and a feeling for the material will be developed that is difficult to obtain across the scream of an electric tablesaw. When, however, this feeling has been developed, then the tablesaw may be used with discrimination to great advantage.

DIFFERENT STROKES FOR DIFFERENT FOLKS

THIS BOOK WILL SHOW YOU HOW TO MAKE A VARIETY OF furniture. While being very explicit regarding tools and techniques, especially in the beginning, it is the principle of construction that is most important. There is, however, more than one way to skin a cat, so if you discover another technique that you prefer, use it. *Traditional Woodworking Techniques* represents what I have learned over the years, and is founded largely on fundamental traditional techniques, which will often be found to complement very nicely a more modern approach. Ultimately, how you practise woodworking depends on your goals and what you enjoy the most. My own story is a case in point.

I come from a long line of woodworkers, but my parents made every effort to see that I did something else. Nevertheless, it seems blood will out. My grandfather was a joiner who walked to work every day of his life, my father was a builder who was reserved from the military during World War II to check on the structural integrity of bombed buildings in London, which involved him in a lot of nasty crawling about in partially collapsed buildings, and several uncles had a hard time of it after the postwar bomb-damage boom slumped in the mid-fifties. So I was sent off to university to study for a supposedly more reliable profession.

Nevertheless, the appeal of wood, building, and especially tools, was too strong, and all through college and especially at vacations I worked part-time with an old cabinetmaker in the north end of London gaining a firm grounding in tools and techniques long outmoded even then. When I arrived in America (to continue my education in New York) and had the chance to build a house in the Catskills it was all over with academe. I never went back to England, but instead built houses and eventually started my own custom furniture shop.

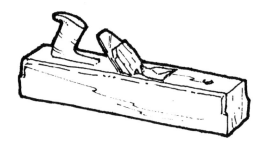

With regard to my use of handtools, this was originally an economic necessity, and most of my toolkit was put together with purchases at second-hand stores and fleamarkets. Tool collecting as a hobby in the nineteen-sixties was a rare sport, and when I ran into it, it often bemused me. When I grew up so much was still common knowledge that it was not even discussed. My school workshop had twenty double-benches with full-length leg vises, and wooden bench planes were the order of the day. Our first term was spent turning a square block of wood into an identical square block half as big. There was no discussion of chatter, back-bevel, wedge trimming, and other matters; the master demonstrated, and students planed away with occasional corrections from above, absorbing the fine points without question. It was simply a question of 'this is how it's done'.

Times change, and today much tradesman's lore that was once common knowledge is now become as arcane as ancient Egyptian embalming techniques. Now we feel the need to discuss and analyze every detail in order to reinvent the past. One refreshing aspect of this, however, is that, free of the blind dogmatism of the past, new ideas can surface, which is part of the reason I am still totally absorbed by woodworking.

Some progress is undoubtedly good, but I must admit that I do what I do because I like it, not because it is necessarily better, faster, or more economical. The books and articles that I have written over the years are primarily an attempt to share and explain what I enjoy. Most of all I like the feeling of connexion I get when planing by hand with a tool that has earned several generations of tradesmen their daily bread. My most treasured possession is an old carriagemaker's T-rabbet plane made by Moon in St. Martin's Lane, the same street in London in which Chippendale worked (I found the plane in San Diego!). It gives me hope that the past is not totally gone, and that the future is not totally without hope.

BEYOND THE FUNDAMENTALS

ALTHOUGH I HAVE AIMED TO COVER THE FUNDAMENTALS, AND you would be kept busy for a considerable length of time if you were to make everything described in PART ONE, there are yet other areas of woodworking not discussed. Therefore I have appended a bibliography for those who would know more about such subjects as turning, veneering, carving, and finishing.

Your most valuable assets will be patience and care. Although "in good carpentry everything depends on accuracy of measurement" (*Elementary Carpentry and Joinery,* 1870), remember that it has also been said that "there is no such thing as accuracy" — and enjoy your woodworking.

Graham Blackburn
Bearsville, New York, 2004

PART ONE

NINE PIECES *of* FURNITURE

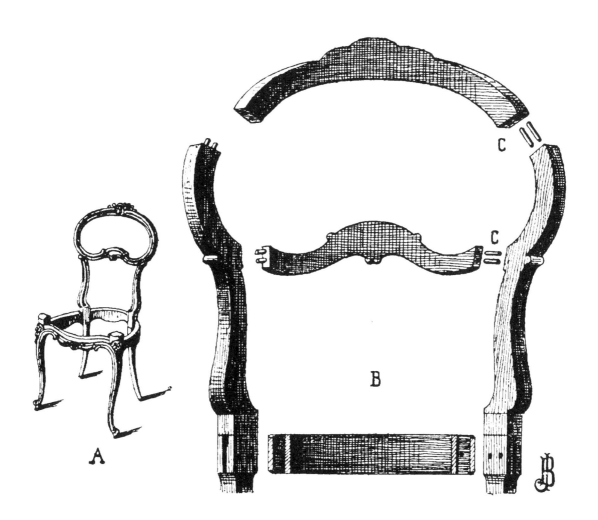

A progressive series of projects introducing basic techniques

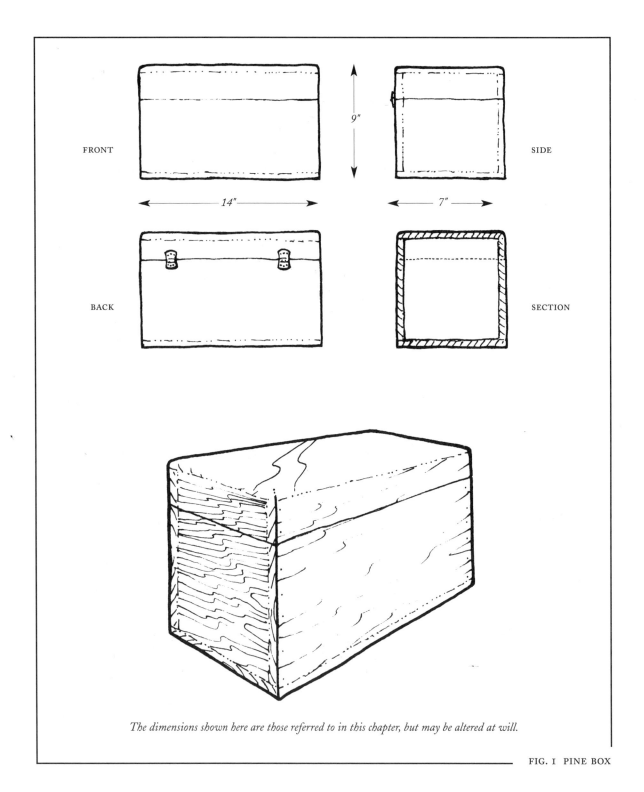

FRONT

SIDE

9"

14"

7"

BACK

SECTION

The dimensions shown here are those referred to in this chapter, but may be altered at will.

FIG. 1 PINE BOX

1

PINE BOX

Lumber Dimensions & Grades • Jointing • Trying an Edge •
The Shooting-board • Crosscut Sawing • Gluing • Nailing •
Clamping • Sanding • Hinging • Finishing

ALTHOUGH THIS IS THE EASIEST EXERCISE IN THE SERIES
SO FAR AS JOINTS AND DESIGN ARE CONCERNED, THE
TECHNIQUES REQUIRED TO MAKE THIS SIMPLE PINE BOX
successfully will demand as much care as will more complicated
processes. While it is true that once you have understood a particular
technique success requires nothing more than care, yet the proper exercise
of care is itself something that requires attentive practice. So take care,
take care in everything you do, but do not be discouraged if, despite
all your best efforts, you do not get it quite right the first time. Once
you fully understand what you are trying to do, practice will make
perfect — or as near to it as woodworking will allow.

One other point to remember: be as careful as you can at the very
beginning of this and every other project, because a mistake made early
on rarely becomes less important as you continue; on the contrary, its
effects are usually magnified by each successive operation.

In many ways, the two main processes required for this box, sawing
and planing, though less complicated than those that follow, are rather
more important. One reason is that they are fundamental to many more

complicated techniques. In the old days, apprentices were expected to labor long perfecting precisely these abilities before being allowed to do anything else. The ability to saw to a straight line and to plane a piece of wood to square requires a certain amount of practice. The task is made a great deal easier than it was formerly, however, because of the way in which wood is now generally obtained, that is, pre-dried and cut to standard sizes.

LUMBER DIMENSIONS & GRADES

THE OVERALL HEIGHT OF OUR BOX, INCLUDING THE THREE-QUARTER inch-thick top and the ¾ in.-thick bottom, being approximately 9 in. (see FIG. 4), we may conveniently buy wood from the lumberyard referred to as 'one-by-eight'. This is a nominal measurement only, because although it may have measured precisely 1 in. by 8 in. at the sawmill, when it was cut from the tree, it has since been seasoned (dried) and milled (planed smooth), and has consequently lost a certain amount of material so that its measurements are now closer to ¾ in. by 7½ in. Even though lumber may be ordered cut to an exact size, it is more economical to buy wood in the standard dimensions used by the lumber industry.

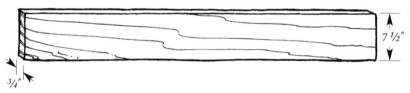

7½"

¾"

FIG. 2 ONE-BY-EIGHT BOARD

As well as the dimensions, you also need to know the grade required when buying wood. There are various sytems of grading in use, but they all refer to the clearness, or freedom from knots, of the wood. Grading also reflects the different ways in which boards are cut from the tree. This process is known as 'conversion'. Some methods produce boards that are more stable and less liable to warp or twist, and this, of course, is reflected in the price. Grading can also reflect the process by which wood has been seasoned. Air-dried wood, for example, which takes longer to season and is consequently more expensive, may have better color and be more stable than wood which has been kiln-dried.

The seasoning or dryness of wood is often expressed in terms of 'percentage moisture content'. Ultimately, it will pay to become familiar with actual numbers and the rate at which different species are likely to expand or contract under particular circumstances, but to begin with, regular kiln-dried wood will suffice.

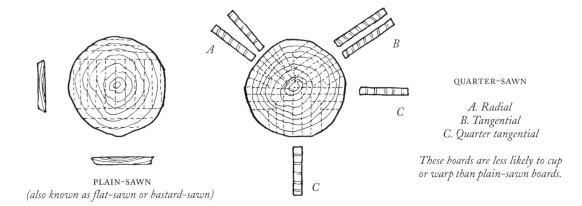

QUARTER-SAWN

A. Radial
B. Tangential
C. Quarter tangential

These boards are less likely to cup or warp than plain-sawn boards.

PLAIN-SAWN
(also known as flat-sawn or bastard-sawn)

FIG. 3 CONVERSION METHODS

The common pine that you may buy at the average lumberyard is typically graded as follows: 'clear', meaning there are no knots in it; 'number one', meaning there are only a few knots, relatively small and tight; or 'number two', meaning there are more and bigger knots. Additional classifications exist, but these three are the most useful.

Remember that this pine, known as deal in England, is the eastern white pine that you may buy at the local lumberyard. If you go to a specialist furniture-wood supplier you will find that there are many species that go under the name 'pine', including woods such as Baltic pine, fir, larch, loblolly pine, pitch pine, ponderosa pine, red pine, Scots pine, spruce, white pine, and yellow pine, all of which have different characteristics and whose prices may vary considerably.

Our box may be made satisfactorily with number one pine, but it is worth the slight extra expense to obtain a clear board, free of all knots. The dimensions of the box are shown in FIG. 4, from which it can be seen that all the pieces required may be got from one 6 ft. length of one-by-eight.

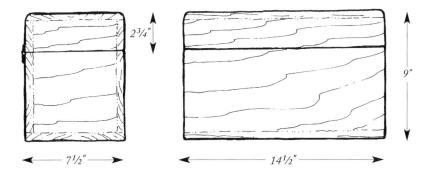

FIG. 4 DIMENSIONS OF PINE BOX

PINE BOX

The board you choose should be as straight and as true as possible, and not warped, bent, bowed, propellored, or twisted in any way. However, if you hold it up to the light, you will observe a succession of tiny ridges on all surfaces, especially on the edges. These ridges were formed by the blades of the big planers and jointers that milled the wood smooth from its rough-sawn state. The marks on the faces of the wood can be taken care of after the box has been assembled, but those on the edges must be removed now if you want to make neat joints.

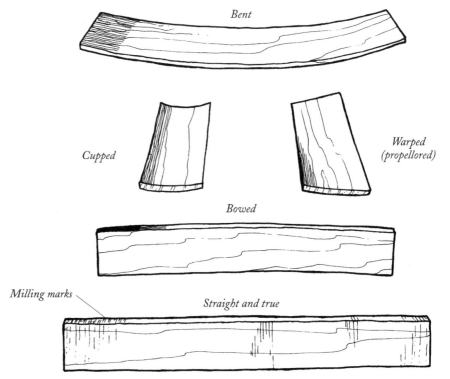

Bent

Cupped

Warped
(propellored)

Bowed

Milling marks

Straight and true

FIG. 5 BOARD DEFECTS

JOINTING

PLANING THE EDGE OF A BOARD STRAIGHT AND TRUE, WHETHER by hand or machine, is known as 'jointing'. A well-sharpened and properly set-up handplane should be able to cut in any direction without tearout*, but it will not hurt to place the 6 ft. board, edge uppermost, in the vise, with the grain running away from you (see FIG. 6). Set the cutting iron of your longest plane to take a very fine shaving, and run the full length of the board.

* For an in-depth discussion of how to set up and sharpen a plane,
see *Traditional Woodworking Handtools*, chapters 13–16.

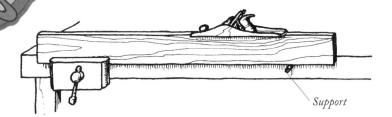

Support

FIG. 6 JOINTING BY HAND

The jointer plane, being the longest of all the bench planes, is the best plane to use since it will bridge the low parts and not cut them until the high parts are removed. Shorter planes, such as jack planes and fore planes, may also be used effectively, but you will be working at a disadvantage if you are forced to use the much shorter smooth plane.

A short plane will follow the curves, but a longer plane will bridge the low parts and not cut them until the high parts have been removed.

FIG. 7 JOINTING WITH A SHORT PLANE & A LONG PLANE

TRYING AN EDGE

TO TEST WHETHER YOUR JOINTED EDGE IS TRUE, USE A straightedge, or sight along the edge from one end. Any hollows or rises will be immediately apparent. To correct any imperfections, mark the high spots with a pencil while sighting along the board, and then take a

Slight rise

FIG. 8 SIGHTING ALONG THE EDGE OF A BOARD

few shavings from just those areas, finishing with a shaving taken right through, from one end to the other.

Be especially careful to keep the plane centered over the edge, as well as to hold it at right angles to the face of the board so that the edge remains perfectly square. If, assuming you are right-handed, you keep the fingers of your left hand tucked under the sole of the plane so that they act as a fence running against the face of the board, you will find it much easier to keep the plane centered and square.

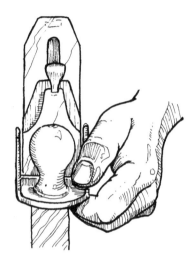

FIG. 9 USING THE FINGERS AS A FENCE

To test the edge for squareness, use the trysquare as shown below throughout the length of the board.

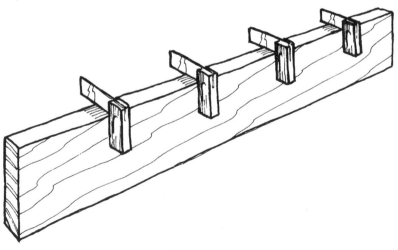

FIG. 10 TESTING THE EDGE FOR SQUARENESS

If the edge should prove to be out of square, holding the fingers as shown in FIG. 9 will also assist the manipulation of the plane necessary to correct the defect. By moving the plane to one side or the other you can take advantage of the slight crown that should be formed on the plane's cutting iron and so take a shaving that is thicker on one side, thereby adjusting the squareness of the edge.

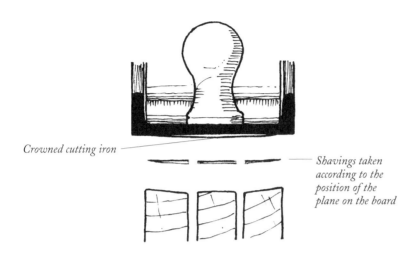

Crowned cutting iron

Shavings taken according to the position of the plane on the board

FIG. II CUTTING-IRON PROFILE

THE SHOOTING-BOARD

ONE WAY TO GUARANTEE SQUARE EDGES WHEN PLANING shorter lengths is to use an easily made device known as a shooting-board. A convenient size for bench-top use is about 3 ft. to 4 ft. long, with a lower platform, or 'bed', wide enough for a common jack plane and a top platform, or 'table', about 8 in. wide.

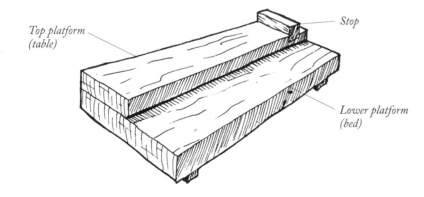

Top platform (table)

Stop

Lower platform (bed)

FIG. I2 SHOOTING-BOARD

The wood lies on the upper platform and the plane runs on its side on the lower platform. The wood overhangs slightly and is planed square by virtue of the squareness of the plane's own sole.

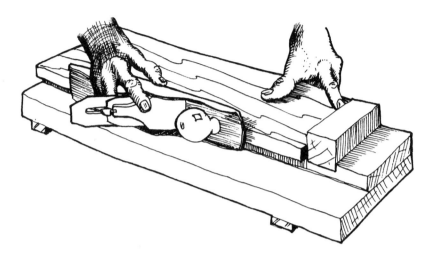

FIG. 13 SHOOTING AN EDGE

When one edge has been jointed, turn the wood over and joint the other edge, taking care to plane 'with the grain', as at B in FIG. 14. If your plane is not properly set and the grain is against you, as shown at C, tearout may result. If the direction of the grain alternates, as at D, it may be necessary to turn the board around from time to time. Difficult grain is something you should look for when buying the board. Until your planes are in perfect condition it will be better to obtain a board in which the grain runs consistently in one direction.

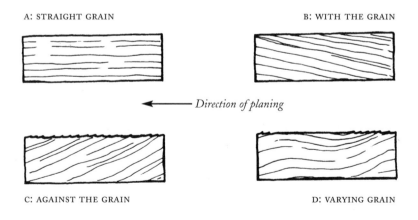

A: STRAIGHT GRAIN

B: WITH THE GRAIN

← *Direction of planing*

C: AGAINST THE GRAIN

D: VARYING GRAIN

FIG. 14 GRAIN DIRECTION

When both edges have been jointed, measure across the board at various places throughout its length to check that the edges are always exactly the same distance apart. If they are not, one edge must be rejointed until both edges are indeed parallel.

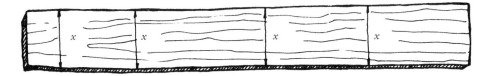

All xs should be equal.

FIG. 15 CHECKING THE WIDTH

CROSSCUT SAWING

WHEN BOTH EDGES OF THE BOARD ARE CLEAN, SQUARE, AND parallel, you may mark out and saw off the various parts of the box. Do this, however, one piece at a time, for if you mark out all the pieces end-to-end, you will have failed to allow for the width of the sawcut, known as the 'kerf'. Start at one end, and, using the biggest square you own, check that the end is square to the sides. If it is not — and it is doubtful that it will be — square off the end as shown in FIG. 16. Make the mark at least ½ in. from the end in order that the saw may make a firm cut. If the kerf is too close to the end, the saw may break out from the line.

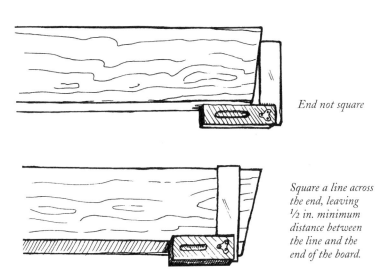

End not square

Square a line across the end, leaving ½ in. minimum distance between the line and the end of the board.

FIG. 16 SQUARING THE END

Rest the board on the bench, on trestles, or on sawhorses, whichever is most convenient, and, starting with the saw held at a low angle, the better to check that its blade is in alignment with the line you have drawn, lightly draw the blade towards you a few times to start the kerf. Once the kerf is well defined, begin sawing. When the saw is a little way into the wood, increase the angle to about 45° and take as long a stroke as possible, using the whole length of the blade. Do not force the saw; if it cuts badly or slowly or wanders from the line despite your best efforts, it probably needs attention*. Take care to hold the saw so that its sides are at right angles to the wood, and check frequently with a square as in FIG. 17 to make sure of this. As you gain experience, you will be able to keep the saw vertical simply by keeping your eye directly above the blade so that you can see both sides equally.

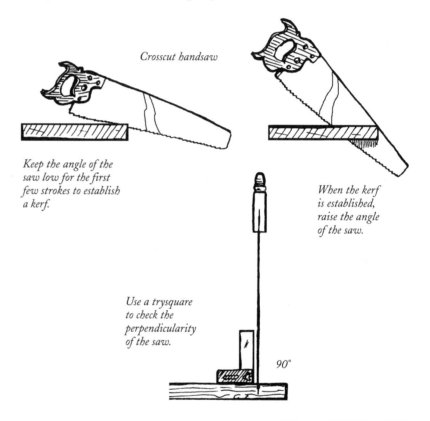

Crosscut handsaw

Keep the angle of the saw low for the first few strokes to establish a kerf.

When the kerf is established, raise the angle of the saw.

Use a trysquare to check the perpendicularity of the saw.

90°

FIG. 17 CROSSCUT SAWING

The actual cut should be made slightly to one side of the line so that it can be trimmed down perfectly, later. Always cut on the waste side of the line and have the line visible as you saw. This generally means sawing to the right of the line. If you are right-handed, hold the wood with your left hand close to the saw, and extend the thumb of this hand to help

* For an in-depth discussion of sawfitting and use, see
Traditional Woodworking Handtools, chapter 9.

Steady the blade for the first few pulled strokes. As soon as the kerf is sufficiently established to allow normal push strokes, be sure to move your left hand away from the saw in case the saw should jump out of its kerf and cut your thumb.

Guide the saw with the thumb for the first few upstrokes only.

FIG. 18 FIRST STROKES

When crosscutting a board like this, arrange the work so that the piece to be cut off overhangs the support. If you have supported the work between two sawhorses and you make the cut between the horses, the wood will bend as you saw and bind the saw in the kerf. As the cut nears completion, support the piece about to be cut off with your left hand, or the wood will splinter if you allow it to fall, especially if the piece being cut off is more than an inch or so long.

When the end has been cut square, check it again with the trysquare, from both the edge and the face, as shown in FIG. 19.

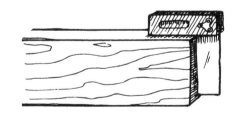

Check both the squareness and the perpendicularity of the cut.

FIG. 19 TRYING THE END

If the grain of your board is at all pronounced, the best effect will be achieved by continuing the grain around the box just as it runs in the uncut board. Therefore start by cutting one side rather than the front; then cut the front, then the other side, and finally the back.

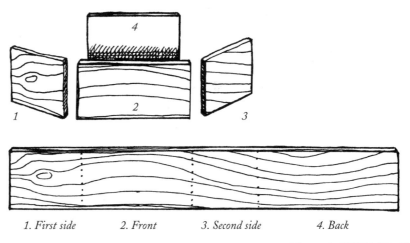

1. First side   2. Front   3. Second side   4. Back

FIG. 20 CUTTING ORDER

The overall width of the side of the box is the same as the width of the board. The length of the side pieces *(x)*, therefore equals the exact width of the board *(y)*, less twice the thickness of the board, since both the front and the back of the box butt up against the sides.

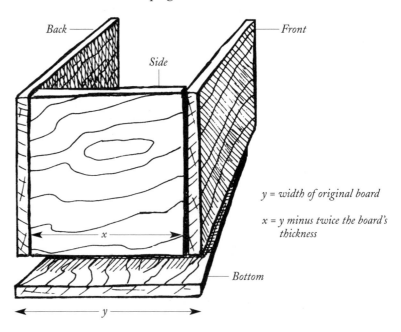

y = width of original board

x = y minus twice the board's thickness

FIG. 21 WIDTH OF THE SIDES

Carefully measure the thickness of the board. A nominal 1 in. board is generally about ¾ in. thick, but may vary by as much as ¹/₁₆ in. more or less. Subtract twice the true thickness from whatever the width of the board may be. Mark this distance (*x*, in FIG. 21) on your board, square off a line, and saw off the piece as before, taking care to saw on the waste side of the line.

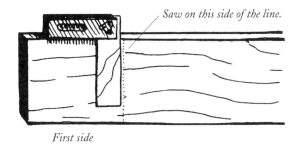

Saw on this side of the line.

First side

FIG. 22 SIDE PIECE LAYOUT

Mark the sawn-off piece to indicate which side is intended to be the face side and which edge is intended to be at the top, as shown in FIG. 23, in order that the grain will match when all four sides are joined together. Then lay out the front piece on the board, which should measure exactly 14½ in. (see FIG. 4). Saw this and mark as before, and proceed to the next side, which should measure exactly the same as the first side. Lastly, lay out, saw off, and mark the back piece, which, like the front, should also measure exactly 14½ in. When all four pieces are cut, assemble them on top of the bench and look to see how well you have cut the side pieces. If you have sawed neatly and consistently to the line, all should be well, and the ends of the sides will butt up closely to the front and back, as at A in FIG. 23.

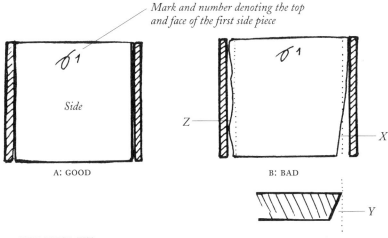

Mark and number denoting the top and face of the first side piece

Side

Z

X

Y

A: GOOD   B: BAD

FIG. 23 SIDE PIECE FIT

If your sawcut is irregular and it is only a matter of removing excess wood, as at *Z* in FIG. 23, then you must trim down to the line. Ideally, this should be done on a shooting-board to guarantee a square edge, using a jack plane, a smoothing plane, or a block plane. Since, when planing end grain, the far corner is liable to splinter out, you should either plane halfway in from each corner (which necessitates continuing the line around the wood with the trysquare) or plane all the way across, using a scrap block as in FIG. 24.

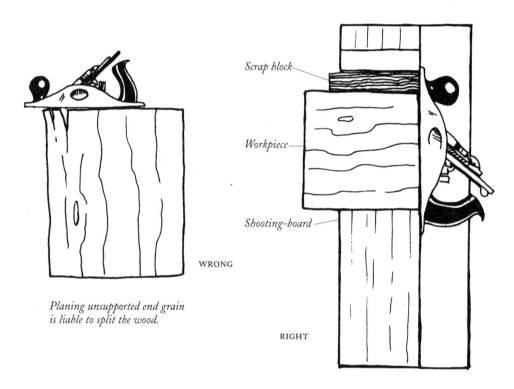

Scrap block

Workpiece

Shooting-board

WRONG

*Planing unsupported end grain
is liable to split the wood.*

RIGHT

FIG. 24 TRIMMING END GRAIN

If, however, you have removed part of the line by sawing across it as at *X* in FIG. 23, or have undercut the line through not having held the saw at right angles to the wood, as at *Y* in FIG. 23, then you must either cut another piece — and in so doing lose the effect of the grain being continuous around the box — or, if you have no more wood, recut the piece to a smaller width, which means, of course, that you will also have to recut the other side piece to match.

Should the ends of the front and the back pieces also need trimming, this may be done after the box is assembled.

Finally, measure and lightly mark with a pencil the exact spots where the nails will go in the front and back pieces, as shown in FIG. 25.

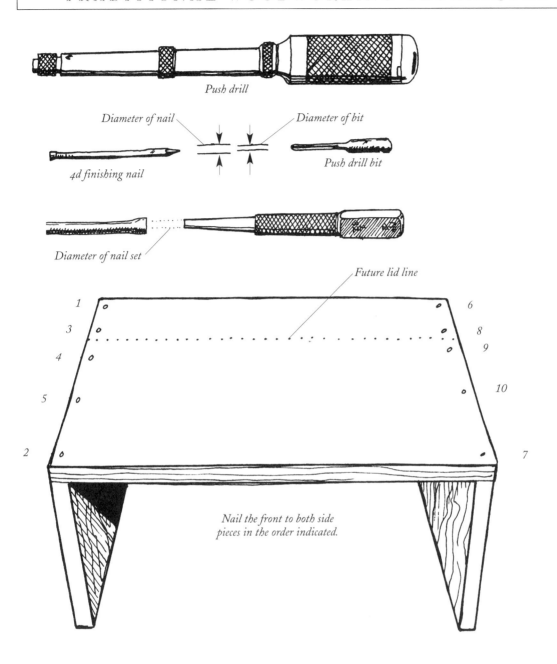

Push drill

Diameter of nail

Diameter of bit

4d finishing nail

Push drill bit

Diameter of nail set

Future lid line

1
3
4
5
2

6
8
9
10
7

*Nail the front to both side
pieces in the order indicated.*

FIG. 25 NAILING DETAILS

GLUING

NEXT SQUEEZE OUT A CONTINUOUS BEAD OF WHITE OR YELLOW
woodworking glue onto the front ends of the sides, and then spread the
bead evenly using a piece of scrap as a spatula. Now stand the sides up on

the bench, glued ends uppermoſt, as shown in FIG. 26. Experience will teach you how much glue to use. It muſt be enough to cover the surface completely, but not so much that moſt of it oozes out when the parts are pressed together, for this is merely waſteful and results in a lot of cleaning up.

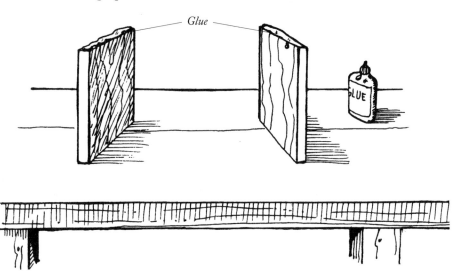

Glue

FIG. 26 GLUED SIDES

Place the front piece on top of the side pieces, making sure you have all the marks indicating top and face in order, and position it perfeĉtly. White or yellow glue does not set immediately, so you will have plenty of time to adjuſt the pieces and wipe off any excess glue that may run down the sides.

NAILING

THE NEXT STEP INVOLVES BORING HOLES FOR THE SMALL NAILS that will help hold the box together. A push drill is a particularly convenient tool to use for this job since it can be used with one hand. Seleĉt a bit with a diameter a little smaller than the diameter of the nail you are going to use. A 4d finishing nail, about 1½ in. long, is ideal. Holding both the top and the side, and being very careful to see that they remain in proper alignment, bore through the top, and then, ſtill holding the parts together, remove the drill and insert a nail. Hammer the nail juſt to the surface — you may use a regular nail hammer, although the joiner's Warrington hammer, or even a tack hammer, is more convenient — and then set the nail ⅛ in. below the surface using a nail set whose tip is no bigger than the head of the nail.

Pre-boring ensures that the wood will not split, which it is very liable to do when nailed so close to its end. Pre-boring also helps you to drive the nail vertically and so avoid having the nail suddenly emerge through the side. When the first nail is home, continue with the second, and so on in the order shown in FIG. 25, wiping off any extruded glue as you go. It is most efficient to set all the nails at one time, after all have been inserted.

With the front piece thus glued and nailed, turn the assembly over and repeat the process with the back piece.

The nails should hold the pieces together tightly enough so that clamping is not needed. But should there be a slight bow in the front or back pieces, then you may use a couple of clamps, taking care to insert pieces of scrap wood between the work and the jaws of the clamp to avoid marring the work. Be careful not to pull the work out of square as you tighten the clamps.

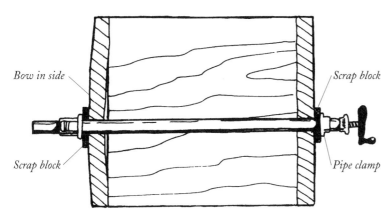

Bow in side

Scrap block

Scrap block

Pipe clamp

FIG. 27 CLAMPING

Cut the top piece and the bottom piece from what remains of the original board. These pieces, like the front and back pieces, should measure exactly 14½ in. long, but should you have cut the front and back a little short then you must cut the top and bottom to match. While it is an excellent idea before beginning any project to make an exact drawing and generate a cutting list in order to estimate how much material will be needed, it is ultimately more important that the components of a piece fit each other than match the drawing. Therefore, cutting each piece as you go along rather than all at once is the safer course.

True up the ends of the top and bottom if necessary, and, placing the assembled sides on the bottom so that the front of the box is flush with the front of the bottom, mark with a pencil any projection of the bottom at the back as shown in FIG. 28. This projection may then be planed away down to the line you have drawn, once again using the shooting-board.

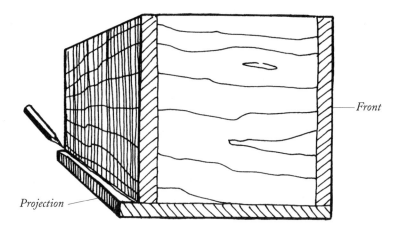

Front

Projection

FIG. 28 MARKING THE BOTTOM

Similarly mark, cut, and fit the top. Then glue and nail the bottom, and glue and nail the top, as shown in FIG. 29. Try to space the nails evenly. Use the experience you gained while gluing the sides of the box to judge how much glue is needed, because this time, if you use too much, you will not be able to wipe away any excess that may squeeze out into the interior of the box.

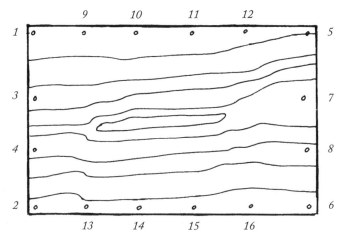

FIG. 29 NAILING ORDER

CLAMPING

IF THE EDGES OF THE SIDES WERE CUT PERFECTLY SQUARE, THEN the assembled box should form a perfect rectangle. And if the top and bottom were also cut square they should fit perfectly. The reason for the particular nailing order shown in FIG. 29 is that if for some reason the box is not absolutely square, you may be able to adjust it somewhat as you proceed by pulling or pushing the sides to meet the edges of the top and bottom.

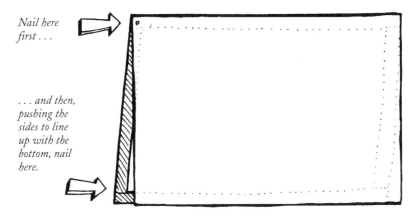

Nail here first . . .

. . . and then, pushing the sides to line up with the bottom, nail here.

FIG. 30 SQUARING THE BOX

Unless you have been fortunate enough to obtain a quarter-sawn board (see FIG. 3) for your box, fit the top and bottom pieces so that the faces of these pieces which were nearest the center of the tree are towards the outside of the box. This is because the outside of a plain-sawn board will become concave as the board dries and it will be easier to keep the center of the board flat than to keep the ends flat. This is best understood by looking at FIG. 31. It will also have been a good idea to bear this in mind when deciding which side of the board is to be used as the face side for the sides of the box.

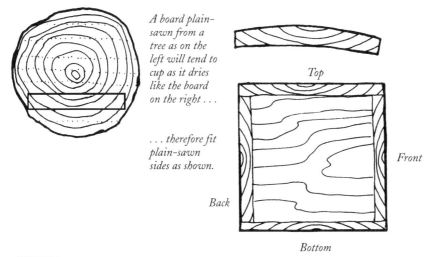

A board plain-sawn from a tree as on the left will tend to cup as it dries like the board on the right . . .

. . . therefore fit plain-sawn sides as shown.

Top

Front

Back

Bottom

FIG. 31 CUPPING

Once again use the clamps, if necessary, to make sure all edges touch. If you have used clamps, leave them on for half an hour or so. Otherwise begin immediately to check that all nails have been set. Fill the resultant holes with a suitable wood filler, and as soon as this is hard, usually in a minute or so, plane the ends of the front, back, top, and bottom, if this should still be necessary. Use a block plane, working always in from the edges as shown in FIG. 24 to avoid splintering the ends, and hold the plane at a 45° angle in order to minimize tearing the grain of the adjacent side.

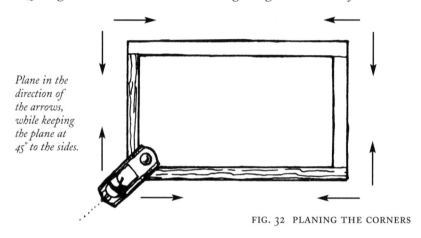

Plane in the direction of the arrows, while keeping the plane at 45° to the sides.

FIG. 32 PLANING THE CORNERS

The next step is to separate the lid. Set your marking gauge to 2¾ in., position the stock on the top of the box, and scribe a line around all four sides as shown below.

Stock (head)

2¾"

FIG. 33 MARKING GAUGE

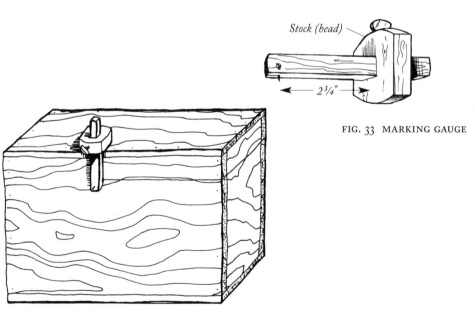

FIG. 34 MARKING THE LID

Having scribed all around once lightly, but with the ſtock pressed firmly againſt the top of the box, go around again, this time making the mark a little deeper. The scribed line will not only indicate clearly where to saw but will also help guide the saw teeth. The backsaw, also known as a 'tenon saw', is the beſt saw to use since the ſtiffener keeps the blade rigid. Use a bench hook — another easily made accessory — to secure the work; otherwise it may shift about.

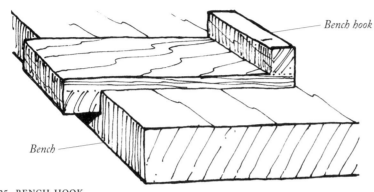

FIG. 35   BENCH HOOK

Holding the box firmly againſt the back of the bench hook, carefully saw in a little way from each corner in turn, being sure to saw in the groove made by the marking gauge. If you keep a sharp eye on both the front and the back of the saw as you saw, the kerfs should eventually meet.

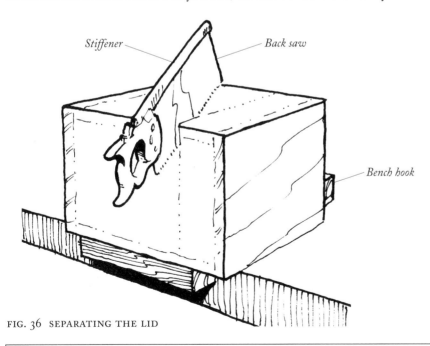

FIG. 36   SEPARATING THE LID

PINE BOX

With a sharp blade set to take a fine shaving, use the block plane to remove the saw marks from the two parts you have separated. When planing at the corners, take care to hold the plane so that the cutting edge remains at a 45° angle to each piece, since a shearing cut is less likely to result in any tearout of awkward grain. Do not attempt anything more than the simple removal of the saw marks from both parts or you risk making the two edges uncomplementary. Even if the line you sawed was not quite straight, the two parts of the box will still fit perfectly together so long as you remove the same light amount from each part.

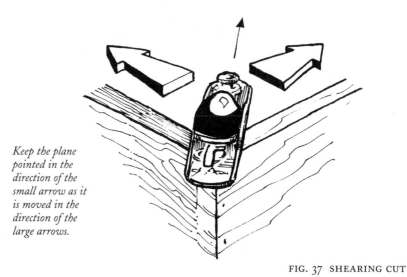

Keep the plane pointed in the direction of the small arrow as it is moved in the direction of the large arrows.

FIG. 37 SHEARING CUT

The top edge of the lid is to be rounded, and rather than do this by eye and risk an uneven profile, it will be better to first mark the limits of the rounded corner by drawing a couple of pencil lines. Use your fingers as a fence against the side of the lid and lightly pencil a line a little less than ¼ in. in from the side. Then, holding your fingers against the top of the lid, mark a similar line around the side of the lid, as in FIG. 38.

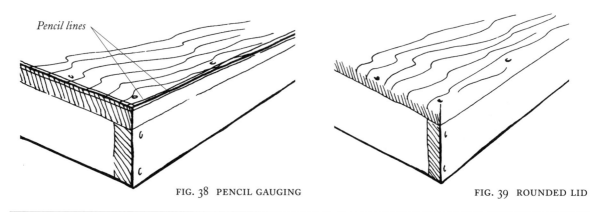

Pencil lines

FIG. 38 PENCIL GAUGING

FIG. 39 ROUNDED LID

Once again using the block plane, round the edges of the top as evenly as possible, just barely removing the gauge lines, and remembering always to work in from the corners.

On no account should you exceed the pencil line or you will be in danger of damaging the cutting edge of your plane on the nails holding the top to the sides! FIG. 40 shows clearly the limits of the radiused corner.

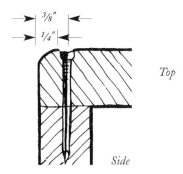

FIG. 40 RADIUS DIMENSIONS

SANDING

BEFORE HINGING THE LID YOU SHOULD CLEAN UP THE OUTSIDE of the box to remove all traces of glue, pencil marks, excess wood filler, and any other marks. The ideal tool to use is a smooth plane, or possibly a scraper, but for this first project a light sanding is acceptable. A properly planed surface is always superior to a sanded surface since it leaves the surface of the wood cleanly cut and clear. Sanding, no matter how fine a grit is used, by its very nature abrades the ends of the fibers and deadens the surface. If you do decide to sand, start with a medium-grit production paper and finish with a finer grade. Work always with the grain, lightly rounding all the sharp edges.

HINGING

NOW LAY THE BOX AND ITS LID FACE-DOWN ON THE BENCH and lightly clamp the two parts together, just enough so they stay put. Two hinges of the sort illustrated, designed to be face-mounted rather than mortised into the edges, may now be affixed. Since no mortise is necessary, simply position both hinges on the back of the box so that each hinge is 3 in. in from the side. Take care that the centers of the hinge knuckles lie exactly over the crack between the two parts of the box, and that both hinges are in line, as shown in FIG. 41. Make pilot holes for the screws using an awl centered in the screw holes of each hinge leaf, and make sure the hinges do not change position as you insert the screws.

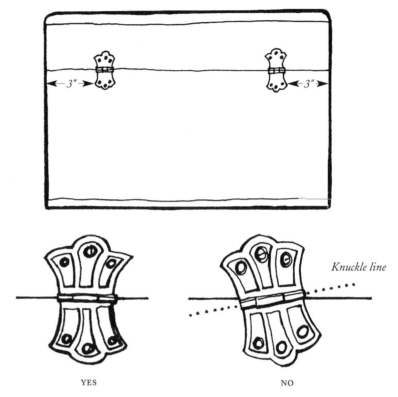

Knuckle line

YES   NO

FIG. 41 HINGE POSITION

Hinges are usually sold with screws to match, but be sure to check that the screws are not longer than the wood is thick, or they will penetrate the inside of the box. If this should be the case you must use shorter screws, but mind that the heads of the screws fit as nicely in the hinges as did the original screws.

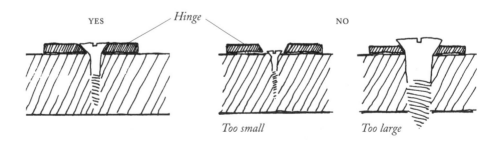

YES   *Hinge*   NO

Too small   *Too large*

FIG. 42 SCREW SIZE

FINISHING

FINALLY, WHEN THE BOX IS TOTALLY CLEAN, INSIDE AND OUT, and the lid is securely hinged, wipe a very light coat of linseed oil into all surfaces. A linseed oil finish will slowly deepen the color of the pine and eventually result in the mellow orange shade typical of much Shaker furniture. Without any such protective coating, pine will remain white but quickly become shabby and soiled. For continued good looks, or to repair any damage that the box may sustain, you may repeat this oiling at intervals. Alternatively, after the first oiling, polishing the box with a hard furniture wax will produce good results. One traditional recipe for caring for this type of finish calls for polishing the piece once a day for a week, once a week for a month, once a month for a year, and then once a year for life. Nothing is superior to the patina developed by years of such care. The only things to beware of are excessive wax buildup, which can be prevented by moderate applications of polish and vigorous rubbing, and the opposite condition of inadvertently removing the finish by the promiscuous use of spray-type furniture polishes containing petroleum distillates.

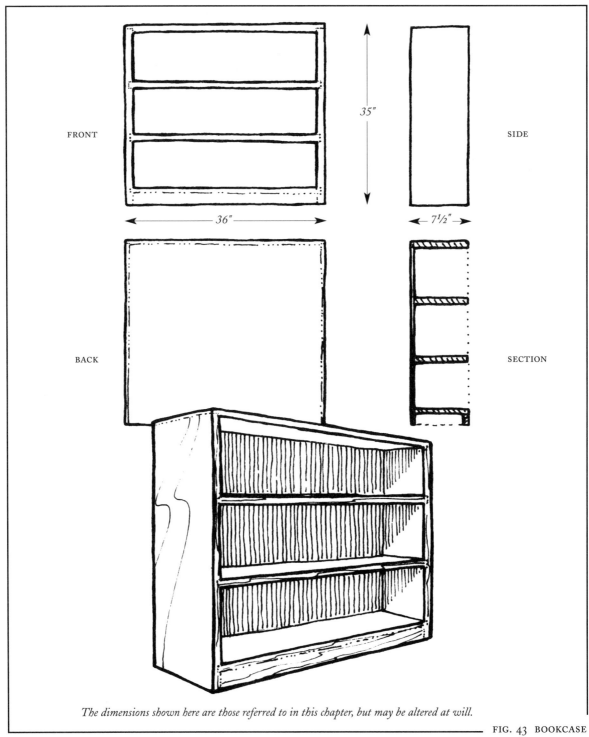

FRONT

SIDE

35"

36"

7½"

BACK

SECTION

The dimensions shown here are those referred to in this chapter, but may be altered at will.

FIG. 43 BOOKCASE

2

BOOKCASE

Surface Planing • Dadoing • Rabbeting

THE BOOKCASE IS A PIECE OF FURNITURE THAT MAY BE BUILT IN AN ALMOST INFINITE VARIETY OF DESIGNS PROVIDING THE BASIC PRINCIPLES ARE UNDERSTOOD. IT is essentially nothing more than a convenient arrangement of shelves supported by two sides, the whole held square by a plywood back. In addition to the sawing and planing techniques discussed in chapter 1, construction of this bookcase involves the related operations of rabbeting and making a housed joint.

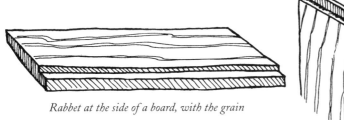

Rabbet at the side of a board, with the grain

Rabbet at the end of a board, across the grain

FIG. 44 RABBETS

For the purposes of this chapter we shall work with the dimensions illustrated in FIG. 45, but remember, changes may be made according to the size of the books to be shelved. For most medium-sized books, one-by-eight pine from the local lumberyard will be sufficient. For larger books you might have to use one-by-ten or even one-by-twelve. Weight is another consideration: shelves much over 3 ft. in length may sag if made with ¾ in.-thick pine, so you may need to use something thicker, such as five-quarter pine, or something stronger, such as ¾ in.-thick oak. When buying wood remember that lumberyard measurements are nominal, so material described as 'five-quarter' (which implies lumber 1¼ in. thick) is actually closer to 1⅛ in. thick. 'One-by' material, sometimes referred to as 'four-quarter', is actually closer to ¾ in. thick.

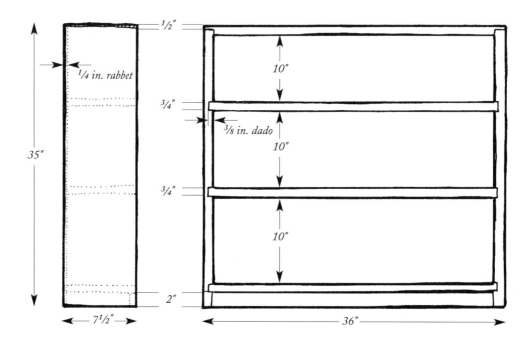

FIG. 45 DIMENSIONS OF BOOKCASE

All the material needed for the dimensions as given may be got from one 18 ft. length of number one, one-by-eight pine, one 3 ft. length of one-by-four pine, and one 3 ft. by 3 ft. piece of ¼ in.-thick plywood.

If you live in a small apartment or have limited transportation, you may wish to have the wood pre-cut into 3 ft. lengths. Many lumberyards will do this for a small charge, but try to buy your material in lengths as long as possible. Make sure that the lengths you specify, if longer than the finished parts, are complete multiples of one or more parts. Even if you have the wood pre-cut, you will still have to make just as many sawcuts yourself, so you will not be saving any labor, and more importantly you will lose the opportunity of choosing a good board free from the defects illustrated in FIG. 5, chapter 1.

Lastly, when ordering lumber for any project, always figure exactly what is required, then allow ten to twenty percent extra. Unless you are buying top-quality, expensive hardwood, which may be ordered almost to the inch, most lumber is generally only available in certain stock sizes. As a result, it is usually most economical to bear in mind what is available when designing a piece.

SURFACE PLANING

UNLIKE THE PINE BOX OF THE PREVIOUS CHAPTER, MOST OF which can be finished after having been assembled, the bookcase will be harder to prepare for finishing if you leave the removal of sawmill stamps, lumber company marks, or milling marks (see FIG. 5, chapter 1) until after the piece is assembled. If the wood is already impeccable, or if you intend to paint the piece, then perhaps all that will be necessary is a little sanding, although this might be better done after construction. Otherwise it will be easier to plane the surfaces of the various parts now, while your material is still in a few parts, than later, when it has become a bookcase consisting of all manner of corners and tops and bottoms.

Planing an edge, and testing for straightness, squareness, and parallelness, has been discussed in chapter 1. The wood for the bookcase requires the same treatment, and this should be done now before beginning work on the faces.

Planing the face of the wood is usually done on the top of the bench, which may not always be perfectly flat. This may not only make the job difficult, since the board may insist on moving around, but actually cause you to plane the surface out of true.

This difficulty may be overcome by the use of a planing board, which is nothing more than a board a little longer than the one being planed, and

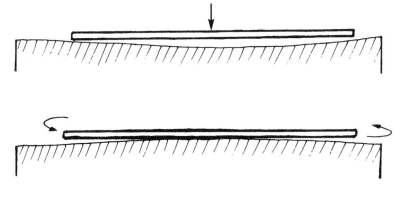

A hollow bench makes it hard to plane the middle of a board.

A rounded bench makes it hard to prevent the board from swiveling.

FIG. 46 DIFFICULTIES IN PLANING

which is already perfectly flat and true. At one end, to prevent the board being planed from being pushed off, a cleat is attached, either with screws or small clamps.

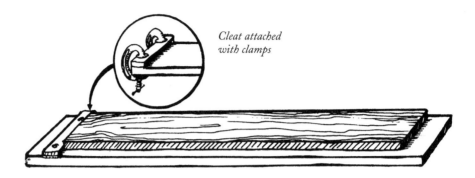

*Cleat attached
with clamps*

FIG. 47 PLANING BOARD

Even with the help of a planing board it is still a good idea to place a very thin piece of wood beneath the center of the board being planed. This helps to counteract any tendency to plane hollow.

Be careful not to plane the ends of the board round through incorrect pressure on the plane. You can avoid this by remembering to apply pressure to the toe (front) of the plane at the beginning of the stroke and to the heel (back) of the plane at the end of the stroke, as shown in FIG. 48. In any event, your material is assumed to have been obtained fairly true, so all that should be necessary is the removal of the milling marks. This only requires that a very thin shaving be taken.

*Press here at the
beginning of the
stroke.*

*Press here at the
end of the stroke.*

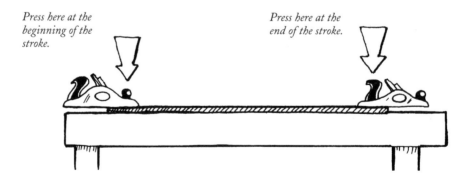

FIG. 48 PLANING PRESSURE

Until you have gained enough expertise in tuning your plane to be able to plane in any direction without tearout, it will be easiest to plane with the grain rather than against it. This will involve turning the board end-for-end as you plane first one side and then the other.

When all your lumber is clean and true, cut the two sides of the book-case. These measure 35½ in. long. Determine which is to be the top end and the outside of each, and mark lightly with a pencil accordingly.

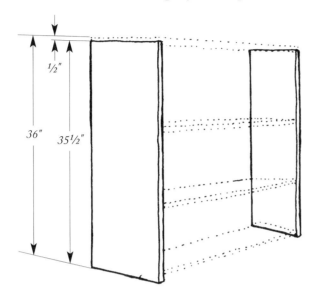

FIG. 49 THE TWO SIDES

DADOING

THE SIMPLEST FORM OF MECHANICAL JOINT (ONE THAT connects two pieces of wood by means of a certain degree of mutual support) is known as a housed joint. The bookcase shelves are let into grooves (known as dados, because they are grooves formed across the grain rather than with the grain) cut in the sides of the case. These simple square-shouldered dados constitute one of the simpler forms of housed, or housing, joints, some variations of which are shown in FIG. 50, overleaf. These and many other varieties have been devised for different purposes over the centuries by various woodworking trades to answer their own particular needs.

To lay out the dado joints required for this bookcase, first square off the inside of the side pieces at the places where the shelves are to fit (FIG. 51). The distance between shelves is 10 in., and the width of the grooves into which the shelves are to fit must equal the exact thickness of the shelves. In the dimensions given in FIG. 45 this has been estimated as ¾ in. If the actual thickness is a little more or less make all measurements from the top of the board and let the difference be absorbed at the foot, since the bottom piece (shown in FIG. 67) may be cut to fit.

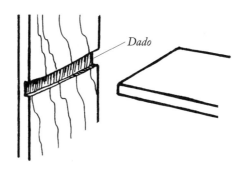 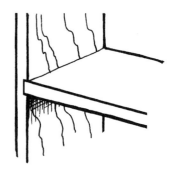

THROUGH HOUSED JOINT

This is often the easiest form to cut, since the groove is taken all the way across.

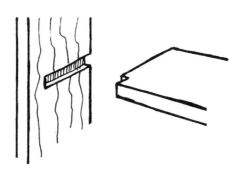 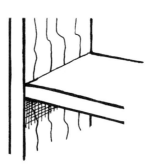

STOPPED HOUSED JOINT

Although this form preserves the line of the uprights and presents a neater appearance, it entails more work to stop the groove.

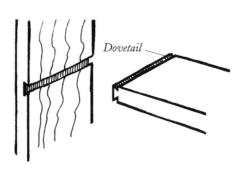 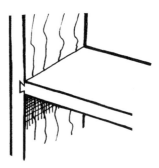

THROUGH DOVETAILED HOUSING

Mechanically stronger than a plain housed joint, a dovetailed housing resists any outward tendency of the sides.

THROUGH HALF-DOVETAILED HOUSING

A simpler form of dovetailed housing requiring less work, this variety is commonly used in case construction where multiple shelves share the job of holding the sides.

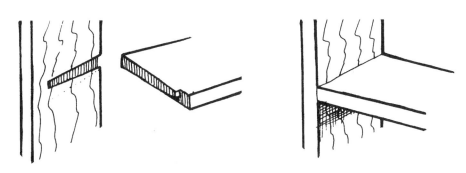

TAPERED AND STOPPED DOVETAILED HOUSING

This form is easier to cut than a regular dovetailed housing, especially for wide work, since the dovetail may be slid into position more easily, only making contact at the last moment.

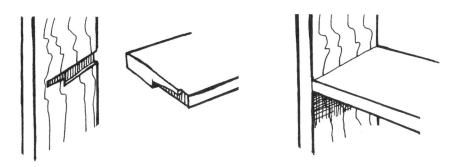

STOPPED DOVETAILED AND HOUSED JOINT

Easier to make than the fully tapered dovetailed housing, this variety is used in casework where a back shares the work of keeping the sides together.

FIG. 50 HOUSED JOINTS

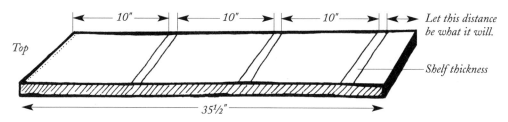

FIG. 51 SHELF LOCATIONS

After laying out the dados, use a marking knife or a chisel against a trysquare to cut a groove on the waste sides of the mark (the side that will be excavated) in order to provide a channel in which the saw may run, as in FIG. 52. Only the waste side of the groove should be sloped; the outside, which will form the shoulder of the dado, should be vertical.

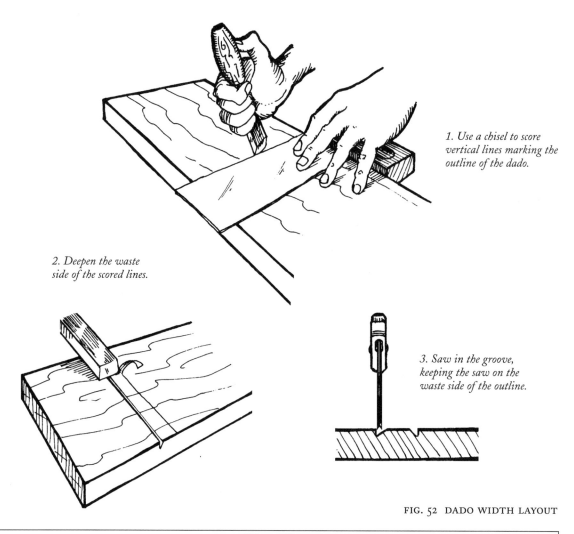

1. Use a chisel to score vertical lines marking the outline of the dado.

2. Deepen the waste side of the scored lines.

3. Saw in the groove, keeping the saw on the waste side of the outline.

FIG. 52 DADO WIDTH LAYOUT

The finished dado will be ⅜ in. deep. Therefore carefully square the sides of the dado around the edges of the board to a depth of ⅜ in. and then mark the bottom of the dado on both sides, as in FIG. 53.

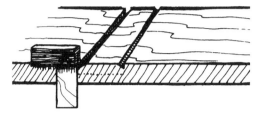

Square the dado around the edges to a depth of ¾ in.

FIG. 53 DADO DEPTH LAYOUT

Next, use a backsaw to deepen the grooves, keeping the saw at right angles to the board and cutting down to, but not below, the lines marking the bottom of the dado. The wood at *A*, FIG. 55, can now be chiseled away, using a chisel slightly narrower than the width of the groove. To finish, use a router plane set to the exact depth to make the bottom of the groove perfectly flat and equally deep across the entire width of the dado, as shown overleaf. Just as when using the block plane to plane end grain, you must plane in from each side with the router plane, for the wood will split at the far end of the groove if you continue right across. Finally, test the fit of the housed joint by trying the end of another piece of the board into the dado, chiseling away any unnecessary wood if necessary.

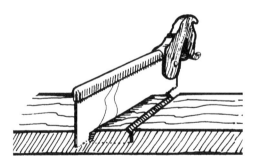

FIG. 54 SAWING THE SHOULDERS

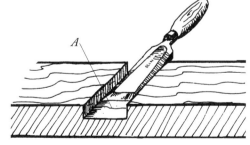

FIG. 55 REMOVING THE WASTE

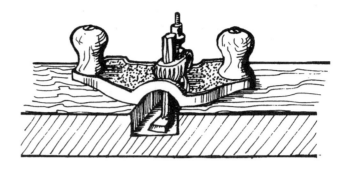

FIG. 56 ROUTER PLANE

Incidentally, until the invention of the electric router, which is now so common as to have usurped the unqualified title 'router', it was the hand router or router plane that was meant by the term 'router'.

Cut all six dados at once, checking as you do so that the dados on the one side are in the same position as the dados on the other side, and that you have, indeed, laid out the dados on the insides of the side pieces.

Leaving the router set at the exact depth required will automatically ensure that all the dados are of uniform depth. It would, of course, be possible to remove all the wood in each dado with the router, but this would necessitate constantly having to adjust the depth of the blade, since you can only take relatively thin shavings with the plane, and in so doing you would lose the guarantee of equal depth.

A slightly more sophisticated form of housing can be achieved by stopping the dado as shown in FIG. 57. This produces a neater appearance at the front of the bookcase.

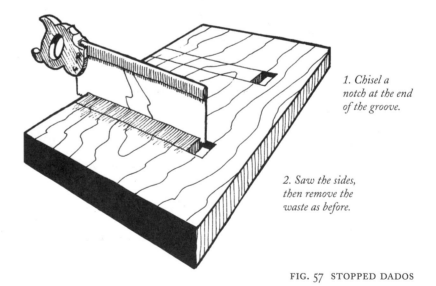

1. Chisel a notch at the end of the groove.

2. Saw the sides, then remove the waste as before.

FIG. 57 STOPPED DADOS

RABBETING

THE BACK INSIDE EDGES OF THE SIDE PIECES MUST NOW BE rabbeted to receive the plywood back. The dimensions of the rabbet are shown in FIG. 58. The ⅜ in. measurement is needed to align the back edge of the rabbet with the bottom of the grooves, which are also ⅜ in. deep. The ¼ in. measurement is required so that the face of the ¼ in.-thick plywood will be flush with the back of the bookcase.

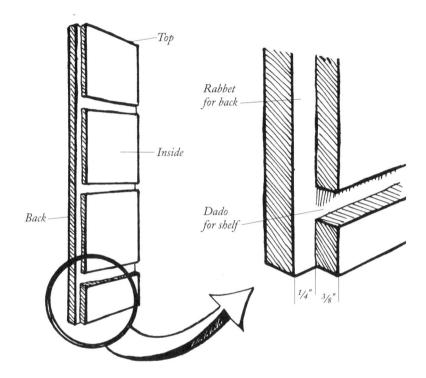

FIG. 58 DIMENSIONS OF RABBET FOR PLYWOOD BACK

The best handtool for rabbeting is either a wooden or a metal fillister plane. A fillister is simply a rabbet plane fitted with an integral depth stop and an adjustable fence. All that need be done is to set the depth stop to

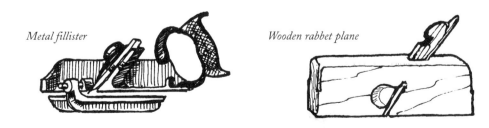

FIG. 59 RABBET PLANES

BOOKCASE

¼ in. and the fence so that ⅜ in. is removed from the inside face of the board. Lacking a fillister you must mark the rabbet on the board with a marking gauge and use a plain wooden rabbet plane, or any other plane whose blade extends across its entire sole.

The rabbet may be adjusted, if necessary, with a side rabbet plane. This little plane is also useful for widening the dado. Alternatively, a plain rabbet plane of any size, or even a shoulder plane, may be used on its side. The side pieces are now ready for assembly and may be put to one side while the shelves are cut.

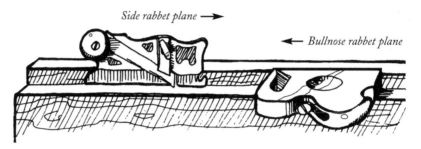

Side rabbet plane →

← *Bullnose rabbet plane*

FIG. 60 RABBET ADJUSTMENT

Cut first the top piece of the bookcase, which measures exactly 36 in. This piece must also have rabbets equal to the exact thickness of the side pieces cut into the bottom edge of both ends to receive the tops of the sides. These rabbets may be worked with the fillister plane or cut similarly to the grooves in the side pieces: with a saw and chisel, as in FIG. 61. In either event, observe all precautions against splitting the wood by planing in from both ends.

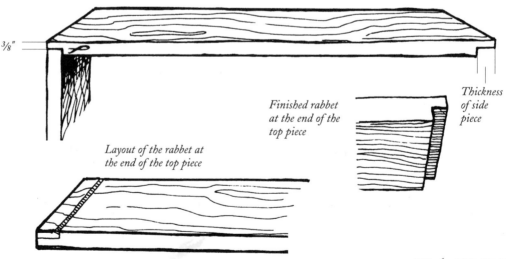

⅜″

Finished rabbet at the end of the top piece

Thickness of side piece

Layout of the rabbet at the end of the top piece

FIG. 61 TOP PIECE

When both ends have been rabbeted, another rabbet must be made along the back edge to take the plywood back, as was done in the side pieces.

The three lower shelves, which ideally should still comprise a single board, must now be reduced ¼ in. in width to allow for the plywood back. Use the marking gauge to lay out this reduction along whichever edge you choose to be the back, and then plane the waste away, preferably using a shooting-board in order to keep the edge square.

Now compute the exact length of each shelf as follows: The total width of the bookcase from outside to outside is 36 in., and the length of each shelf is therefore 36 in. less the thickness of the wood remaining at the bottom of the grooves on each side. Carefully measure x and y as shown in FIG. 62, add these amounts together, and subtract the total from 36 in. This then will be the length to which you should now cut the shelves.

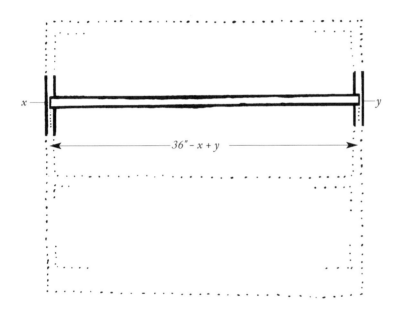

FIG. 62 SHELF LENGTH

Having first tested the fit of all the shelves in their respective dados, adjusting where necessary, glue the grooves and assemble the sides and the shelves. Place one or two bar or pipe clamps on each side to hold the whole together, not forgetting to insert scraps under the jaws to protect the wood being clamped, and wipe off any excess glue that may be forced from the joints.

Do not forget that only the front edges of the shelves are flush with the sides; the backs are necessarily recessed flush with the inside edge of the rabbet formed in the sides to accommodate the back of the bookcase.

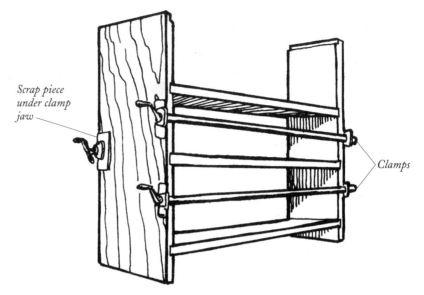

Scrap piece under clamp jaw

Clamps

FIG. 63 CLAMPING THE SHELF ASSEMBLY

If all the joints are tight, and glued and clamped well, the piece should hold together, but if you are at all nervous you may nail through the sides into the ends of the shelves, using 4d finishing nails. It is not necessary to pre-bore the nail holes, since there is no danger of the wood splitting, but be careful to nail directly into the shelf ends, angling the nails as shown in FIG. 64. This is made easier by laying the piece on its side.

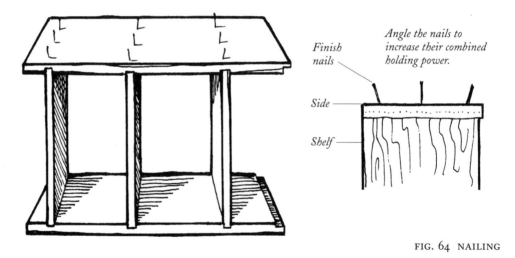

Finish nails

Angle the nails to increase their combined holding power.

Side

Shelf

FIG. 64 NAILING

Glue the end rabbets on the top piece and assemble this to the sides. Since its function is to hold the sides together this piece should definitely be nailed, having been first pre-bored. It should, moreover, be nailed from both top and sides. Finally, set all nails and fill the holes with wood filler.

When the main body of the case has been thus assembled, measure across the case from the insides of the rabbets on the sides *(x)*, and from the inside of the top rabbet to the bottom *(y)*, to determine the exact width and height of the back. Take care to cut this piece with perfect right angles, for it is the back that will ensure that the whole case is square.

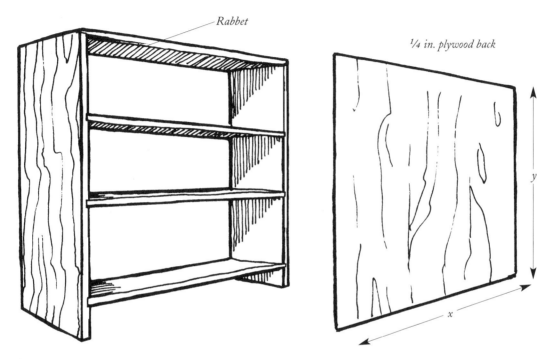

FIG. 65 DIMENSIONS OF BACK

Cut and insert the backing as soon as possible after the case has been assembled in order that the case may still be racked or twisted into square, if need be, before the glue sets.

The back may also be set into its rabbet with a bead of glue, or it may be fixed with ¾ in. tacks every 4 in. or so around the perimeter. This will be more than adequate.

FIG. 66 TACK

With the back secured in place all that remains is to measure and cut the bottom piece from the remaining piece of one-by-four, according to the previously explained techniques.

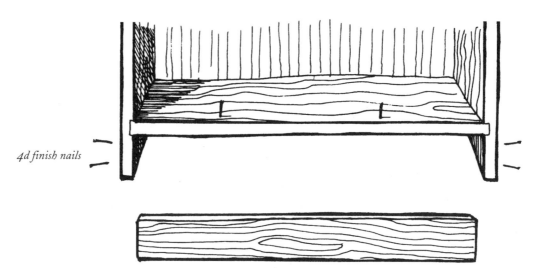

4d finish nails

FIG. 67 BOTTOM PIECE

The bottom piece, when cut, is glued and nailed in from the ends, and further secured to the bottom shelf with a couple of finishing nails driven through the shelf, as shown in FIG. 67. It may be fixed flush with the front of the case, as shown, or set back ½ in. or so to add a little interest.

When all the nails, with the exception of the tacks holding the back in, have been set and the holes filled, the entire case may be lightly sanded if necessary and all edges lightly rounded. Clean up any glue that may have seeped out of any of the joints, and the bookcase will be ready to be painted, oiled, stained, or varnished, as you prefer.

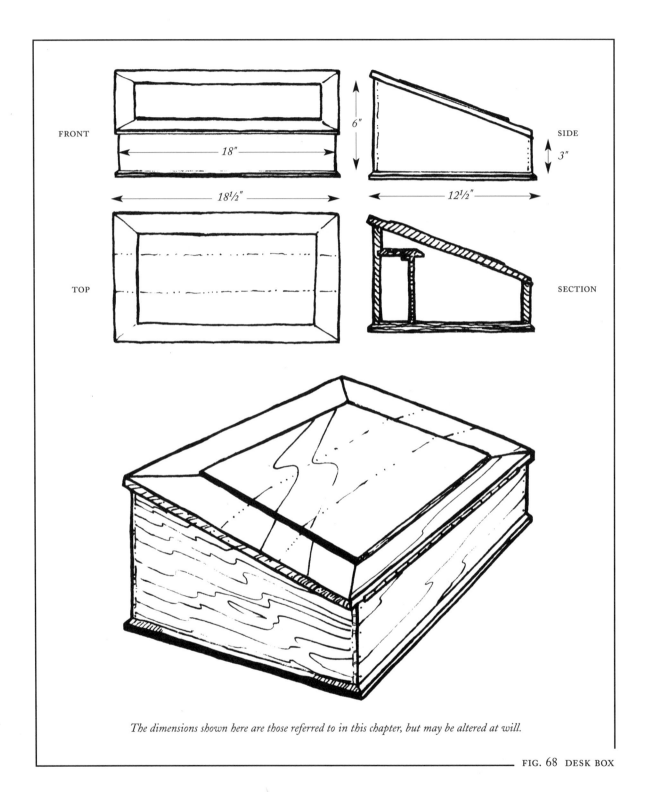

FRONT

SIDE

TOP

SECTION

6"

18"

3"

18½"

12½"

The dimensions shown here are those referred to in this chapter, but may be altered at will.

FIG. 68 DESK BOX

3

DESK BOX

Making Wider Stock • Butt Joints • Beveling • Grooving •
Chamfering • Scraper Use • Reeding • Raised Fielding

THE PINE BOX OF CHAPTER ONE AND THE BOOKCASE OF
CHAPTER TWO WERE DESIGNED TO ILLUSTRATE THE BASIC
TECHNIQUES FOR SAWING AND PLANING, AND TO PROVIDE
practice at making rabbets. The desk box described in this chapter is
rather more special, and so may be profitably made with a hardwood such
as walnut or mahogany.

Select your boards to suit the dimensions shown in FIG. 68. Unlike pine,
which was used for the two previous pieces, walnut and mahogany,
although readily available, are not always sold in standard sizes, so you
may have to do a little figuring to see how you can get what you need out
of whatever is available. The front and the back, as well as the pieces
required for the sides and the interior, should present no problem, as these
are not very large pieces. Both the lid and bottom, however, will more
than likely have to be made from several pieces joined together. If this
should prove to be the case, you can save some time by obtaining lumber
long enough so that, when joined together to provide the required width,
the piece thus joined may be sawed in half to make both the lid and the
bottom.

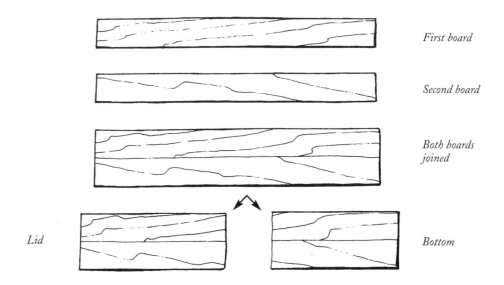

First board

Second board

Both boards joined

Lid

Bottom

FIG. 69 PROVIDING LID & BOTTOM

MAKING WIDER STOCK

THE WAY TO JOIN BOARDS TOGETHER IN ORDER TO MAKE A wider piece is as follows: Start by selecting as many boards as necessary to make up the required width. Obviously, the wider the pieces the fewer will be needed, but the principle in joining them is always the same, and there is really no limit to how many pieces you may join together.

Secondly, while remembering to use pieces long enough so that both the lid and the bottom may be cut from the joined piece, pay attention to the grain, and arrange the joints in such a way that the pattern of the grain either tends to render the joint imperceptible, or contrasts in a balanced way. Walnut sometimes has blond areas in its otherwise chocolaty color; use these to best effect if they occur. But whatever you do, think about the desirability of alternating the grain of adjacent pieces, as shown

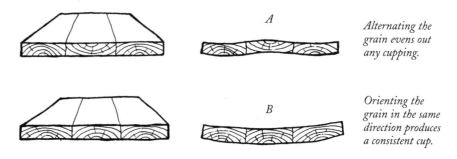

A

Alternating the grain evens out any cupping.

B

Orienting the grain in the same direction produces a consistent cup.

FIG. 70 JOINING PLAIN-SAWN BOARDS

at *A* in FIG. 70, since this helps to maintain an overall flatness, although it is sometimes easier and more useful to join flat-sawn boards so that all cupping occurs on the same side, as at *B*. Boards joined in this fashion can be kept flat simply by securing the center, with the added advantage of leaving any dimensional change to take place at the edges.

Even if you have been able to obtain quarter-sawn wood, which is much less susceptible to warping than plain-sawn (see FIGS. 3 and 31), it is still good practice to alternate the pieces according to the direction of the grain, as shown in FIG. 71.

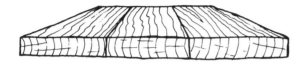

FIG. 71 ALTERNATING QUARTER-SAWN BOARDS

BUTT JOINTS

THERE ARE VARIOUS METHODS OF JOINING BOARDS EDGE TO edge involving the use of splines and dowels, but all that is required here is a plain butt joint, held together by nothing more than glue and the truth of the edges. Since there is no inherent mechanical strength in a butt joint, it is of the utmost importance that the edges be planed as perfectly as possible. This is possible using the techniques outlined in the previous two chapters. When you are able to plane two edges to match perfectly*, simply sliding their glued surfaces together for an inch or so will produce a joint, properly known as a rubbed glue joint, that will not need clamping. Indeed, if you try to break the joint after the glue has cured, the chances are that the wood will break somewhere other than at the glue line.

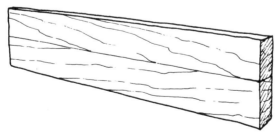

FIG. 72 BUTT JOINT

* For an in-depth discussion of how to set up and sharpen a plane, see *Traditional Woodworking Handtools,* chapters 13–16.

DESK BOX

A 3 ft.-long machinist's straightedge, properly cared for, is ideal for checking the straightness of an edge. Use it continually as you plane. Before gluing the joint, make sure that both edges match by placing one board on top of the other, edge to edge, and looking to see if there is any light visible between the edges, or if the boards will swivel. If you see light then it is clear that one or both edges are hollow at that point. If the boards swivel then it is clear that one or both edges are rounded.

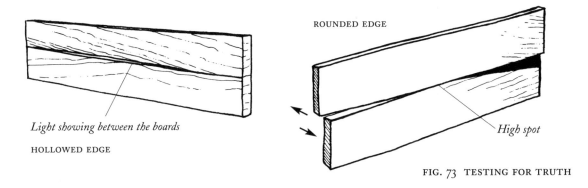

ROUNDED EDGE

Light showing between the boards

HOLLOWED EDGE

High spot

FIG. 73   TESTING FOR TRUTH

If the joint is tight along its entire length, the next step is to check the alignment. This means seeing whether the boards lie in the same plane.

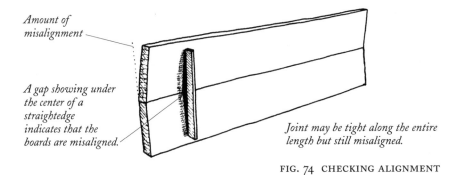

Amount of misalignment

A gap showing under the center of a straightedge indicates that the boards are misaligned.

Joint may be tight along the entire length but still misaligned.

FIG. 74   CHECKING ALIGNMENT

If the joint is out of alignment there are two ways to correct it: the first is to plane the offending edge square; the second is to plane both edges together on the shooting-board, for even if the edges are not perfectly square to the face of the board, the difference will be the same on both edges, and one error will cancel out the other, as in FIG. 75.

When it is seen that all the edges to be joined match, they may be glued and, if desired, clamped. If there are three pieces, clamp them all at one time; do not clamp two and then wait before adding the third. For short lengths one clamp may be sufficient. If you use two or more clamps, alternate the from one side of the wood to the other so that the stresses are

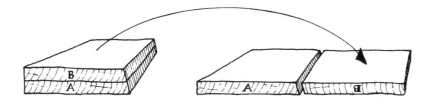

FIG. 75 EQUAL MISALIGNMENT

equalized and the wood is not clamped into a bowed position. Wipe off any excess glue and stand the glued boards to one side to set up. The length of time needed for this is usually indicated on the glue container; be sure to allow at least this amount of time and, if possible, leave the joint to cure overnight.

If pipe or bar clamps are unavailable, boards can be held tightly together after gluing by wedging them between blocks, which may be nailed to the floor or clamped to a bench.

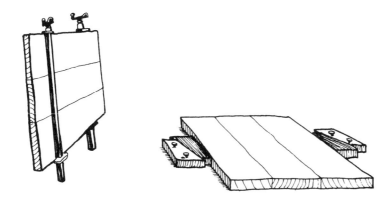

Cut the front and back pieces to length first (18 in.). The back piece should be a little more than 6 in. wide and the front piece should be a little more than 3 in. wide, so that after the top edges have been beveled the outside faces can measure exactly 6 in. and 3 in. respectively.

Next, make ½ in.-deep rabbets, as wide as the thickness of the stock you are using, at both ends of the front and back, as explained in the previous chapter.

Measure the amount of wood left at the bottom of the rabbet (if you have made a ½ in.-deep rabbet in ¾ in.-thick stock you will have ¼ in. left here) and subtract twice this amount from 12½ in., which is the overall length of the side of the box. The result will be the actual length of the side pieces.

Cut two side pieces, as wide as the back piece is high, a little more than 6 in., to this length, and then clamp all four sides of the box together dry — with no glue.

Draw a pencil line from a point exactly 6 in. up from the bottom of the back piece on its outside face, to a point exactly 3 in. up from the bottom of the front piece on its outside face. Saw the resultant sloping top edge of the sides. Make sure to saw on the waste side of the line so that you can finish exactly to the line with a plane, removing all the saw marks.

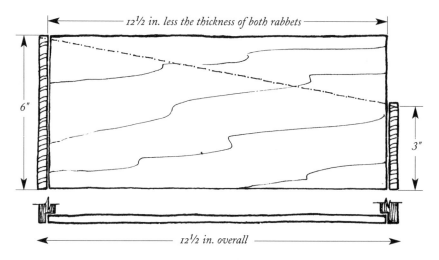

12½ in. less the thickness of both rabbets

6"

3"

12½ in. overall

FIG. 77 SIDE PIECE LAYOUT

BEVELING

USE A BEVEL TO TRANSFER THE ANGLE OF SLOPE OF THE SIDE pieces to the ends of the front and back pieces as shown in FIG. 78. After marking both ends of each piece, connect the lines on both faces so that there is a line to plane to.

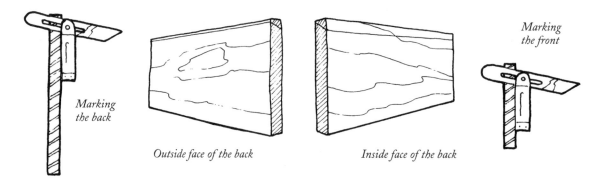

Marking the back

Outside face of the back

Inside face of the back

Marking the front

FIG. 78 MARKING FRONT & BACK BEVELS

You may place the front piece in the vise and carefully plane down to the lines you have drawn to establish the bevel, but before beveling the back piece you should first plough the groove for the compartment lid as described below, since it will be easier to keep the plough's fence against a square edge than a beveled edge.

FIG. 79 BEVELING

GROOVING

THE GROOVE TO RECEIVE THE BACK OF THE COMPARTMENT lid is made ¼ in. wide and ¼ in. deep, 4½ in. up from the bottom. You may mark this out with a marking gauge and then saw or chisel out the groove, but such a groove is more easily made with a plough plane, as shown in FIG. 81.

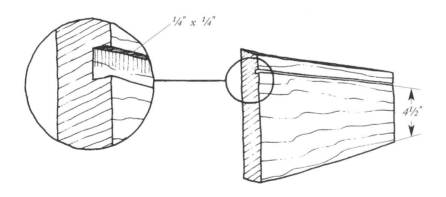

¼" x ¼"

4½"

FIG. 80 COMPARTMENT LID GROOVE

DESK BOX

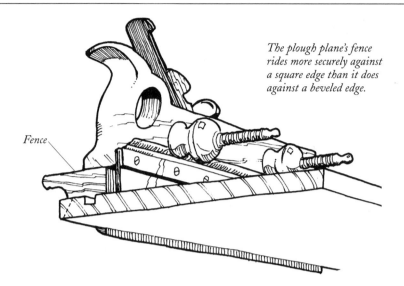

The plough plane's fence rides more securely against a square edge than it does against a beveled edge.

Fence

FIG. 81 PLOUGHING

The grooves needed in the side pieces to receive the partition are stopped at 4½ in., that is, they do not continue all the way across the board, and are consequently best made in the manner shown in FIG. 57, chapter 2. These grooves, like the compartment lid groove, are also ¼ in. wide by ¼ in. deep.

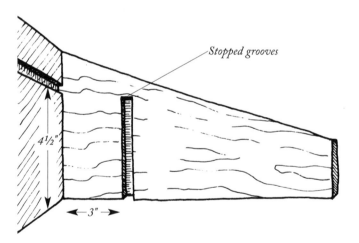

Stopped grooves

4½"

←3"→

FIG. 82 COMPARTMENT GROOVES

When all the beveling and grooving is complete it is time to glue and assemble all four sides. While still clamped, check the squareness of the assembly at each corner using a trysquare.

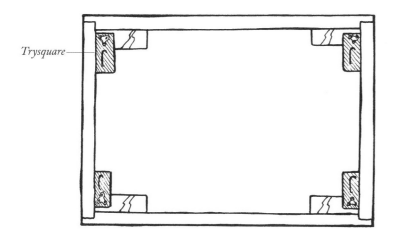

Trysquare

FIG. 83 CHECKING SQUARENESS

Pre-bore the front and back pieces and nail them to the sides with small finishing nails in the same manner as was used for the pine box of chapter 1.

The inside partition is most easily made from ¼ in.-thick stock. This only needs to be cut to the right height and length, and then slipped into the grooves in the side pieces. Do not glue the partition, for if it shrinks and is fixed it may split; left unglued it is free to move in its grooves and may shrink at will without splitting.

To save the labor of planing or resawing a piece of ¾ in.-thick stock down to ¼ in. you may instead cut ¼ in.-thick rabbets at each end.

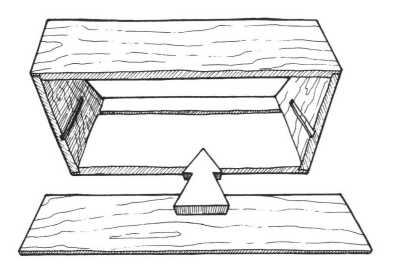

DESK BOX

CHAMFERING

THE NEXT STEP IS TO FIT THE BOTTOM, THE TOP EDGE OF WHICH is sloped so as to form either a bevel or a chamfer. It is interesting to note here the nice difference between a chamfer and a bevel: both refer to a slope, usually along the edge of a piece of wood, but the chamfer extends an equal distance from the original arris (the edge formed by the meeting of two surfaces), whereas the two edges of a bevel may extend an unequal distance from the original arris. The top edges of the front and back pieces of the box were beveled, because the sloped surface formed on an originally square edge extends farther across the top than it does down the side.

The same distinction is true for edges formed by the junction of two surfaces not at 90° to each other: if the edge is beveled so that the distance to each edge of the bevel from the original arris is equal, then this is called a chamfer; if not then it is a bevel.

The bottom piece should be approximately ¼ in. larger all round than the outside of the box. Cut the base to this size and then, after having trimmed the end grain with a block plane (using the shooting-board), set the marking gauge to ¼ in. and lightly scribe a line around the edge, from the underside up.

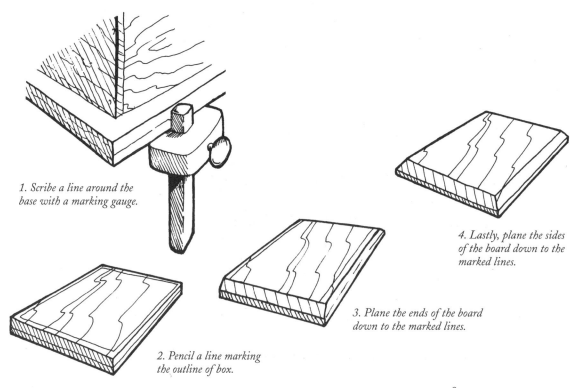

1. Scribe a line around the base with a marking gauge.

2. Pencil a line marking the outline of box.

3. Plane the ends of the board down to the marked lines.

4. Lastly, plane the sides of the board down to the marked lines.

FIG. 85 BEVELING THE BASE

Now set the assembled box on top of the base and position it equidistant from all edges of the base, using a pencil to mark what will become the upper limit of the slope. If this slope should prove to be at 45° to the side, it may properly be called a chamfer. Since it may not equal this exactly, we shall refer to it from here on as a bevel. With the bevel thus marked, reduce it with the block plane, following the steps shown in FIG. 85.

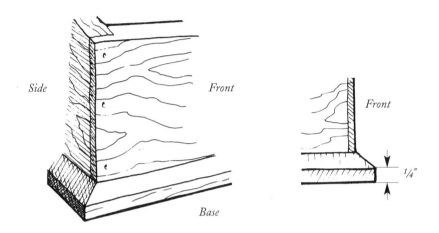

FIG. 86 DETAIL OF A BEVELED BASE

SCRAPER USE

AS SOON AS EVERYTHING HAS BEEN PLANED CLEAN AND SMOOTH you may nail the base to the sides from underneath, using 4d finishing nails. Rather than sanding, or even planing, you may prefer to use a scraper at this point to achieve a really smooth surface.

Scrapers are made in various shapes, the most usual being a simple rectangle, about 5 in. wide. Once you have mastered the sharpening process, they become very useful tools, especially for finishing hardwoods with awkward grain. FIG. 87 illustrates the various stages in sharpening a scraper, and FIG. 88 shows how to use a scraper.

IT IS NOW TIME TO MAKE THE COMPARTMENT LID TO THE dimensions shown in FIG. 89. The first step is to cut the piece to the correct length and width. The second step is to make a rabbet on the top edge at the back so that the piece fits easily into the groove in the back of the box. The third step is to bevel the front edge using a block plane. The fourth step is to glue a small strip underneath, close enough to the front edge to prevent the little lid from slipping out of the groove in the back

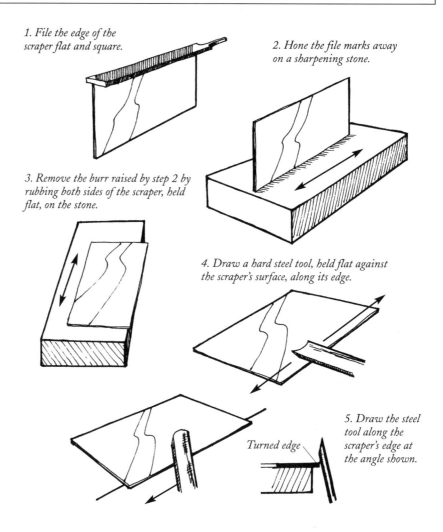

1. File the edge of the scraper flat and square.

2. Hone the file marks away on a sharpening stone.

3. Remove the burr raised by step 2 by rubbing both sides of the scraper, held flat, on the stone.

4. Draw a hard steel tool, held flat against the scraper's surface, along its edge.

5. Draw the steel tool along the scraper's edge at the angle shown.

Turned edge

FIG. 87 SHARPENING THE SCRAPER

The scraper may be pushed or pulled, adjusting the angle at which it is held, while bowing it slightly by pressing in the center with one or both thumbs.

FIG. 88 USING THE SCRAPER

of the box and falling down into the compartment, but not so close that the lid cannot be inserted or removed easily. The fifth and final step is to cut the pencil grooves as explained below.

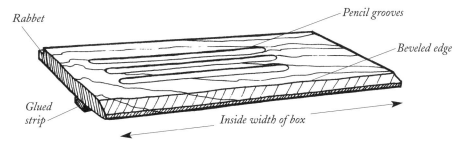

FIG. 89 COMPARTMENT LID DETAILS

REEDING

THE PENCIL GROOVES MAY BE THOUGHT OF AS THREE WIDELY spaced reeds. Lay them out by lightly scribing their outside edges to match the width of a convenient gouge. For a neat appearance be sure to make the ends of the grooves even. Staying within the scribed marks, first make a series of downward cuts with the gouge along the entire length of the groove. Then remove the waste with the gouge held as flat as possible, and finally clean up with a piece of sandpaper folded over a piece of wood (called a rubber) rounded to the same shape as the groove.

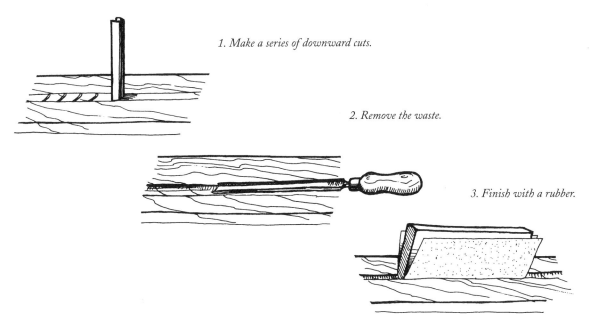

1. Make a series of downward cuts.

2. Remove the waste.

3. Finish with a rubber.

FIG. 90 MAKING PENCIL GROOVES

RAISED FIELDING

THE LAST MAJOR OPERATION IS TO MAKE THE LID. CUT THIS from the previously glued-up boards to the dimensions shown in FIG. 68. The central area is defined by a raised field that is formed as follows: Start by marking the central raised area with a marking gauge set at 2 in. Then deepen the marks left by the pin of the marking gauge with a knife and a straightedge, followed by a chisel, and then the backsaw, as illustrated in chapter 2 when cutting dados. Hold the saw perfectly level, and take care not to cut deeper than ⅛ in.

Now mark the outside edge of the lid in the same way as the outside edge of the base, and then plane away the waste. There are one or two ways to do this, including using special panel-raising planes and other relatively uncommon handtools, but good results can be achieved for your first panel raising using very simple tools such as a block plane to remove the bulk of the waste and a small metal bullnose rabbet plane, or even a shoulder plane, to clean up the inside corner of the central field.

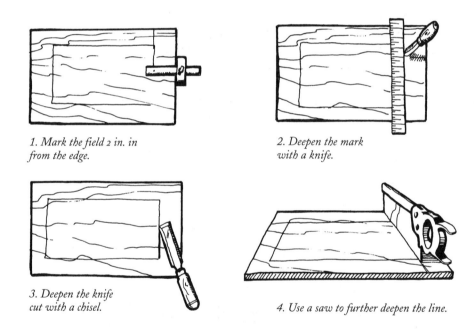

1. Mark the field 2 in. in from the edge.

2. Deepen the mark with a knife.

3. Deepen the knife cut with a chisel.

4. Use a saw to further deepen the line.

FIG. 91 STEPS IN MARKING RAISED FIELD

Whatever kind of plane you use, plane the short ends first, working across the grain and using a scrap block at the end of the cut to prevent splitting the end. Any splitting that does occur will then be removed when planing the sides, since the plane will be running with the grain. At the same time, pay close attention to keeping the beveled edge flat and making sure that the arris formed at the corners is perfectly straight and runs from the very corner of the field to the very corner of the board.

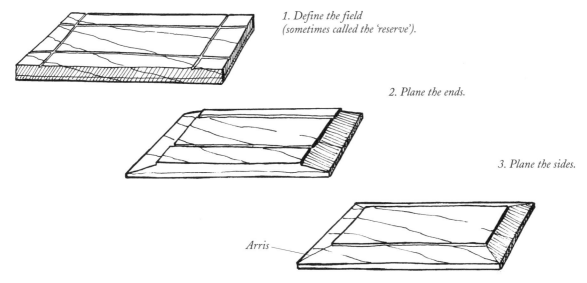

1. Define the field (sometimes called the 'reserve').

2. Plane the ends.

3. Plane the sides.

Arris

FIG. 92 PANEL RAISING

When the raised field has been cut and cleaned, lay the lid on top of the box and use an adjustable bevel to mark a vertical line on the front edge of the lid. Plane to this line so that the front edge of the lid lies flush with the front of the box.

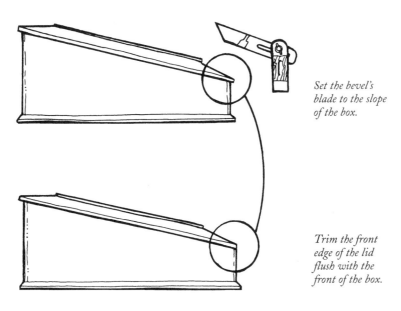

Set the bevel's blade to the slope of the box.

Trim the front edge of the lid flush with the front of the box.

FIG. 93 BEVEL LAYOUT

DESK BOX

To attach the lid to the box, cut a 15 in. length of ½ in. piano hinge and center the hinge along the front edge of the box so that the knuckle overlaps the front as you carefully mark around it with a knife, as shown at *A*, FIG. 94.

Then make a rabbet for the hinge as deep as one flap, as shown at *B*. Finally, make pilot holes, and screw the hinge to the box with no more than a couple of screws in case any adjustment is necessary, and then, supporting the lid as at *C*, repeat the whole procedure on the lid. When you are sure the hinge is properly positioned, insert the remainder of the screws, and the construction of the desk box will be finished.

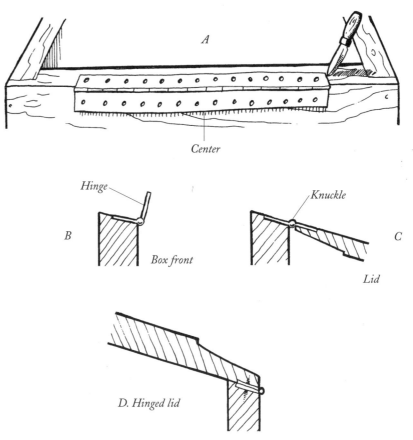

Center

Hinge

B

Box front

Knuckle

C

Lid

D. Hinged lid

FIG. 94 HINGING THE LID

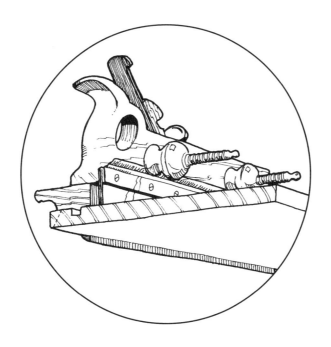

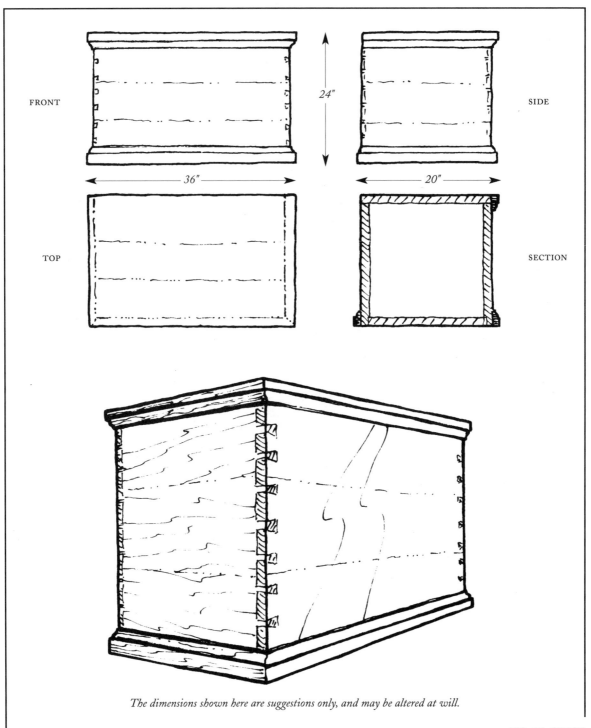

FRONT

SIDE

24"

36"

20"

TOP

SECTION

The dimensions shown here are suggestions only, and may be altered at will.

FIG. 95 CHEST

4

CHEST

Doweled Edge Joints • Dovetail Joints •
Moulding • Mitering

CHESTS WERE ONE OF THE FIRST TYPES OF FURNITURE TO BE MADE. NEARLY EVERY GREAT HOUSE OF THE EARLY MIDDLE AGES HAD A CHEST OR TWO EVEN IF IT HAD little else. With such a long history it is not surprising that there are now many ways of constructing chests. The chest described in this chapter is a development of the so-called six-board chest, and has been chosen in order to demonstrate the use of doweled edge joints and dovetails.

While it may have been possible a hundred years ago to find wood wide enough to make the sides of a chest measuring 18 in. to 24 in. high out of single pieces, today this is largely impossible. The original 'six boards' that comprised the two ends, the top and bottom, and the back and front, therefore, must needs each be made up of two or more boards, edge-jointed together. The exact dimensions may vary considerably, but so long as you understand the principles of the construction, you should be able to build the chest in a variety of sizes as the occasion demands.

In the same way that the pine box of chapter 1 was made from one length of wood, so may the six basic pieces of the chest be got from one length of common pine, except that the length in this case must first be made up to the required width by joining two or more boards together. Since the principle is the same no matter how many boards are being joined, the instructions are limited to joining two pieces.

Having first determined the total length necessary, choose and mark the face sides of the two boards and then plane the edges that are to be joined, perfectly straight and square, as explained earlier. Now mark approximately the places where the joined boards will be sawed into the component parts of the chest.

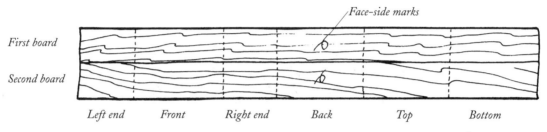

FIG. 96 BOARD LAYOUT

DOWELED EDGE JOINTS

SUCH MARKING, EVEN THOUGH ONLY APPROXIMATE, IS VERY important because the two boards are going to be joined with dowels whose position may not coincide with the places at which the board will be sawed. Mark the lateral position of the dowels now by squaring across the edges to be joined at intervals of 8 in. or so.

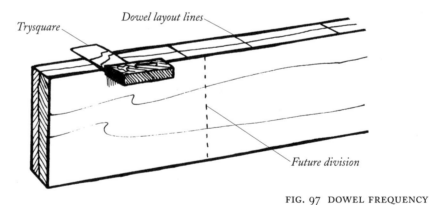

FIG. 97 DOWEL FREQUENCY

Next, separate the two boards and, working consistently from the face side of each board, use the marking gauge to bisect each of the lines you drew across the edges to locate the dowel centers.

Make all marks for the dowel centers with the stock of the marking gauge held against the face side of the board.

FIG. 98 MARKING DOWEL CENTERS

Choose dowels having a diameter no more than half the thickness of the board. Using a twist bit of commensurate diameter, bore holes no deeper than 1 in. in each edge. If a doweling jig is available there will be no problem in making all the holes equally deep and ensuring that they are all perfectly upright, since these adjustments may be made on the jig.

If you do not have a jig, stand at the end of the boards when boring rather than at the sides, since it is much easier to judge whether the brace is leaning to the left or right than it is to judge whether it is leaning away from or towards you. This is important because a hole that slopes to and from the ends is less of a problem during assembly, for it will only involve a certain amount of strain, whereas if the hole slopes to and from the faces of the wood the boards will be out of square when joined. Furthermore, if you bore without the aid of a jig you should also use some kind of depth gauge, such as a piece of tape wrapped around the bit, to ensure holes of an equal depth.

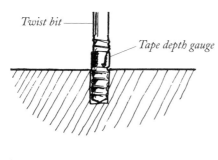

Twist bit ——

—— *Tape depth gauge*

Better that holes slope like this . . . . than this.

Side view *End view*

FIG. 99 BORING DOWEL HOLES

CHEST

When all the holes have been bored, lightly countersink them to ensure that no fibers left by the drill at the entrance prevent a close fit, as well as to provide a place for surplus glue. Then cut the dowels slightly shorter than the combined depth of two holes. The ends of the dowels should be slightly rounded to ensure easy entrance into the holes.

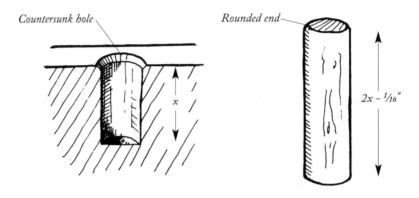

Countersunk hole

Rounded end

$2x - \frac{1}{16}''$

FIG. 100 DOWELING DETAILS

It is possible to buy hardwood dowels that are spirally grooved, thereby providing an escape channel for any glue which, becoming trapped at the bottom of the hole, might, under pressure, cause the wood to split. However, if these are not available you must provide a groove in the side of the dowel yourself. This can be done either by running a saw kerf down the length of the dowel, or by knocking the dowel through a hole in a scrap piece of wood that has a nail sticking into it, as shown in FIG. 101.

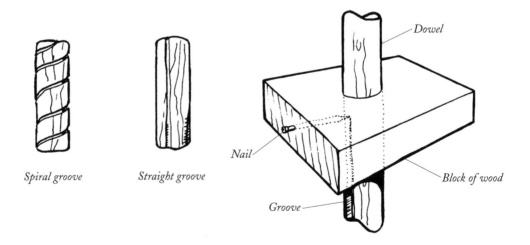

Spiral groove   *Straight groove*

Dowel

Nail

Groove

Block of wood

FIG. 101 GLUE-GROOVES IN DOWELS

To assemble the joint, squirt a little glue into each hole and also put a little glue on the business end of each dowel before gently knocking it into its hole with a mallet. Then glue the second board's edge, making sure not to use too much glue and being careful to spread it evenly over the entire surface, similarly squirting a little glue into each of its holes, before fitting it over the dowels already inserted in the first piece. Wipe off any surplus glue as you clamp up the two boards.

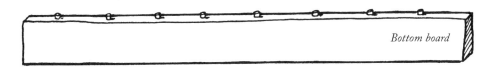

1. Insert lightly glued dowels into the glued holes of the bottom board, and tap them home.

2. Place the top board, with glued edge and glued holes, onto the bottom board.

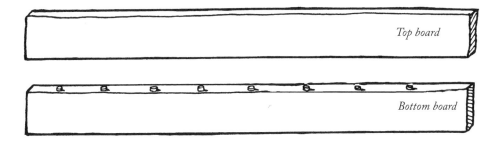

3. Clamp both boards together, alternating the clamps.

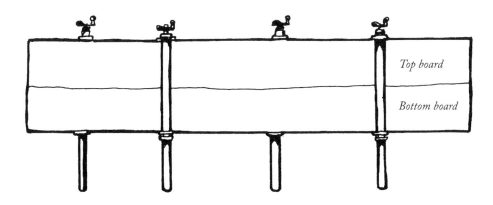

FIG. 102 ASSEMBLY OF BOARDS

Assembly will be a lot easier with an assistant, since, if the chest is about 2 ft. long, the total length of the boards being joined will be about 10 ft. Do not forget to alternate the position of the clamps and to use scraps to prevent the jaws of the clamps from marring the edges of the wood.

When the glue has set and the clamps have been removed, the joined board may be sawed into sides, back, and front. Remember to make the width of the chest a little less than the width of the board so that the lid will cover the chest, and to mark the face and top of each part.

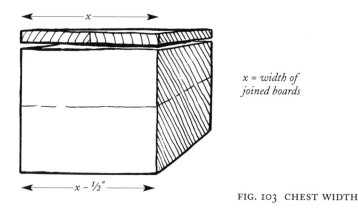

x = width of joined boards

FIG. 103   CHEST WIDTH

DOVETAIL JOINTS

ALL FOUR SIDES OF THIS CHEST ARE DOVETAILED TOGETHER. Dovetailing is a very strong form of joinery, and although it may seem dauntingly complicated when approached for the first time, the process is relatively simple if a few basic facts are borne in mind. Numerous varieties of dovetail joints, each designed for a specific purpose, are described in chapter 13; the one to be used here is one of the simplest, and is known as a through dovetail.

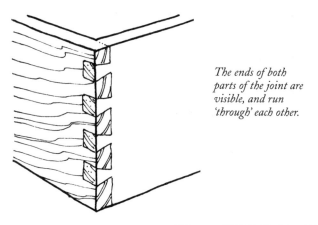

The ends of both parts of the joint are visible, and run 'through' each other.

FIG. 104   THROUGH DOVETAIL

The two parts of the joint are easily distinguished if you remember that the tails look like dovetails from two sides, but the pins only look like dovetails from the end. When viewed from either side the pins are square. FIG. 105 also shows the approximate angle at which the dovetails used for this pine chest should be cut.

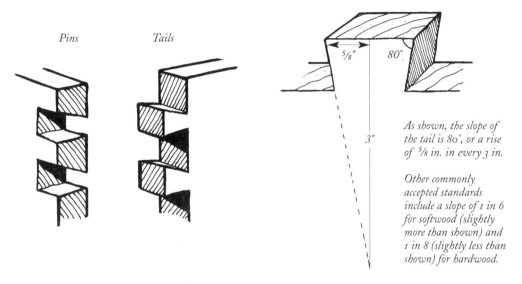

Pins   Tails

⅝"

80°

3"

As shown, the slope of the tail is 80°, or a rise of ⅝ in. in every 3 in.

Other commonly accepted standards include a slope of 1 in 6 for softwood (slightly more than shown) and 1 in 8 (slightly less than shown) for hardwood.

FIG. 105 TAILS, PINS, & SLOPES

Although for the strongest possible joint the tails should be as thick as the piece they are cut in, and the pins should equal the tails, for most purposes the tails may be made twice as wide as the pins. An even nicer proportion, often found in old work, consists of the widest part of the pins being a little more than half the thickness of the wood being used.

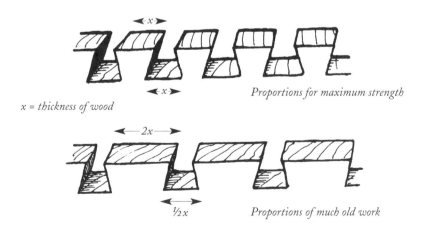

x

x

Proportions for maximum strength

x = thickness of wood

2x

½x

Proportions of much old work

FIG. 106 PROPORTIONS

    CHEST

Two important points to remember when laying out the dovetails for the chest are: one, that the tails should be cut in the front and back pieces of the chest; and two, that it is a pin which forms the top and bottom corner of the front and back.

Firstly, having made sure that the ends of each section are perfectly square and straight, having been planed thus using a block plane with a shooting-board, square off a line around all the ends equal to the exact thickness of the wood.

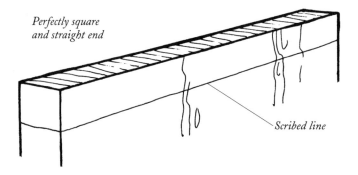

Perfectly square and straight end

Scribed line

FIG. 107 SQUARING THE ENDS

Secondly, having decided on the approximate proportions to be used, lay out the dovetails on the front and back pieces of the chest, using a bevel set to the proper angle, making sure that tails are evenly spaced and that you begin and end with a pin. Thirdly, square across the ends of the boards with a trysquare.

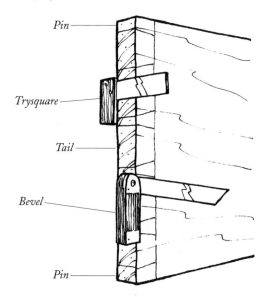

Pin

Trysquare

Tail

Bevel

Pin

FIG. 108 LAYING OUT THE TAILS

Now, using a dovetail saw, cut carefully between the tails, just on the waste (pin) side of the line, being careful not to saw below the scribed line that you initially squared around the ends on either side. For the sake of ease and greatest accuracy, position the wood so that the cuts can be made vertically, and to save time, saw two pieces at once, as in FIG. 109.

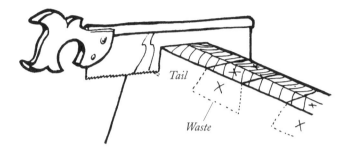

FIG. 109 SAWING DOVETAILS

Remove the waste wood between the dovetails by first sawing along the waste side of the scribed line with a coping saw, being careful not to cut into it. Place a chisel with its cutting edge on the pin waste with its bevel facing towards the end of the wood, and draw it back until it catches in the scribed line. Start paring away the waste by pushing in at a slight upward angle, then gradually lower the angle until you can make a cut parallel to the end. Work from alternate sides to avoid splitting out the wood. Your chisel should be very sharp, and ideally be a paring chisel, characterized by having wide bevels on each side of the face, which will allow it to reach into acute angled corners.

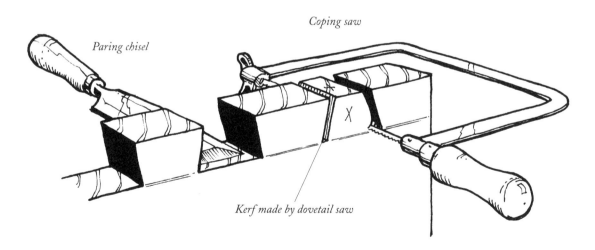

FIG. 110 REMOVING THE WASTE

Mark the pins on the ends of the side pieces by laying the appropriate end of the front or back piece over them as shown in FIG. 111. Making sure that the ends of the tails are perfectly flush with the faces of the sides, use a sharp marking knife or a fine-pointed scratch awl to scribe around the tails. Using a trysquare, continue the lines you have just scribed down to the line originally squared around the ends of the sides, and then saw the sides of the pins, being careful to saw exactly to the line.

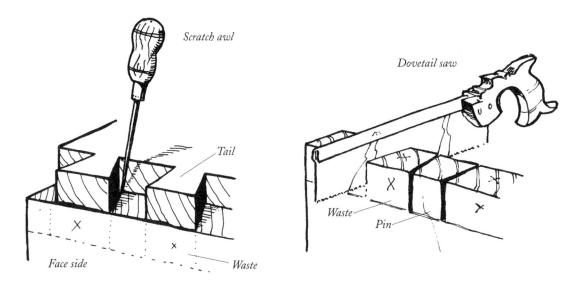

FIG. 111 MARKING & SAWING PINS

Remove the waste wood between the pins in the same way as you removed the waste between the tails.

Before assembling the joint, relieve the inside edges of the dovetails a little so that the pieces will go together more easily and there will be less danger of anything splitting. The perfect fit should require the assistance of a mallet tapping lightly on a piece of scrap placed over the tails. If the piece of scrap used to prevent the mallet from marring the work is long

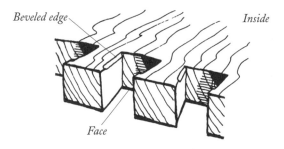

FIG. 112 RELIEVING THE INSIDE EDGES

enough to cover the entire joint, this will help seat the tails evenly. If the joint is too tight, be careful where and how much you pare away; you can always remove a little more, but it is harder to replace wood.

When all four corners of the chest have been successfully jointed and individually dry-fitted, you may glue and assemble the entire chest. Assemble the sides to the front first, then assemble the back to the sides. Clamp if necessary to remove any bowing or cupping, but be sure to maintain the squareness of the box.

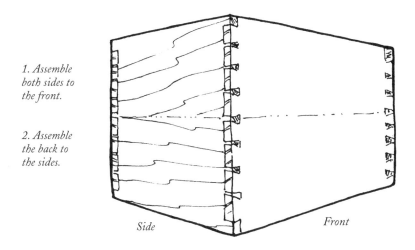

1. Assemble both sides to the front.

2. Assemble the back to the sides.

Side   *Front*

FIG. 113 THE FOUR SIDES ASSEMBLED

Ideally, the bottom should be fitted into rabbets cut in the bottom of all four sides so that any shrinkage will be hidden by the rabbets. For a basic pine chest simply fitting the bottom within the four sides and nailing it in place through the sides will be sufficient. This method will carry more weight than nailing from underneath (as at B in FIG. 114), and avoid any splitting that might occur should the bottom shrink.

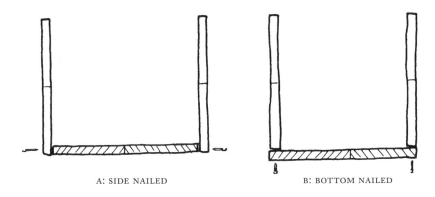

A: SIDE NAILED   B: BOTTOM NAILED

FIG. 114 POSITION OF CHEST BOTTOM

     CHEST

MOULDING

ONCE THE BOTTOM HAS BEEN NAILED IN PLACE THE PLINTH MAY be made. This is simply a length of one-by-four, or any other dimension that looks right with the size chest you have made, sufficient to run around the entire base. The top edge of the plinth not only looks good but is also less likely to splinter if it is moulded. The moulding can be anything from a simple chamfer, made in the manner described in chapter 3, to a complicated series of coves, rounds, and quirks, made either with an electric router or shaper, or with one or more moulding planes*. If a shaper is used, nothing more is required than to choose an appropriate bit and run the wood through the machine. But if you prefer the nicer feel of a hand-planed moulding, bear the following points in mind.

First, since the moulding plane is a plane like all other planes you should plane with the grain if possible. And since you are planing on an arris you must take into account not only the grain on the face of the wood but also the grain on its edge.

Second, a moulding plane is used in the reverse direction from a bench plane. That is to say, you do not start at the back end of the wood and plane towards the front; rather, you must begin close to the front end of the wood, and while still planing in a forward direction start each stroke from progressively farther back as the wood is cut away. By working into a profile already formed or partly formed, the task of keeping the plane's fence close to the workpiece is made easier. If you observe this precaution success is virtually guaranteed, since between the fence and the integral depth stop the majority of these planes are completely self-regulating. There is, however, one other point to observe. Most moulding planes are designed to be worked while being held tilted somewhat to the left of vertical. The exact degree at which the plane should be tilted is usually marked on the toe (front end) of the plane as a scribed line. When held at the correct angle this scribed line, known as the 'spring line', should remain vertical.

It is also advisable to plane a piece of wood somewhat longer than the actual length required, since you will lose much of the planed piece when cutting miters for the corners, and also because it is difficult to plane the extreme ends of a piece to an exact shape, resulting in a little of the length being lost there, too.

* For more information on particular moulding profiles, see chapter 15. For an in-depth discussion on the preparation and use of moulding planes, see *Traditional Woodworking Handtools*, chapter 25.

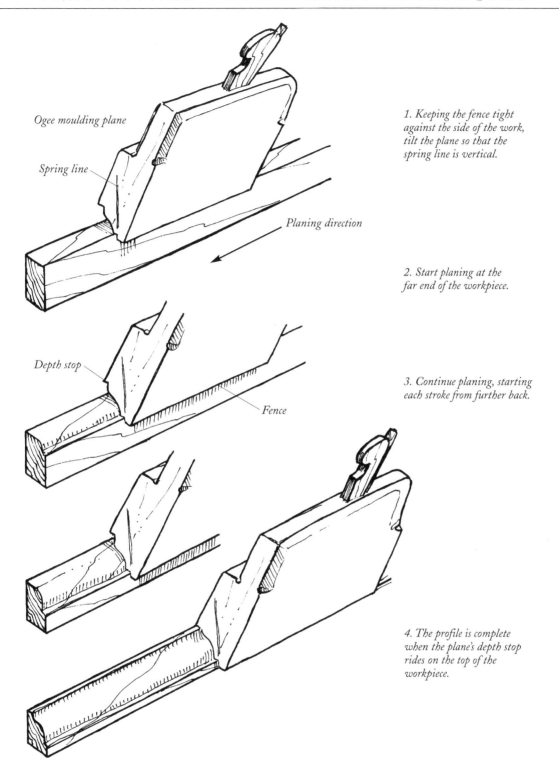

Ogee moulding plane

Spring line

Planing direction

Depth stop

Fence

1. Keeping the fence tight against the side of the work, tilt the plane so that the spring line is vertical.

2. Start planing at the far end of the workpiece.

3. Continue planing, starting each stroke from further back.

4. The profile is complete when the plane's depth stop rides on the top of the workpiece.

FIG. 115 PLANING A MOULDING

MITERING

WHEN SUFFICIENT LENGTH HAS BEEN PLANED, IT MAY BE CUT TO length. The corners of each piece should be mitered so that no end grain is visible. Rather than attempting to mark a miter line on each piece with a bevel set to 45°, or even by using a miter square, it will prove easier to mark the inside length of each piece (which, of course, will equal the outside length of the corresponding chest side), and use a miter box, sawing into the miter to avoid a ragged edge.

x = the outside measurement of the chest and the inside measurement of the moulding

FIG. 116 MEASURING THE PLINTH

Place the moulding at the back of the miter box and saw into the profile to avoid a ragged edge.

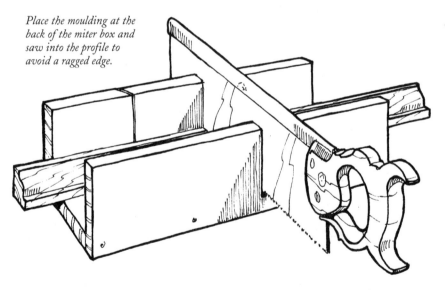

FIG. 117 MITERING

Be sure to cut on the waste side of the line when sawing the miters. Trim down to the line to make a perfect fit with a block plane and a donkey's ear miter shooting-board. This is a straightforward piece of equipment to make, and the only safe way to plane tall miters.

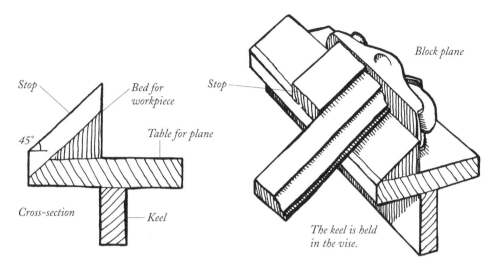

FIG. 118 DONKEY'S EAR MITER SHOOTING-BOARD

Cut the front piece first, and fix it with finishing nails. In this way, if the chest is slightly out of square, you will be able to adjust the side miters to fit, which is an easier business than vice-versa. The moulding may be cleaned up, if necessary, with a small rabbet plane, or wooden rubbers, according to the shape.

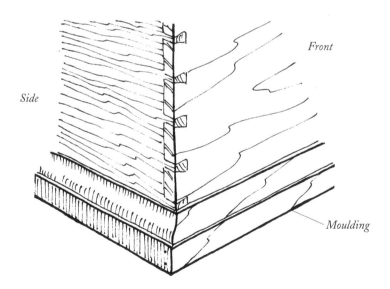

FIG. 119 FIXING MITERED PLINTH

All that now remains to be made is the chest lid. This should be sawed ½ in. longer than the chest is wide, for a little wood will be lost when the ends are planed smooth, and, moreover, a small overhang must be left so that the moulding going around the lid will clear the sides of the chest when the lid is opened and closed.

Not only should the lid be sawed somewhat longer than the chest is wide, it should also be made somewhat wider than the chest is deep. The reasons for this are the same, plus the fact that since wood shrinks most across the grain, should a softwood like pine have been used a certain amount of shrinkage is inevitable, so allow a good ½ in. more for the finished lid's width.

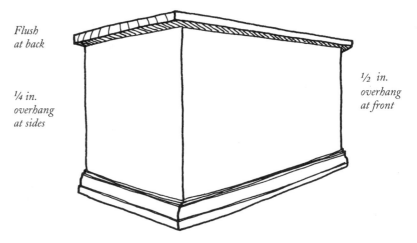

Flush at back

¼ in. overhang at sides

½ in. overhang at front

FIG. 120 SIZE OF LID

The moulding attached to the front and sides of the lid performs three functions: the side pieces prevent the lid from warping; the moulding as a whole forms a lip around the edge of the lid, thereby closing the chest more effectively; and if the moulded profile echoes the moulding of the plinth the chest will gain in coherence.

The lid moulding need be made from nothing larger than one-by-two, and, as just mentioned, looks most effective if given the same profile as the moulding used for the plinth. Miter and fit the pieces in the same manner as before, remembering that the side pieces are cut off flush with the back of the chest, since in order for the lid to open, the lid moulding, unlike the plinth moulding, does not go all the way around.

Note that a strip of moulding nailed long grain to the end grain of a wide top will eventually, if nailed securely enough, cause cracks in the top. This is because the top will shrink more across the grain than the moulding will shrink along the grain. If you would avoid this eventuality you must make allowance for the different rates of shrinking of the two pieces by fixing the moulding so that it can accommodate the greater movement of the top. One method of doing this is to fix the moulding beneath the lid (which will require the lid to be cut long enough to accommodate the width of two pieces of moulding), nailing or screwing the moulding securely at the front end, and allow the back end of the top to move relative to the moulding by slot-screwing the back end of the moulding. The process is illustrated in chapter 6. The top will remain flat and free from any checking should it indeed shrink, but you will, of course, see the end grain of the top.

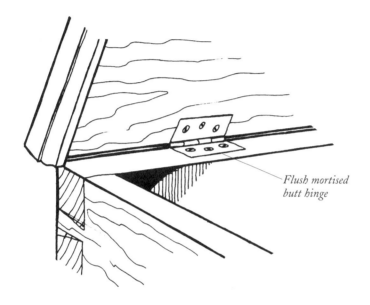

Flush mortised butt hinge

FIG. 121 RABBETED BUTT HINGE

The lid may be hinged in a variety of ways, including the use of outside decorative strap hinges, but the least obtrusive method is to use plain butt hinges rabbeted into the underside of the lid and into the top edge of the chest back.

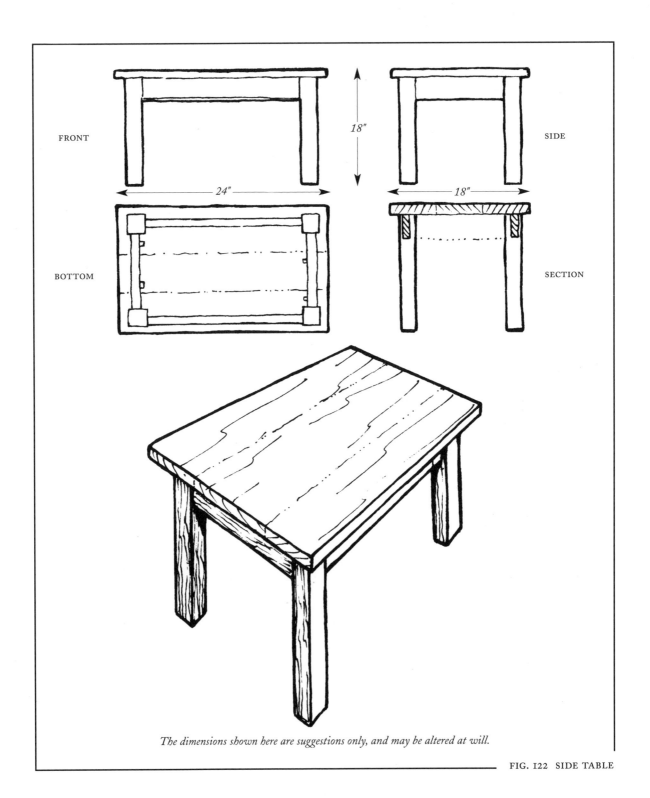

FRONT

SIDE

18"

24"

18"

BOTTOM

SECTION

The dimensions shown here are suggestions only, and may be altered at will.

FIG. 122 SIDE TABLE

5

SIDE TABLE

Legs • Aprons • Dowel Joints • Corner Blocks • Buttons

THE SIDE TABLE IS A SIMPLE SHAKER-STYLE PIECE, BEST MADE FROM CLEAR PINE AS WERE MANY SHAKER PIECES, ALTHOUGH OTHER WOODS SUCH AS CHERRY, MAPLE, AND birch were also commonly used. In common with many Shaker pieces, there is no carving, moulding, or other ornamentation involved in this table, but if carefully made and carefully finished it will be possessed of its own simple beauty and dignity.

As with the chest of the previous chapter, the dimensions given are merely suggestions and may be changed at your own discretion. The important thing is to understand the general construction, and, taking into account the stock from which the table is to be constructed, to adjust measurements where necessary to suit your own specific needs.

LEGS

ASSUMING THE TABLE TO STAND ABOUT EIGHTEEN INCHES HIGH, and the top to be about 2 ft. by 1 ft. 6 in. — good proportions for a side table intended for use by a bed, at the end of a couch, or even as a small coffee table — the legs will be best made from two-by-two clear pine. If all four legs are to be cut from the same length, square them up while they are still in one piece, thereby more easily guaranteeing uniformity. When the two-by-two is nicely squared and cleaned up, it may be sawed into four equal lengths of approximately 17 in.

Orient the legs so any distinctive grain pattern (figure) faces the same way on each leg. This is most noticeable on flat-sawn or quarter-sawn material. To produce legs with an even figure on all four sides, use rift-sawn material and orient each leg to face outwards. Mark the tops of the legs when sawed as shown in FIG. 123 so that you can maintain the chosen orientation.

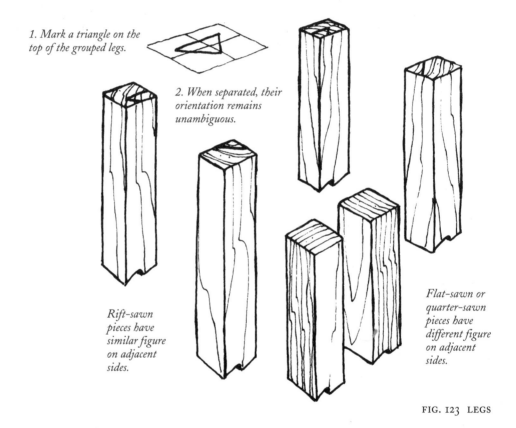

1. Mark a triangle on the top of the grouped legs.

2. When separated, their orientation remains unambiguous.

Rift-sawn pieces have similar figure on adjacent sides.

Flat-sawn or quarter-sawn pieces have different figure on adjacent sides.

FIG. 123 LEGS

APRONS

AFTER THE LEGS HAVE BEEN CUT, MAKE THE APRONS. THESE are horizontal rails — sometimes called the skirts or skirting (or, more properly in the case of older furniture, the frieze) — that connect the legs. The actual length and depth of these rails is a matter of personal preference, but as regards thickness, use five-quarter stock — wood that is nominally 1¼ in. thick. This will offer advantages when making for the first time the dowel joints that connect the aprons to the legs.

Once again, you may calculate the total length required and cut the pieces from a single board. As with the legs, it may be easier to prepare the aprons while they are still in one piece, according to the principles explained in chapters 1 and 2. If, indeed, all the aprons are made from one board, then when it has been planed square and true, and grooved to receive the buttons that will secure the top (see FIG. 136), cut it into the right lengths and mark the faces and top edges as shown in FIG. 124.

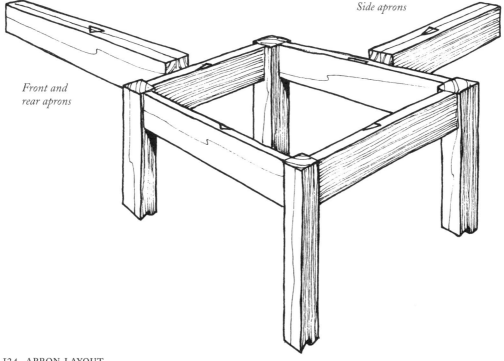

Side aprons

Front and rear aprons

FIG. 124   APRON LAYOUT

It is a very good idea to form the habit of systematically marking the various parts of any piece of furniture you may be building. It avoids the disappointment of finding that you have joined the wrong two parts, especially after having lavished all your care on a particular joint. It can be difficult to remember in the middle of a job precisely which face or edge of a piece you had earlier decided would look best facing outward or inward, and more than annoying to realize when it is too late that you had wanted that knot to be on the bottom, not on the top! But do not get carried away with the marking and be left with unreadable marks on finished surfaces. Try to make your marks on surfaces that eventually will be hidden. If this is impracticable, then take care to make the marks lightly. Chalk is usually preferable to pencil, since it can be removed more easily. There are various systems of marking, one of the more useful being the triangle system used in the previous two figures. This consists of drawing a triangle that covers several parts so that only when each part is correctly oriented will the triangle be complete. All the marks made so far on the piece in this chapter have been made on surfaces that will be completely hidden, and yet everything has been sufficiently indicated: the relationship of one piece to another, the upward facing surfaces and the outward facing surfaces.

Although some antiques may be cherished more if the craftsman's working marks are still to be seen, as, for example, when the lines scratched into the wood for marking dovetails remain visible, this should not be taken as a licence to be sloppy with your own layout marks. The object should not be to impress someone with the difficulties of making a piece, or even to demonstrate that it was, indeed, handmade, but to produce something beautiful.

DOWEL JOINTS

THE APRONS ARE JOINED TO THE LEGS WITH STRAIGHTFORWARD dowel joints. Everything that was said about dowels in chapter 4 remains applicable here. Since the surfaces to be joined must be perfectly square, trim the ends of the aprons (as in FIG. 24, chapter 1) after sawing them to length. Trim both ends of one piece first and then use this piece as an accurate pattern for the exact length of its opposite partner. Then trim the remaining two pieces in the same manner.

Mark the position of the dowel holes in the ends of the aprons using a trysquare and a marking gauge so that the holes are positioned in the center of the wood.

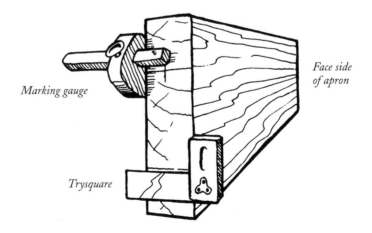

Marking gauge

Face side of apron

Trysquare

FIG. 125 LAYING OUT THE DOWEL POSITIONS

The top edge of each apron should be flush with the top of the legs, therefore these too must be cut perfectly flat, trimming if necessary on the shooting-board.

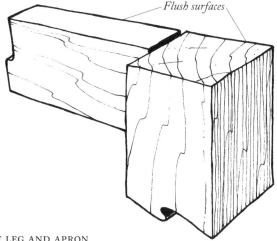

Flush surfaces

FIG. 126 TOP OF LEG AND APRON

It is, however, a matter of personal preference where the aprons join the leg laterally; that is, they may be flush with the front of the leg, flush with the back of the leg, or positioned anywhere in between.

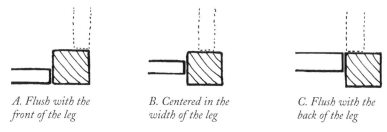

A. Flush with the front of the leg

B. Centered in the width of the leg

C. Flush with the back of the leg

FIG. 127 LATERAL POSITIONS OF APRONS

The aprons of most tables are set back at least a little from the front of the legs, and if indeed they are so joined as to be flush with the back, as at *C* in FIG. 127, then laying out the dowel holes in the legs will be made easier since these holes will then be exactly the same distance from the inside face of the leg as they will be from the inside face of the apron.

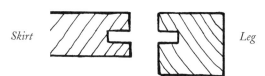

Skirt   *Leg*

FIG. 128 DOWEL LAYOUT

SIDE TABLE

Lay out the dowel holes in the ends of the long aprons only, and then use these marks to locate the matching dowel holes in the appropriate faces of the appropriate legs, as shown in FIG. 129.

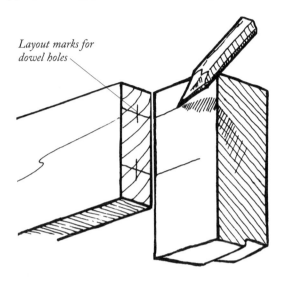

Layout marks for dowel holes

FIG. 129 TRANSFERRING DOWEL LAYOUT TO LEGS

If the marking gauge was used from the inside face of the apron, as shown in FIG. 125, then it may be used on the legs in the same manner,

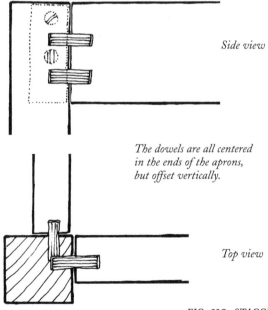

Side view

The dowels are all centered in the ends of the aprons, but offset vertically.

Top view

FIG. 130 STAGGERED DOWELS

since if the apron is to be flush with the inside face of the leg then the holes in both the leg and the apron will be the same distance from the inside, as shown above in FIG. 128.

The reason for first laying out the long aprons only, is that the short aprons must be laid out so that the dowels are staggered in relation to the holes in the long aprons, as shown in FIG. 130. If all the dowels were laid out at the same height, they would attempt to occupy the same space!

To repeat the caution mentioned earlier, if you do not use a doweling jig, exercise the utmost care when boring in order to ensure holes of uniform depth and reciprocal perpendicularity, as explained in chapter 4.

Make sure that the ends of the dowels are lightly rounded, and that every dowel is grooved to provide an escape channel for any excess glue. Lightly countersink the bored holes and then glue the dowels into the ends of the long aprons. Now glue the legs to these long aprons and clamp up the resultant pairs of legs.

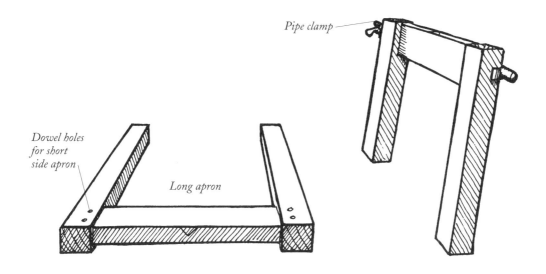

FIG. 131 LONG APRON ASSEMBLY

Next, glue dowels into the ends of the two remaining aprons, and then assemble both short aprons into one of the glued-up pairs of legs. Lastly, fit the other pair of legs onto the remaining ends, as shown overleaf, and then clamp the entire assembly, being careful not to rack the legs out of square.

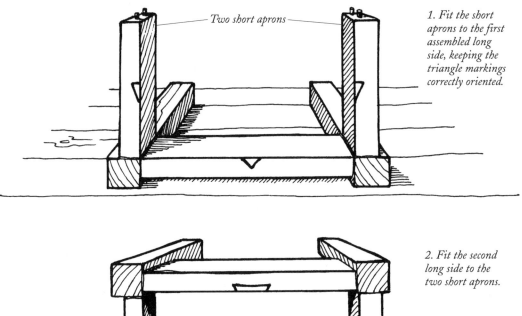

—— *Two short aprons* ——

1. Fit the short aprons to the first assembled long side, keeping the triangle markings correctly oriented.

2. Fit the second long side to the two short aprons.

FIG. 132 SHORT APRON ASSEMBLY

CORNER BLOCKS

A SMALL TABLE WHEN THUS JOINTED AND GLUED UP SHOULD BE sufficiently ſtrong, but larger tables, tables with more delicate legs, or tables designed to carry more weight may need additional support.

One way to provide this is to use a ſtronger joint, such as some form of mortise-and-tenon (see chapter 11), since these will take much more ſtrain before coming loose or breaking.

But whatever the joint, the use of corner blocks is well advised for larger pieces. Corner blocks are one or more additional pieces of wood inserted in the angle of the corner, designed to ſtrengthen the framework. They may be fashioned and fixed in a variety of ways depending on how the basic carcase or framework of the particular piece is conſtructed.

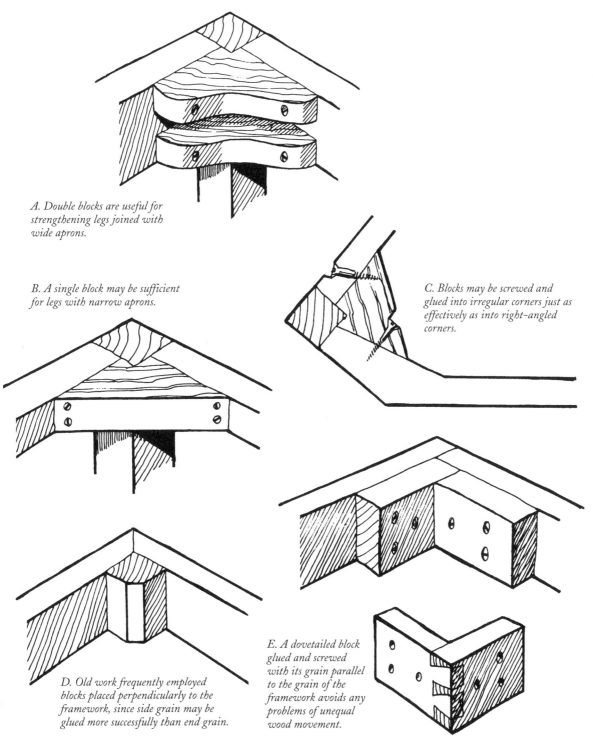

A. Double blocks are useful for strengthening legs joined with wide aprons.

B. A single block may be sufficient for legs with narrow aprons.

C. Blocks may be screwed and glued into irregular corners just as effectively as into right-angled corners.

D. Old work frequently employed blocks placed perpendicularly to the framework, since side grain may be glued more successfully than end grain.

E. A dovetailed block glued and screwed with its grain parallel to the grain of the framework avoids any problems of unequal wood movement.

FIG. 133 CORNER BLOCKS

When the legs have been assembled, it is time to think about the tabletop. If the table is small enough it is conceivable that the top may be made from a single board. It is more likely, however, that you will have to join two or more pieces together in order to obtain the required width. So far as proportions go, a top that is made from five-quarter material will look better with 2 in.-square legs than will a top made from material that is only 1 in. thick. Furthermore, a relatively small top made from five-quarter material will be less likely to cup than would a thinner top, although this difficulty could be overcome with the use of end cleats, such as will be discussed in chapter 6.

If you join several pieces together to form the top, remember that one of the cabinetmaker's biggest problems is movement, and that wood moves much more across the grain than with it. Therefore arrange the several boards comprising the top so that they run the length rather than the width of the table.

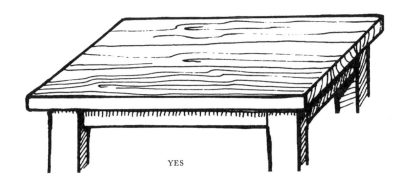

If the tabletop boards are oriented lengthwise, cross-grain movement — which is greater than long-grain movement — will be limited to the smallest dimension.

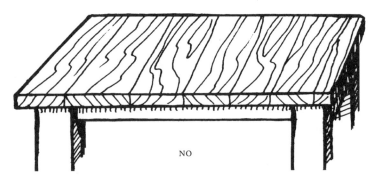

FIG. 134 TABLETOP ORIENTATION

The various boards may be joined with plain edge joints, as described in chapter 3, or, if you prefer, with dowel joints, as discussed in chapter 4. In either event, allow for a substantial overhang of the tabletop on all sides when cutting the boards, and remember to alternate the grain as illustrated in FIG. 70, chapter 3.

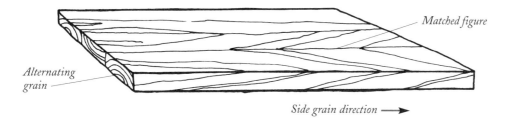

Matched figure

Alternating grain

Side grain direction ⟶

FIG. 135 OPTIMUM GRAIN ARRANGEMENT

When the boards have been jointed and glued together, plane the top and the sides. The process of doing this will demonstrate the virtue of careful arrangement when selecting the pieces to be joined. While it may have been useful to arrange the parts of the top so that the grain at the ends of the boards alternates, and while the figure (grain pattern) on the top surface should have influenced your choice in attempting to arrive at a pleasing design, you will now observe just how useful it can be to have arranged the boards so that the lengthwise grain runs in or out of the top surface in the same direction in all the pieces.

That all these conditions be met is, however, not always possible, and a compromise is often necessary. But bear in mind that this is the optimum arrangement, and your work will be made as easy as possible.

If, because of alternating grain on the top surface, it proves too difficult to obtain a smooth finish by planing, you may use a scraper, as explained in chapter 3. A scraper is most effective on close-grained hardwoods, but careful and judicious use of a well-sharpened scraper on troublesome pine can also yield good results.

BUTTONS

THE LAST OPERATION IS TO FIX THE TABLETOP TO THE BASE. Here again the main factor influencing how you do this is the inevitable expansion or contraction of the wood as it adjusts to any changes in the ambient moisture content. Because you cannot prevent any such movement without dire results such as cracks or burst joints, the top must not be rigidly fixed, since any movement would be opposed by the frame upon which it rests.

One way to fix the top securely yet allow for any movement is to use buttons. These are small pieces of wood screwed firmly to the underside of the top. They are made with a small projecting tongue that fits into a slightly larger groove cut towards the top edge of the inside of the aprons. Should the top move, the buttons slide in their grooves. The arrangement is illustrated overleaf in FIG. 137.

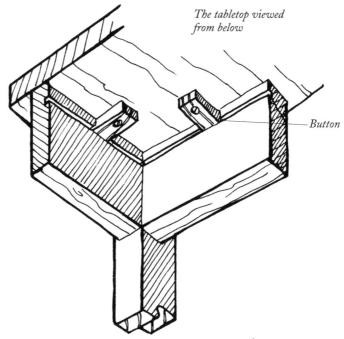

The tabletop viewed from below

Button

FIG. 136 BUTTON ARRANGEMENT

Buttons are best made from scrap pieces of hardwood, such as oak. They should be cut so that the grain runs into the tongue and not across it, otherwise the tongue will break off at the first strain. They need not be larger than a couple of inches, so be sure to pre-bore the screw holes, and be careful not to use screws longer than the combined thickness of button and tabletop.

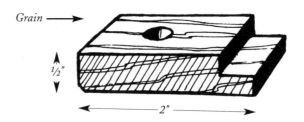

Grain

1/2"

2"

FIG. 137 BUTTON

As mentioned earlier, the grooves to receive the tongues of the buttons are most easily made before the aprons are sawed into separate pieces and assembled to the legs. But if they were not, make short grooves where necessary now.

Button grooves must be sufficiently far from the top edge of the aprons so that the button, when screwed tightly to the underside of the tabletop, pulls the top firmly down upon the aprons. But there must also be a slight gap between the end of the tongue and the groove in order to allow for movement if and when movement should occur.

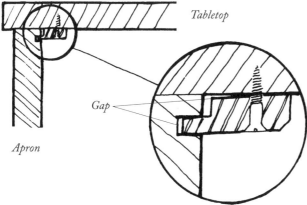

Tabletop

Gap

Apron

FIG. 138 MOVEMENT ALLOWANCE

The number of buttons required is dictated by the size of the tabletop. Use two in every corner, and if the distance between legs is much longer than 18 in., use additional buttons every 10 in. to 12 in.

Finally, make sure the whole table is nicely finished. Lightly sand all edges to relieve any sharpness, and chamfer the bottoms of the legs before fitting them with small metal furniture-glides. These provide the double function of protecting the bottoms of the legs from splintering and allowing the table to be moved easily, smoothly, and silently.

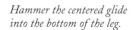

Hammer the centered glide into the bottom of the leg.

FIG. 139 METAL FURNITURE GLIDES

As for finishing, it is best not to leave a pine table raw or it will become quickly dirty and stained. You may apply some kind of varnish, shellac, milk paint, or even polyurethane, but for a beautiful and traditional finish, linseed oil is very acceptable, even though it may take a little longer to apply. Oil finishes should be rubbed in a little at a time, and polished thoroughly and energetically, over all surfaces. This both nourishes and protects the wood, and, to a certain extent, minimizes shrinkage. Linseed oil also turns pine to a most beautifully mellow shade of orange over a period of years, as inspection of any Shaker furniture made from pine will demonstrate.

There are two kinds of linseed oil generally available, raw and boiled. The boiled, being somewhat thinner in consistency, is somewhat more penetrating, and dries more quickly. In the long run, however, it may be just as effective to use raw linseed oil, perhaps applying the first coat thinned down with a little turpentine to effect a more immediate initial penetration. The oiling process should be repeated from time to time over the years, but beware of applying too much too often. It will simply build up and produce a sticky layer that will attract dirt, and you will have to scrape it down and begin again. The secret to a successful oil finish lies in repeated rubbing.

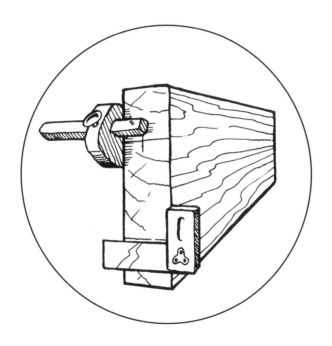

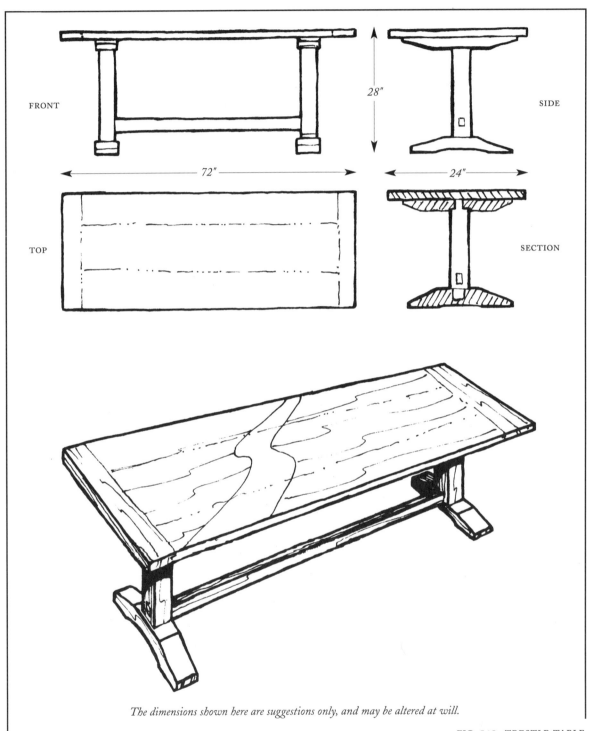

FRONT

SIDE

28"

TOP

SECTION

72"

24"

The dimensions shown here are suggestions only, and may be altered at will.

FIG. 140 TRESTLE TABLE

6

TRESTLE TABLE

Splined Joints • End Cleats • Bridle Joints • Blind Mortise-and-tenon Joints • Through Mortise-and-tenon Joints • Draw-boring

THE DESIGN OF THIS TABLE DERIVES FROM A TYPE KNOWN AS A TRESTLE REFECTORY TABLE. THE TRESTLES IN THIS CASE ARE THE LEGS, WHICH CONSIST OF A PAIR of shoes into which upright posts are set, the posts being connected by a horizontal stretcher. The term 'refectory' refers to the long narrow top, a form common since the Middle Ages. These tabletops were originally supported by a different form of trestle, from which they could be removed easily. Later, fixed legs connected by heavy stretchers, usually located near the floor, were added. Because this type of table was much used in monastery dining rooms, which were known as refectories, any long table, whether supported by four legs, medieval trestles, or the type of trestles used in this design, is now often called a refectory table.

Early refectory tables were typically made from various hardwoods such as oak or walnut. Centuries later, the Shakers became fond of this type of dining table, and theirs were often made from pine, although maple and birch were also used for the legs and stretchers. So feel free to use whatever wood you prefer. Of course, certain woods, having their own peculiar characteristics, are naturally better suited for particular jobs, and this is something that greatly concerns all woodworkers. But almost as important are availability and personal preference, proof of which may be found in the fact that over time furnituremakers have used all kinds of woods for all kinds of furniture.

You might consider the following points when choosing wood for this table: Pine is perhaps more easily worked than oak, since it is softer and lighter, although it requires really sharp tools. Precisely because it is softer, however, it does not wear as well as oak, and will dent and scratch more easily. On the other hand, although certain kinds of oak are more stable than pine, and therefore less likely to distort or shrink as much as pine, it is harder to prevent a piece of oak from moving than it is a piece of pine. Oak is more expensive than pine, but pine is generally more readily available. Also important is the fact that oak is often better seasoned . . . and so on and so on. Of course, if you just happen to have three or four old chestnut barn floorboards, none of the above will apply! The only thing to be really careful about is not to use pieces of wood that have radically different moisture contents, since this will exacerbate problems caused by uneven shrinking as the wood dries out.

A good height for a dining table is around 28 in., but there are plenty of examples of widely varying heights. Let the height of your table be a function of the chairs you intend to use and the size and comfort of the people likely to sit down to it. The dimensions of the top are even more changeable, and will depend on how many people you would like to seat, the size of the table's home, and the wood available from which to make it. An average width might be anything from 2 ft. to 4 ft.; the length could be as much as 20 ft. — there is a 20 ft.-long table made by the Shakers in the Henry Francis du Pont Winterthur Museum.

SPLINED JOINTS

SINCE THE SIZE OF THE TOP IS LIKELY TO BE THE MOST important consideration, start with the construction of this part. Choose your boards and true the edges to be joined, making your arrangements according to the principles outlined in previous chapters. Do not worry about the ends of the boards; these will be cut to the exact length after all

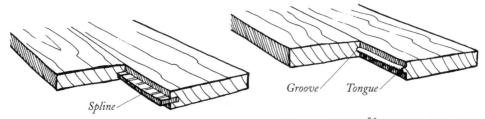

FIG. 141 SPLINE & TONGUE-AND-GROOVE JOINTS

the boards have been joined together. Assuming there are three boards to be joined to make up the required width, there will be two spline joints to be made. A spline joint is an improved tongue-and-groove joint, in which the tongue is made from a separate piece of wood.

A spline joint has several advantages over a tongue-and-groove joint: first, a hardwood spline is stronger than a softwood tongue formed on a softwood board; second, because the spline should be cut with the grain at right angles to the groove it sits in, it is less liable to break off; and third, using a spline to join two boards does not reduce the surface width of either board.

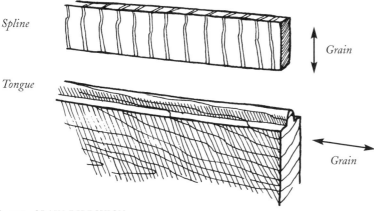

Spline

Tongue

Grain

Grain

FIG. 142 GRAIN DIRECTION

The proportions of the spline in relation to the boards to be joined are as follows: the thickness of the spline should be about a quarter to a third of the thickness of the boards to be joined, and its width should equal a little more than the thickness of the boards.

If the spline is too thin, it will not be strong enough; if it is too thick, it will make the sides of the groove into which it fits too weak, and they will be liable to break off. The spline will cause a similar weakness in the sides of the groove if it is too wide, whereas if it is too narrow there will be insufficient gluing surface for a secure joint.

  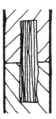 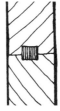 

Too thin   *Too thick*   *Too high*   *Too small*   *Perfect!*

FIG. 143 SPLINE SIZES

TRESTLE TABLE

Bearing all this in mind, work a groove in the appropriate edges of the boards to be joined. If your preferred tool is a plough plane, take care to work with the fence bearing firmly against the face side of each board in order that the groove may be in the same position should there be any variation in thicknesses. The same is true if using machinery to make the groove, such as a router, a shaper, or a circular saw; the wood should always be worked from the face side.

The spline, as mentioned before, should be of hardwood, with the grain at right angles to its length. However, in order to obtain longer lengths of spline, you may cut at 45° across the grain. This will still give the spline sufficient strength but will waste less wood.

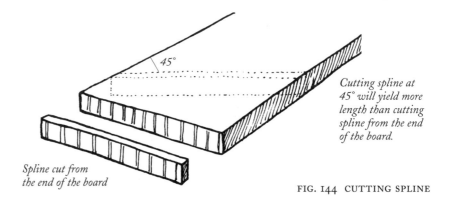

45°

Cutting spline at 45° will yield more length than cutting spline from the end of the board.

Spline cut from the end of the board

FIG. 144 CUTTING SPLINE

Do not make the spline more than hand tight in the groove. If it must be pounded in with a mallet it will ultimately cause the wood on either side to split out, and thus weaken the joint. There should also be a little space between the spline and the bottom of the groove, or the two boards will not come together when glued.

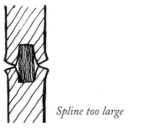

Spline too large

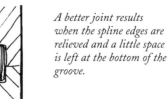

A better joint results when the spline edges are relieved and a little space is left at the bottom of the groove.

FIG. 145 SPLINE DETAILS

When the grooves have been cut and enough spline made, lightly round the edges of the spline and prepare for gluing. If your table is overly long it will be better if you have an assistant to help at this stage. Support one board in the vise and run glue into the groove. Then insert the spline, which should also be lightly glued, and tap it home. Finally, after gluing the groove of the next board, fit it over the spline and clamp the two boards together, alternating the clamps from side to side.

If you have three boards to join, glue and clamp all three together at the same time. Set the joined boards to one side and wait for the glue to set, ideally overnight. If you have arrived at the gluing-up stage early in the day and do not want to quit, then you may proceed with work on the trestle. For clarity's sake, however, the instructions for this job will be completed before beginning another, but you should feel free to plan your schedule to suit yourself. Providing you do not become confused, there is no particular virtue in undertaking only one operation at a time.

END CLEATS

WHEN THE CLAMPS HAVE BEEN REMOVED FROM THE JOINED boards it is time to make the cleats. A cleat is a piece of wood whose grain runs perpendicularly to the grain of the board to which it is attached in order to prevent the latter from warping. When cleats are attached at the end, rather than under (or on top of) other boards, they are known as 'breadboarding' and serve the additional function of hiding the end grain.

The end cleats may be similarly joined to the tabletop with spline joints, which, if neatly cut, provide an interesting detail at the sides.

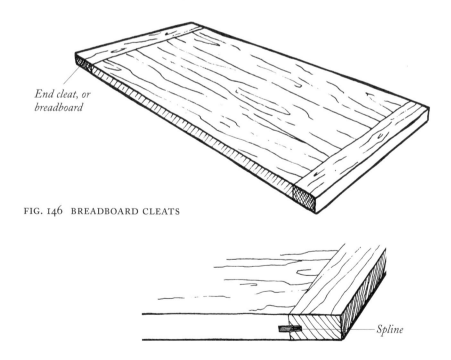

End cleat, or
breadboard

FIG. 146 BREADBOARD CLEATS

Spline

FIG. 147 SPLINED CLEAT

When cutting the ends of the tabletop, include the width of the end cleats in computing the total length of the top. First make sure the end edges are perfectly square, and then, working in from each side so as not to split the corners, cut grooves in both ends of the table. Cut a matching groove in the inside edges of the end cleats. Make sufficient spline to fit, and glue up as before.

Since the spline should be a little smaller than the groove, and since the ends of the spline between the cleats and the tabletop are exposed, there is a little detail which may be made to fill this space. Before fitting the spline, make a sawcut in the middle as shown in FIG. 148. When the spline and cleat are fitted together, insert a short and slim wedge into this cut; in this way there will be no unsightly gaps at the bottoms of the grooves.

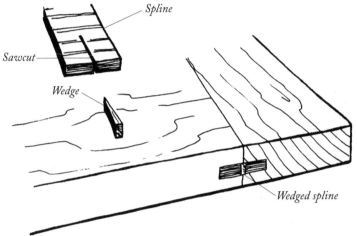

FIG. 148 WEDGING END-CLEAT SPLINE

When fitting the cleats it is unlikely that you will have clamps long enough to reach from one end of the table to the other, so the method of clamping is as follows: fix two pieces of wood to the floor at either end of the tabletop and use wedges, as shown in FIG. 149, to clamp the cleats tightly to the top.

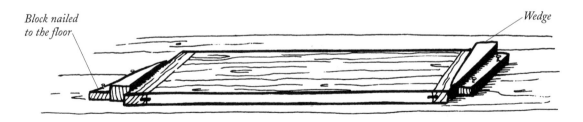

FIG. 149 CLAMPING END CLEATS

The legs consist of three parts: a top rail, bridle-jointed into an upright, which, in turn, is mortised into a shoe.

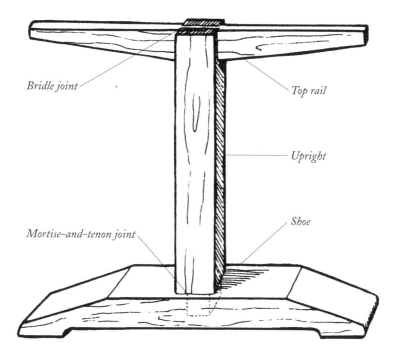

Bridle joint

Top rail

Upright

Mortise-and-tenon joint

Shoe

FIG. 150 LEG

Saw out the shoes to the pattern indicated below. The sloping cuts, if marked out carefully, should present little problem, but the relieved center portion of the bottom of the shoes, necessary to produce a more stable base less liable to rock, will require a little more ingenuity. The relief need not be as great as indicated and may well be accomplished with two sawcuts, each starting at the end of the shoe and meeting in the center.

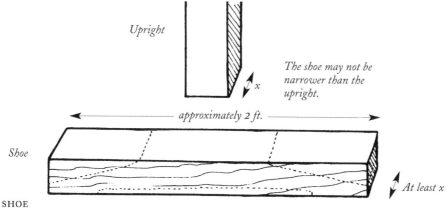

Upright

The shoe may not be narrower than the upright.

x

approximately 2 ft.

Shoe

At least x

FIG. 151 SHOE

TRESTLE TABLE

Cut out the rails according to the pattern indicated in FIG. 152.

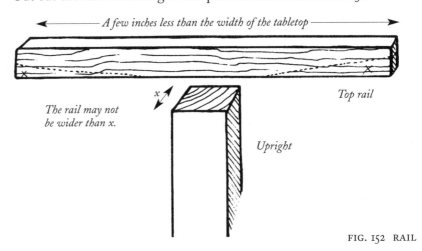

A few inches less than the width of the tabletop

The rail may not be wider than x.

Top rail

Upright

FIG. 152 RAIL

BRIDLE JOINTS

A DISASSEMBLED VIEW OF THE BRIDLE JOINT USED TO JOIN the top rails to the uprights is shown below. The stages involved in its making are illustrated in FIG. 154 and FIG. 155.

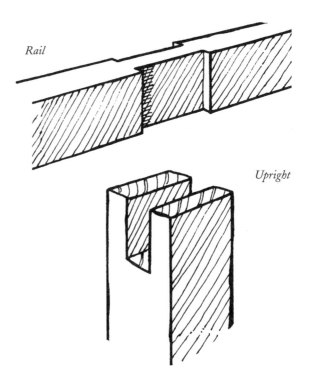

Rail

Upright

FIG. 153 BRIDLE JOINT

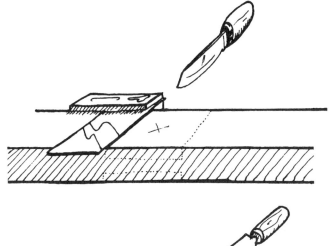

1. Lay out the joint so that its width equals the thickness of the upright, and so that the wood remaining in the center is a little more than a third of the rail's thickness.

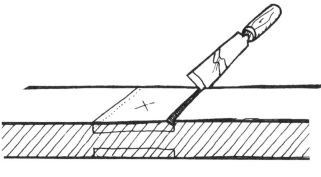

2. Deepen the layout lines with a chisel to provide a guide for the saw. Keep the outside vertical, making a sloping cut only on the waste side.

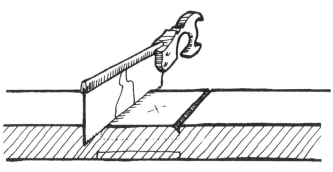

3. Saw down to the horizontal line. Additional cuts, made between the two outside cuts, will make waste removal easier.

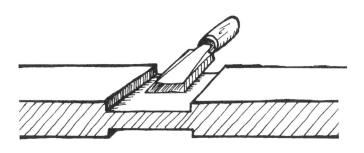

4. Remove the waste with a paring chisel.

FIG. 154 CUTTING THE RAIL

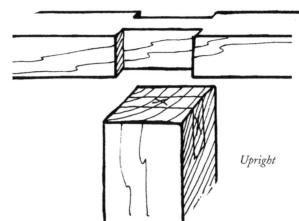

1. Mark the upright directly from the cut rail.

Upright

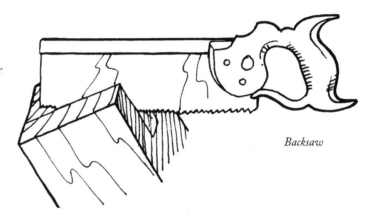

2. Saw on the waste side of the layout lines, tilting the workpiece so that the lines are visible as you saw!

Backsaw

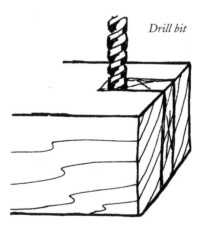

Drill bit

3. Bore a hole (as wide as the waste) at the bottom of the slot in the upright, and clean up the bottom corners with a chisel.

FIG. 155 CUTTING THE UPRIGHT

When both bridle joints have both been cut and tried, and it is found that they fit nicely, disassemble them and lay the rails to one side, but not before having marked the parts using the triangle method so that you will know which rail fits which way into which upright. Later, when the shoes have been fitted, these joints will be glued and pinned with dowels.

BLIND MORTISE-AND-TENON JOINTS

IT IS NOW TIME TO JOIN THE BOTTOM OF THE UPRIGHT TO THE shoe with a simple mortise-and-tenon joint. The mortise-and-tenon joint is perhaps the most used of all woodworking joints, and its varieties and applications are extremely numerous (see chapters 11 and 12). Its main use, however, as here, is for joining two pieces of wood together at right angles. FIG. 156 illustrates and names the various parts of the joint.

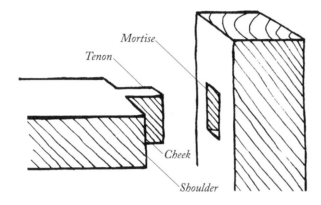

FIG. 156 A SIMPLE MORTISE-AND-TENON

There are two basic types of mortise-and-tenon joints: through and blind, shown overleaf in FIG. 157. The tenon of the through mortise-and-tenon joint passes completely through the piece of wood in which the mortise is cut, whereas the tenon of the blind type does not. Blind mortise-and-tenon joints whose tenons are especially short are properly known as stub mortise-and-tenons.

As well as providing an extra bearing surface, the shoulders of tenons also hide the edges of imperfectly cut mortises. For maximum strength, a tenon should be approximately one third the thickness of the wood from which it is cut. The size of the shoulders, therefore, which may extend around all four sides of the tenon if necessary, is governed by the size of the tenon. To make shoulders bigger than necessary only weakens the joint, but do not make them so small that they have no strength as bearing surfaces.

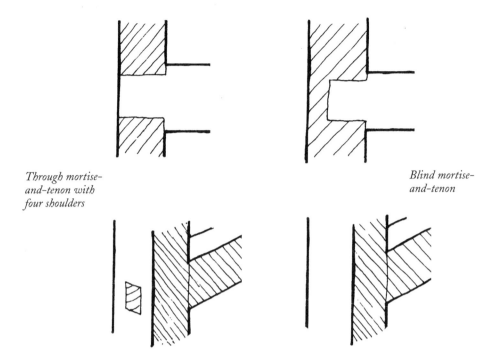

*Through mortise-
and-tenon with
four shoulders*

*Blind mortise-
and-tenon*

FIG. 157 THROUGH & BLIND JOINTS

The tenon of the joint required to join the upright to the shoe should ideally penetrate about two thirds of the way into the shoe. Figure this distance, and square around the bottom of the upright a corresponding measurement, as in FIG. 158.

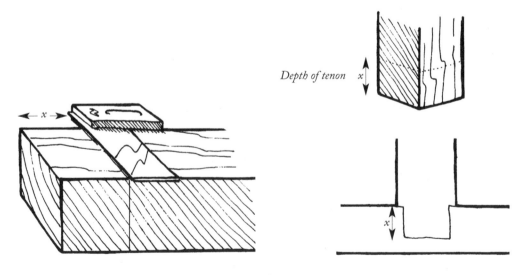

Depth of tenon x

FIG. 158 DEPTH OF TENON

Next, mark the outline of the tenon on the end of the upright and carry these lines up the sides to the previously drawn squared line, as in FIG. 159.

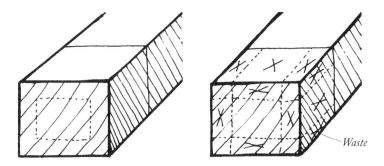

FIG. 159 SIDES OF TENON

Taking care to saw on the waste side of the lines (marked with crosses in FIG. 159), saw out the tenon with a backsaw (known as a tenon saw in Britain). Be especially careful not to saw beyond the lines marking the shoulders of the tenon. You can always remove a little more wood with a chisel, but it is more difficult to replace wood that should not have been removed.

Now use the tenon to mark out the mortise on the top of the shoe.

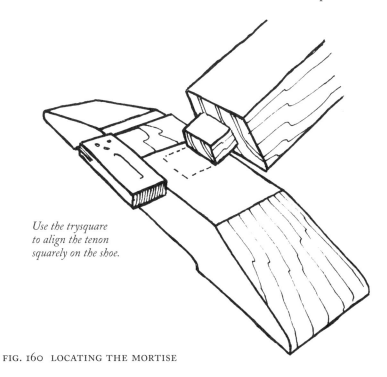

Use the trysquare to align the tenon squarely on the shoe.

FIG. 160 LOCATING THE MORTISE

TRESTLE TABLE

Use a square and a marking gauge to ensure that the sides of the proposed mortise are centered and at right angles on the shoe, otherwise the upright, when fitted, may be twisted in relation to the shoe.

FIG. 161 MORTISE LAYOUT IN SHOE

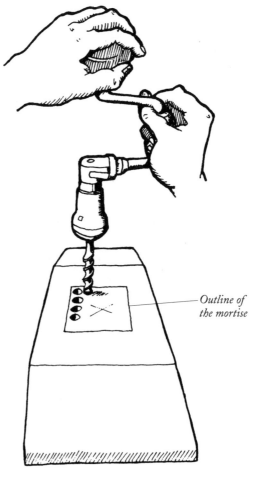

Outline of the mortise

FIG. 162 REMOVING WASTE IN MORTISE

Remove as much of the mortise as possible by boring. Remember to wrap a piece of tape around the auger bit to serve as a depth indicator, and then clean up the sides with a chisel. The mortise should be excavated just slightly deeper than the tenon is long, since the joint is to be draw-bored when pinned.

Before attempting to test-fit the two parts of the joint, relieve the extreme corners of the tenon with a chisel. The fit should be tight enough to require the very light assistance of a mallet, for a loose joint obviously has no strength, but neither should it be too tight or there is the danger that the sides of the mortise might split.

THROUGH MORTISE-AND-TENON JOINTS

AFTER BOTH BRIDLE JOINTS AND BOTH BLIND MORTISE-AND-TENON joints have been made to satisfaction, it will be time to fit the stretcher. Although the position of the stretcher may vary from being right underneath the tabletop to as low to the ground as the uprights will permit, it will perhaps be structurally strongest if it is located a little below the middle of the uprights. Having first determined the length of the stretcher, which will be a function of the length of the table (see FIG. 164), disassemble the uprights from the shoes and the rails, and join the stretcher to the uprights with through mortise-and-tenon joints.

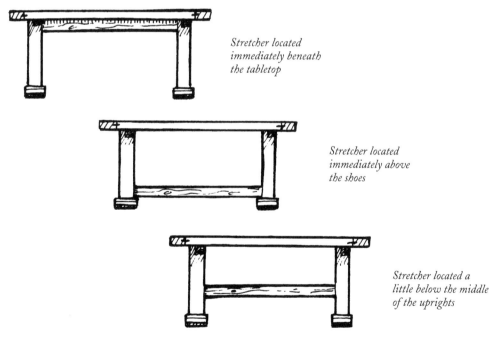

Stretcher located immediately beneath the tabletop

Stretcher located immediately above the shoes

Stretcher located a little below the middle of the uprights

FIG. 163 STRETCHER LOCATIONS

TRESTLE TABLE

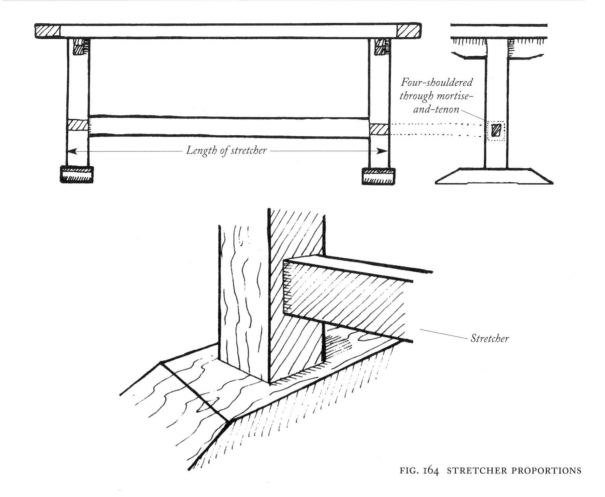

Four-shouldered through mortise-and-tenon

Length of stretcher

Stretcher

FIG. 164 STRETCHER PROPORTIONS

The tenon of the stretcher is marked in the same way as was the tenon of the upright, except that, since it will normally not be seen, it is not absolutely necessary to cut a shoulder on the underside of the stretcher as shown. Note, however, that the length of the tenon must equal the width of the upright it is to penetrate. Indeed, it will help if you cut the tenon a little longer, because then you will be able to plane the projecting end flush with the outside of the upright, which is a better thing to do than to be left with a slightly recessed tenon end.

Lay out the mortise similarly to the shoe mortise, but carry the lines completely around the upright, so that the mortise can be excavated from both sides. If all the work was done from the inside, the wood on the outside would surely split. It should therefore be obvious that you must be very careful when marking, in order that your lines may coincide. It is a little like boring a tunnel through a mountain from both sides at once: not only must the two ends meet in the middle, but also they must be perfectly aligned.

It is usual to wedge through-tenons in the manner illustrated in FIG. 165, especially when joining relatively thin pieces of wood. However, since we are dealing here with more massive pieces, which, moreover, are to draw-bored, the sheer bulk of the joint, if neatly cut, should provide sufficient strength.

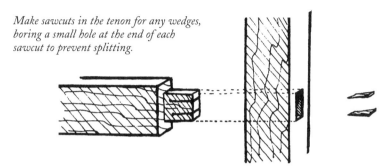

Make sawcuts in the tenon for any wedges, boring a small hole at the end of each sawcut to prevent splitting.

FIG. 165 WEDGED TENON

DRAW-BORING

WHEN ALL THE JOINTS HAVE BEEN MADE, IT IS TIME TO ASSEMBLE the completed trestle. The joints are secured using a technique known as 'draw-boring', which uses pins made from dowels of suitable size.

Draw-boring serves the double function of locking the joint and pulling the tenon right into the mortise. Start with the shoes and then the rails, after which the tops of the uprights may have to be trimmed down in order to make them flush with the tops of the rails, and finally the stretcher. To begin, bore a hole the size of the dowel to be used right through the mortise close to the point where the tenon enters. In order to prevent any splitting it may help temporarily to insert a piece of scrap in

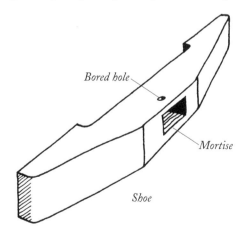

Bored hole

Mortise

Shoe

FIG. 166 DOWEL HOLE IN MORTISE

TRESTLE TABLE

the mortise, and also to clamp a piece of scrap underneath the mortise where the bit will exit.

Next, insert the tenon completely into the mortise and, using a twist bit inserted through the hole you just bored, mark the tenon. Now remove the tenon and through it bore a hole the same size as the one you bored through the mortise, but bore it slightly nearer the shoulder than the mark that was made by the twist bit. When the tenon is reinserted into the mortise and a dowel is knocked through the hole, the effect of the slight misalignment will be to draw the tenon further into the mortise.

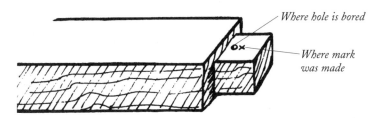

Where hole is bored

Where mark was made

FIG. 167 DOWEL HOLE IN TENON

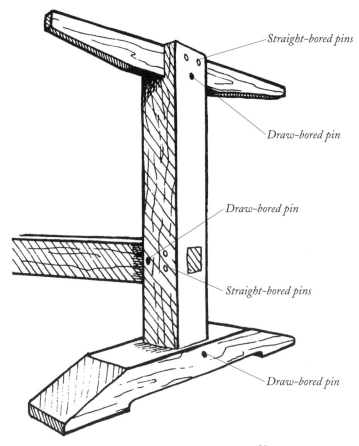

Straight-bored pins

Draw-bored pin

Draw-bored pin

Straight-bored pins

Draw-bored pin

FIG. 168 PINS SECURING JOINTS

In order to get the dowel to pass through, you will have to point the end slightly. Therefore do not cut the dowel to the exact length before driving it home. Use a piece longer than will be necessary and trim it off after it is in place. Furthermore, when draw-boring a blind mortise-and-tenon there must of necessity be a little space at the bottom of the mortise into which the tenon may be drawn. This does not apply to through mortise-and-tenons, nor will it apply to the bridle joints. One pin should be sufficient in the shoe. However, after having fixed the rail and the stretcher with one draw-bored pin each, you will add further stability to the piece by straight-boring two additional holes in a triangular pattern as shown in FIG. 168.

All that now remains is to affix the top. This may be done either by screwing up from underneath through the rails, using a technique known as slot-screwing (explained in greater detail in the following chapter), or by means of the button method explained in the previous chapter. Both methods allow for eventual shrinkage or expansion of the top caused by changing moisture content.

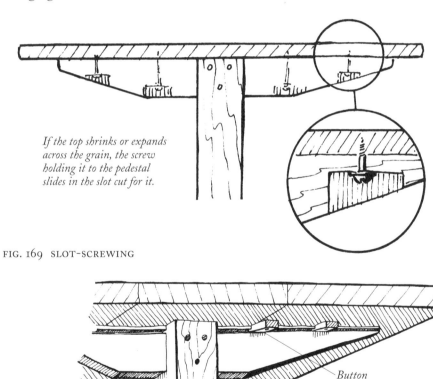

If the top shrinks or expands across the grain, the screw holding it to the pedestal slides in the slot cut for it.

FIG. 169   SLOT-SCREWING

Button

FIG. 170   BUTTONS

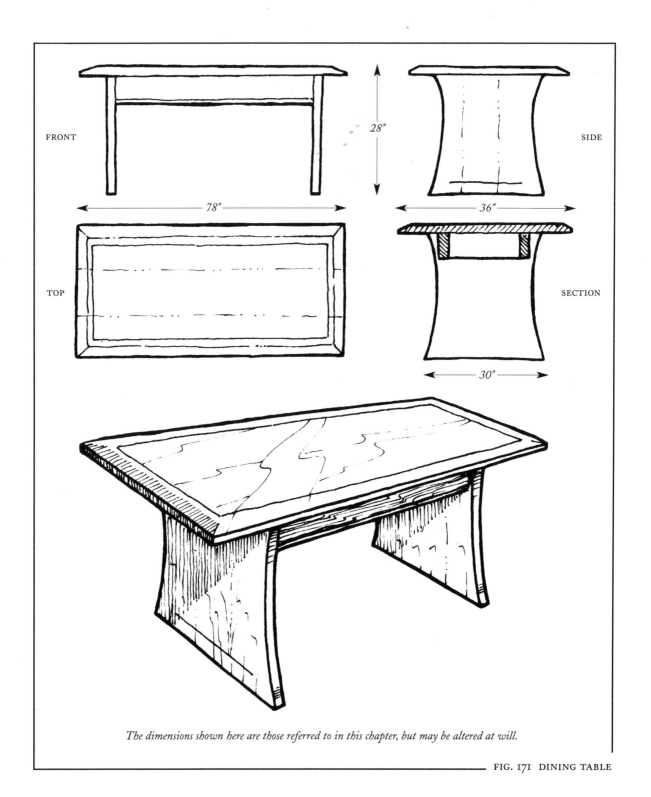

FRONT

28"

SIDE

78"

36"

TOP

SECTION

30"

The dimensions shown here are those referred to in this chapter, but may be altered at will.

FIG. 171 DINING TABLE

7

DINING TABLE

Stringing • Compass-planing • Beveling • Lapped Dovetail Joints • Beading • Slot-screwing • Penetrating Oil Finish

THE DINING TABLE MAY APPEAR TO BE A MUCH SIMPLER CONSTRUCTION THAN THE TRESTLE TABLE OF CHAPTER SIX, BUT THE ELEGANCE WHICH IS THE RESULT OF SUCH apparent simplicity demands greater attention to detail and more careful work than has been necessary up to now, and its construction may be thought of as the first exercise in high-style furniture perfection — or at least, attempted perfection.

The elegance of this table is achieved largely by the shapes and proportions of the three main elements that comprise the table: the top and the two end-supporting pieces. The interesting techniques required in its construction — the beading of the side rails, the beveling and stringing of the top, and the compass-planing of the sides — produce understated elements whose importance only becomes apparent when you begin to explain exactly why the table has such a sophisticated air.

Of course, the choice of material and its finish play a large part in giving the table its distinctive high-toned character. Although the chairs used at this table can play a large part in establishing the tone of the table, the very simplicity of the overall design makes it suitable for use with a wide range of styles, and similarly enables it to feel at home with a wide range of decors and different styles of interior decoration.

Since almost all the joinery for this table is exposed it must be executed as neatly and as finely as possible. Any carelessness will be glaringly obvious. Having already had a certain amount of practice with previous projects, edge-joining a number of boards should not prove too difficult. More important and more interesting is what boards you join. The basic simplicity of the design makes the use of highly figured wood such as the walnut originally used for this table eminently suitable, for the figure will neither detract from nor clash with any other design elements. Consequently, use the figure of the wood to advantage when arranging those boards which form the top and ends. That a certain amount of joining will, indeed, be necessary is inevitable given today's lumber supplies, but providing you choose with some idea of a particular effect in mind — such as alternating light and dark, or emphasizing any vertical flame patterns for the ends — this can work to your advantage.

Having chosen your boards, mill them flat and straight and join them using the method of your choice. This can be by using simple rubbed glue joints, dowel joints (as explained in chapter 4), splined edge joints (as explained in chapter 6), or even biscuits and a plate joiner. Whatever your preferred method, you need to produce three large slabs (see FIG. 172): a top, measuring a little more than 6 ft. 6 in. long by 36 in. wide, and two ends, each measuring a little more than 28 in. high by 30 in. wide.

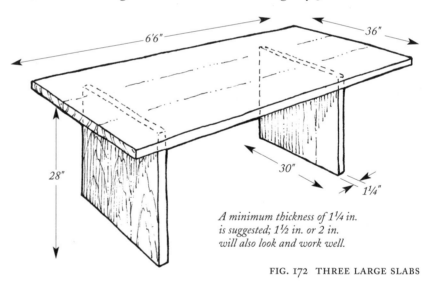

A minimum thickness of 1¼ in. is suggested; 1½ in. or 2 in. will also look and work well.

FIG. 172 THREE LARGE SLABS

The 'little more' is to allow you now to saw and plane the ends of all three pieces perfectly square. Should you decide to cut the ends with a circular saw rather than by hand, run it against a fence clamped to the work. A precaution worth taking when using a circular saw in this way is to apply a strip of masking tape to the top surface of the cut. This helps to prevent any splintering, and so guarantees a clean-edged cut.

The next step is to plane or otherwise surface the faces of the three parts as flat and as smooth as possible. Figured wood will look best if planed or scraped rather than being sanded; the grain will have more clarity if the fibers are cleanly sheared off rather than being abraded and bent over, and the wood will have more depth and more reflectivity.

STRINGING

THE FIRST OF THE SMALL DETAILS DISTINGUISHING THIS TABLE consists of stringing. This is most easily made from ⅛ in. ebonized inlay strips, readily available from a number of suppliers in 3 ft. lengths, and is laid in grooves cut the same width, but just a little shallower. These grooves may be made with a variety of tools, including special veining cutters, simple scratch stocks, or even wooden plough planes, but the simplest method is to use a small rotary tool with a router attachment. This will have an adjustable fence, and it is a simple matter to set the fence and the depth gauge so that the groove is cut approximately 2½ in. from the edge (see FIG. 173), and just a little shallower than the thickness of the stringing. Square up the corners and clean out the grooves with a chisel, and then squeeze a bead of white or yellow glue into the groove. Cut strips of the inlay to length — using square butt joints where lengths

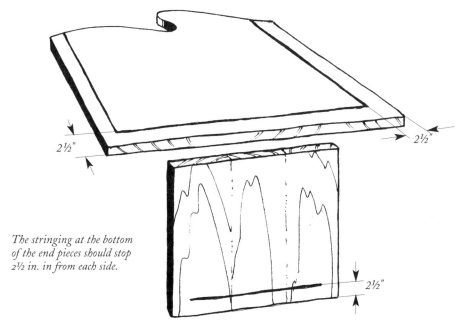

The stringing at the bottom of the end pieces should stop 2½ in. in from each side.

FIG. 173 STRINGING LAYOUT

DINING TABLE

meet along the straight, and mitering the pieces at the corners — and then press them in with a hard rubber or wooden roller. Wipe away any excess glue that may have been squeezed out, and allow it to dry thoroughly before planing or sanding flat. If impatience gets the better of you, and you do not wait long enough, the inlay may end up below the surface of the table when the glue does finally dry and evaporating moisture has caused the inlay to shrink.

COMPASS-PLANING

WITH THIS IN MIND, IT IS A GOOD IDEA AT THIS POINT TO LAY the top aside and focus on the end pieces. These should be similarly surfaced or planed as flat and smooth as possible, and then be marked out for the curvature of the sides. The curve is actually quite shallow, being no greater than 2 in. deep at its deepest point, but in order for the ends to give a feeling of lift to the top and balance at the bottom, this point is located only 9 in. from the top. With the help of clamps or an assistant, position a thin strip of lath, or something else consistently pliable, so that a line may be drawn connecting the top and bottom of the sides with a mark 2 in. in from the side and 1 in. down from the top. Saw as closely to this line as possible, using a bow saw or a bandsaw, and then position the piece in the bench vise so that you can plane the sawed edge.

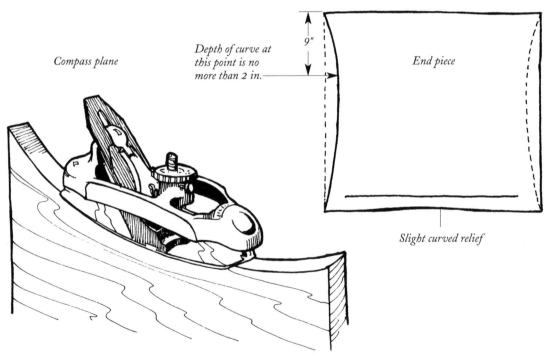

Compass plane

Depth of curve at this point is no more than 2 in.

9"

End piece

Slight curved relief

FIG. 174 SIDES

Compass planes, also called circular planes, have a number of peculiar characteristics, and no amount of reading will take the place of experience with your own particular tool. Nevertheless, a few general tips may be given: In order to avoid chattering, set the iron to take as thin a shaving as possible and make sure that the iron is firmly held against the bed by the capiron, further tightening the screw that holds this piece if necessary. Take extra care that the iron is very sharp and ground straight across — you need no crown on this plane's iron since it invariably overlaps the work, and it is impossible to work the plane at a skewed angle. Although the flexible soles of metal compass planes are designed to form even curves, in reality there is often a flat spot right at the mouth. Therefore resist the temptation to lower the blade, and increase the curvature of the sole instead when you find your iron will not reach the work.

This last point is, in fact, the most important technique to bear in mind when compass-planing: adjust the depth of the iron to take the finest shaving possible only once, but be prepared to adjust the curvature of the sole constantly as you remove more wood. In the case of the ends of this table, this is even truer, since the curve to be planed is irregular and cannot be planed in one pass and with a single setting of the sole. Adjust frequently, and work from different directions according to the changing direction of the grain.

Once you have planed all four curves (two on each end piece), complete the stringing with a stopped length that runs across the bottom outside face of each end, about 2½ in. up from the floor. The stringing is known as 'stopped' because it finishes 2 in. in from each side. The end of the stringing may be left round, shaping the inlay to fit the rounded end of the groove, or it may be squared up with a small chisel.

The final operation necessary to complete the sides is to relieve, very slightly, the center of the bottom so that in reality the end is standing on the ground only at its outside corners. Achieve this relief by compass-planing just enough to form a shallow curve. It should not be noticeable to the casual eye, but it will ensure a non-rocking table base should the floor be less than perfectly flat.

BEVELING

NOW BACK TO THE TOP: USE A PENCIL GAUGE TO MARK A LINE 1½ in. in from the edge on the top surface. It will help considerably if you also make a pencil line around the edge of the top to indicate the depth of the bevel. For a top that is 1¼ in. thick, a bevel that is ¼ in. deep will be very effective since it will leave a vertical edge that is both substantial and in proportion. Secure the top using handscrews or clamps to the top of the bench, and then plane the bevel, starting with the ends.

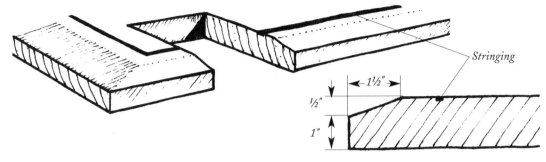

Stringing

1½"

½"

1"

FIG. 175 BEVEL

Although the top should be flat, clamping it to the bench with a few shavings placed under the center of the end will force a slight crown, just sufficient to allow you to plane right to the pencil line. If the top is even slightly cupped you will not be able to do this, and the resulting bevel will have a curved edge. It looks best if the bevel is very crisp and does not consist of a series of facets but rather is all in one plane, so each pass of the tool should be as complete as possible.

To prevent the ends from chipping, plane inwards from the sides. At the same time hold the plane severely skewed. In order to get maximum sole on the work, and yet maintain a skewed approach sufficient to produce a smooth cut, use the longest plane in your toolkit.

When both ends of the top have been beveled — and not before — plane the bevels on the sides of the top. There should be no difficulty in planing to both lines, or even in dealing with contrary grain (simply turn around and plane in the other direction), but the arris at the corners requires a lot of attention. An arris is the junction of two surfaces in different planes, in this case the side and end bevels. As you plane, watch that the outside end of the arris stops exactly at the corner of the table-top, and that the inside end finishes right where the two pencil lines marked on the top intersect (see FIG. 176). Furthermore, make sure that the arris is a straight line. It is all too easy to end up with a curved arris that wanders off the edge of the table completely missing the corner. Go slowly and make each pass of the plane count. If you should overplane the mark you will have to take more off the ends again.

When the bevels are planed to your satisfaction you may turn your attention to the leveling of the stringing. You can sand this flat if you want to, but there is an added advantage in planing: it helps in defining the top edge of the bevel. At this point you are ready for the final preparation of the top before applying the finish. While planing should have been sufficient you may want to touch up a few spots with a scraper, and perhaps also gently round every exterior edge with a gentle wipe of some 400-grit garnet paper.

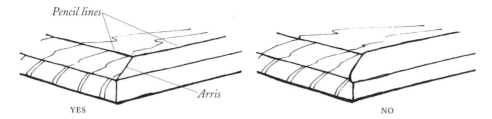

FIG. 176 ARRIS DETAILS

Finish the stringing and edges of the end pieces similarly to the top, and then stack all three pieces safely out of the way; it is time for the undercarriage.

The undercarriage is the structural heart of this table, and yet is the least apparent element in the design. All that is visible when the table is complete are the two relatively narrow sides.

Start by getting out four pieces, each measuring 3 in. deep by at least 1½ in. thick. The side pieces will be 46½ in. long, and the end pieces will be about 27¼ in. long. Any deeper, and people might have difficulty getting their legs under the table. Any shallower or any thinner and the support strength might be compromised.

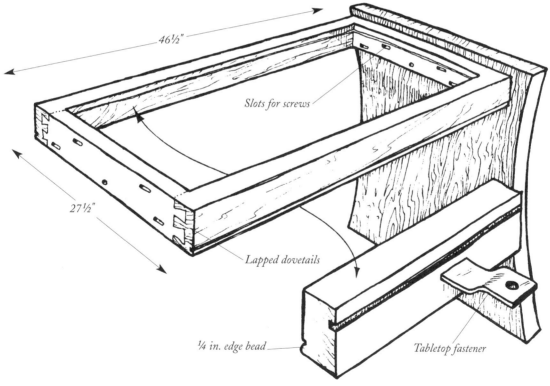

FIG. 177 UNDERCARRIAGE DETAILS

DINING TABLE

LAPPED DOVETAIL JOINTS

PLANE THESE FOUR PIECES TRUE AND SQUARE AND LAY OUT LAP dovetails so that the ends are dovetailed into the sides showing none of the joint on the sides (see FIG. 177). Even though none of this relatively complicated joinery will show, do not get sloppy. Simply because no one will ever see these lapped masterpieces do not think a few loose pins will not matter; you need all the strength a well-cut joint has to offer. The undercarriage provides both support and fixing for the top, as well as lateral stabilization. The pins and tails needed here are fairly substantial, so use your favorite technique to minimize the labor. For example, bore as much of the waste away as possible.

A ¼ in. groove is needed on the inside face of the undercarriage to take the table fasteners. Even though it will not show, take care to lay out the dovetail joint so that this groove, ¼ in. down from the top, runs into a pin cavity and not a tail.

BEADING

THE QUARTER-INCH BEAD THAT RUNS ALONG THE OUTSIDE BOTTOM edge of the side pieces has a dual purpose. Firstly, it softens the edge, presenting a more comfortable surface to a leg pressed up against it, as well as preventing an otherwise sharp corner from being damaged, and secondly, it provides an interesting line of shadow on an otherwise unmoulded piece. It is not immediately noticeable, but is always enjoyable when finally discovered. It is also fun to make. The best way is to use a wooden beading plane of the right size. A universal or combination plane will also do an excellent job, especially if you are lucky enough to possess the auxiliary beading shoe originally supplied with the complete tool. Lacking either of these tools, or any other special-purpose beading plane, you might use a router with a small veining bit and a fence set at ¼ in. As a last resort for the tool-poor you can always improvise a scratch stock, which is simply a piece of scraper steel filed to the shape of the quirk that defines the bead, and set in a wooden handle.

SLOT-SCREWING

BEFORE GLUING THE PIECES OF THE UNDERCARRIAGE TOGETHER, bore the slots for the screws that will hold the sides of the undercarriage to the end pieces. Make the bottom of the slots wide enough for the threaded part and shank of the screw to pass through, but narrow enough for the head to bear against. To guarantee that the head will not be pulled through the slot and to allow it to slide more easily it is usual to add a washer to the screw. If you countersink the slots so that the head of the screw is below the surface, the countersunk part of the slot will need to be wide enough for the washer. Five screws per end are enough. By not slotting the central screw any movement of the end pieces is forced to be equal at both sides. Use the biggest screws compatible with the thickness of the ends. The threads should engage only the end pieces; the shanks should slide in the slots.

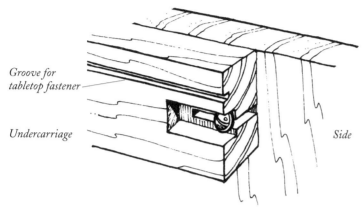

Groove for tabletop fastener

Undercarriage

Side

FIG. 178 SLOT-SCREWING DETAILS

After assembling the undercarriage, make sure that the ends of the long pieces are flush with the shorter side pieces, in order that the ends of the long pieces may butt up tightly to the table ends.

Now clamp the table ends to the ends of the undercarriage and install the screws through the slots. What is important here is to keep the tops of the ends flush with or fractionally below the top of the undercarriage, so that the tabletop will have a perfectly flat surface to sit on.

Making sure that the top is evenly centered on the assembled base is a matter of trial and error. Guess at first, then gently tap the top until the overhangs at each end and both sides are equal. Clamp the top to the undercarriage at this point, and use metal table fasteners to hold it down.

One of the advantages of this particular construction is that it is easily disassembled if necessary for transportation. If you mark the ends and the top with a number or letter punch, reassembly in the same order can be guaranteed.

PENETRATING OIL FINISH

THE SUCCESS OF THE FINISHING DEPENDS LARGELY ON THE CARE exercised in the preparation, but do not overlook the necessity of finishing all surfaces equally, especially the underside of the top. This will minimize

DINING TABLE

any tendency to warp, for any change in moisture content will be the same on both surfaces. One of the easiest treatments for a dining table is repeated thin applications of a penetrating oil like Watco™. Let each coat dry thoroughly before applying the next. Eventually a very durable gloss will build up that will withstand much water and alcohol. Should disaster strike, repairing this kind of finish is relatively easy, requiring only that the damaged area be rubbed with very fine steel wool moistened with a little more oil.

DINING TABLE

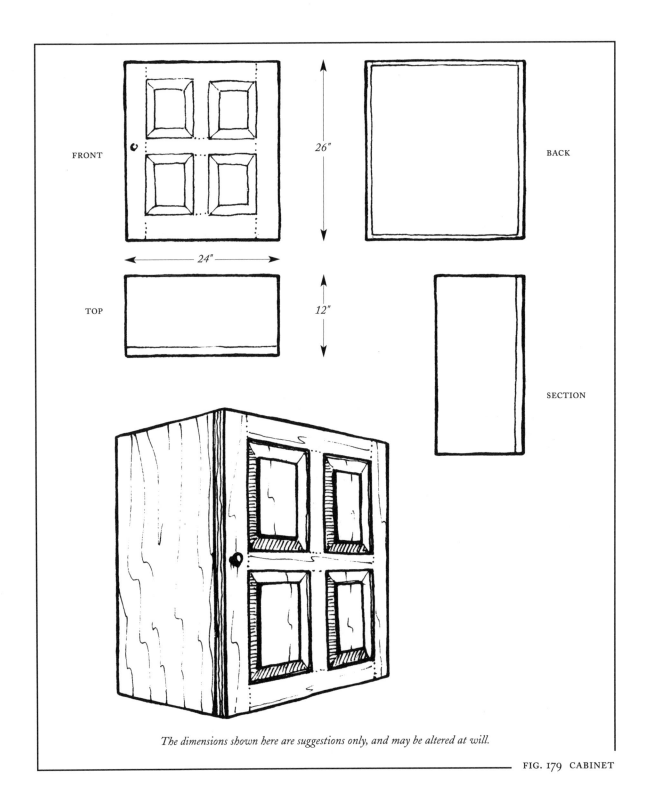

FRONT

BACK

26"

TOP

24"

12"

SECTION

The dimensions shown here are suggestions only, and may be altered at will.

FIG. 179 CABINET

8

CABINET

Carcase Joints • Lapped Dovetail Joints • Partitions & Shelves •
Panel Framework • Haunched Tenons • Fox-wedging • Paneling

THE CABINET IS INCLUDED AS A PRELIMINARY EXERCISE IN CARCASE CONSTRUCTION AND FRAME-AND-PANEL WORK, AND AS SUCH DEMONSTRATES FURTHER REFINEMENTS and uses of mortise-and-tenon joints and dovetail joints. If you build this essentially generic piece as described, you will be better able to appreciate the details and variations described in later chapters. As designed, this relatively small piece might serve as a useful wall-hung cabinet. More importantly, the experience will suggest endless variations for other designs of all sizes and applications.

Frame-and-panel construction involves a rigid frame that holds a panel. Since the panels, which constitute the majority of the width, are fitted without glue into grooves in the framework, and can therefore shrink or expand unrestrictedly, this is an ideal way to create a large area of woodwork that will retain both overall dimensional stability and planar stability. Frame-and-paneling also has the advantage of generally requiring only relatively small pieces of lumber for its construction, no matter how many panels may be involved. In fact, the more panels, and therefore the more pieces that form the frame, the greater is the planar stability.

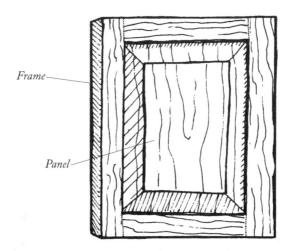

Frame

Panel

FIG. 180 BASIC FRAME & PANEL

A cabinet in its most basic form is simply a box with a door. It may range in size from a small article such as a bathroom wall cabinet to an exceedingly large piece of furniture such as an armoire. But large or small it is essentially a piece of storage furniture fitted with a vertical door as opposed to a horizontal lid. The construction described in this chapter may be applied to any cabinet other than a very small one — which by virtue of its size would not require as much strength in its joints — or a very large one — which, conversely, would require greater strength and a commensurately more complicated construction. Within these two

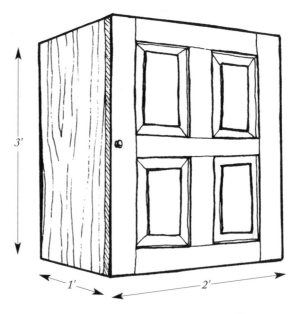

3'

1'

2'

FIG. 181 OVERALL DIMENSIONS

extremes a wide range of sizes is possible, but let us assume this cabinet will measure approximately 2 ft. wide by 3 ft. high by 1 ft. deep, as illustrated in FIG. 181.

CARCASE JOINTS

START BY BUILDING THE CARCASE, WHICH IS THE CASE OR BOX part of the cabinet. The simplest method might consist of nailed butt joints for the sides, top and bottom, as described in chapter 1. A more sophisticated and stronger way would be to join the parts with one of the methods illustrated below in FIG. 182, but arguably the best construction is to use the method illustrated overleaf in FIG. 183.

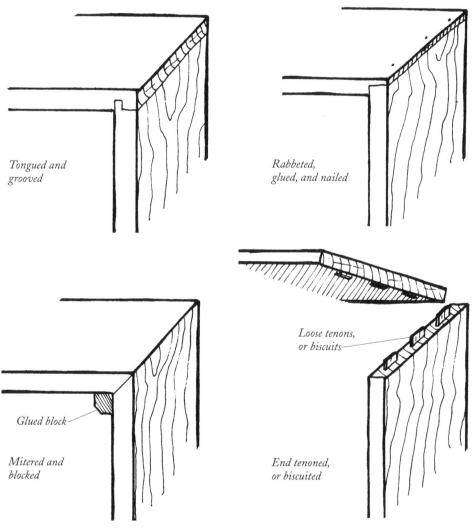

Tongued and grooved

Rabbeted, glued, and nailed

Loose tenons, or biscuits

Glued block

Mitered and blocked

End tenoned, or biscuited

FIG. 182 CARCASE JOINTS

CABINET

The tails are shorter than the thickness of the workpiece which forms the pins — resulting in a lapped, or blind, dovetail.

Tails

Pins

FIG. 183   LAPPED DOVETAILS

LAPPED DOVETAIL JOINTS

THE CHIEF ADVANTAGE OF USING LAPPED DOVETAILS IS THAT the sides are securely prevented from pulling loose or warping, while the joint itself is entirely concealed from the most visible side of the piece. For these reasons it is also one of the joints used in good drawer construction.

The sides of the cabinet may be prepared at once to the finished size of the carcase. The top and bottom pieces will be shorter than the finished width of the cabinet by the amount taken by the lap at each end. The lap itself should approximate a third of the thickness of the stock being used. Therefore, assuming ¾ in.-thick stock, the length of the top and bottom pieces of a 2 ft.-wide carcase will be 23¾ in.

Use the marking gauge as shown in FIG. 184 to mark the length and depth of the pins on the tops and bottoms of the sides. (If the lap equals a third of the thickness of the stock, the length of the pins will equal two thirds the thickness. The depth of the lap will equal the thickness of the stock.) But before continuing with the pins, cut out the dovetails as explained in chapter 4, but to the same length as the pins.

Now finish laying out the pins by positioning the finished dovetails on the ends of the relevant side piece, so that the ends of the dovetails are level with the previously scribed lap, and mark around them with an awl.

1. Scribe the line marking the lap on the ends of the sides.

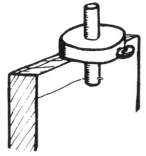

2. Scribe a line equal to the thickness of the stock on the inside of the ends of the sides.

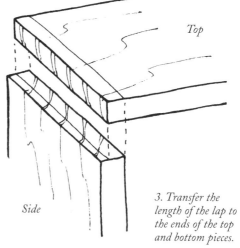

Top

Side

3. Transfer the length of the lap to the ends of the top and bottom pieces.

FIG. 184 PRELIMINARY LAYOUT

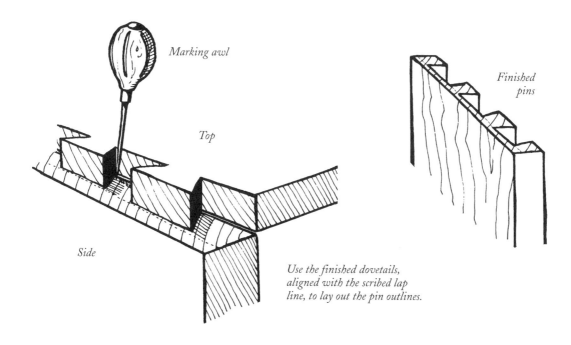

Marking awl

Top

Side

Finished pins

Use the finished dovetails, aligned with the scribed lap line, to lay out the pin outlines.

FIG. 185 MARKING THE PINS

Carry the lines you mark with the awl down the inside of the side piece as far as the depth line shown at *2*, FIG. 184, and, being careful not to saw past this line, saw away part of the waste as shown at *1*, FIG. 186. If a forstner bit is available you may bore away some more of the waste, as shown at *2*. Finally, the dovetails may be cleaned up with a chisel, as at *3*.

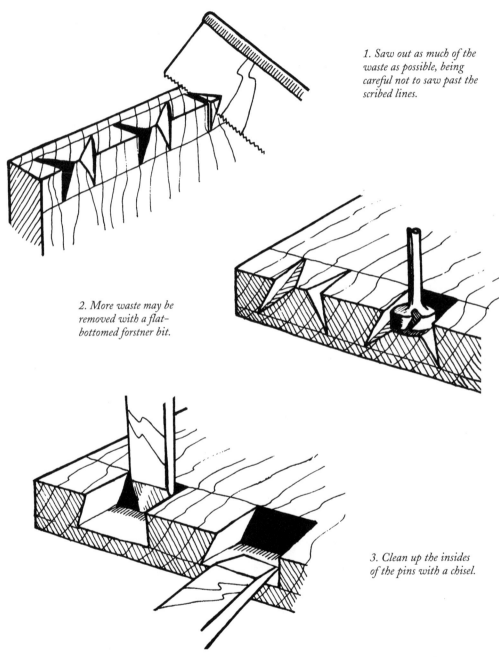

1. Saw out as much of the waste as possible, being careful not to saw past the scribed lines.

2. More waste may be removed with a flat-bottomed forstner bit.

3. Clean up the insides of the pins with a chisel.

FIG. 186 MARKING THE PINS

If the cabinet is to be wall-hung you may not need to provide a back, but if a back is desired you have two choices. The first is simply to nail on a ¼ in.-thick piece of luan plywood cut to the outside dimensions of the finished cabinet. The second and more elegant procedure is to make a paneled back similar to the paneled door. This paneled back may also be fixed onto the back of the cabinet just like the plywood, or perhaps set into a rabbet cut into the back of the cabinet, in the same way as was the back for the bookcase described in chapter 2. If you decide, however, to rabbet the back of the cabinet to receive either a paneled back or a plywood back, note that although a rabbet may be cut across the entire width of the top and bottom pieces of the cabinet, rabbets cut in the back of the sides must be stopped short of the ends by an amount equal to the thickness of the top and bottom pieces.

PARTITIONS & SHELVES

IF THE CABINET IS TO HAVE ANY INTERIOR PARTITIONS OR shelves, construct them as follows: Mortise-and-tenon upright partitions into the top and bottom pieces, and, for maximum strength, wedge the tenons as shown in FIG. 165, chapter 6. Note that the wedges not only secure the partitions, but also serve the additional function of pulling the top and the bottom together. House the shelves into the sides with any of the joints illustrated in FIG. 50, chapter 2, although the best method is to

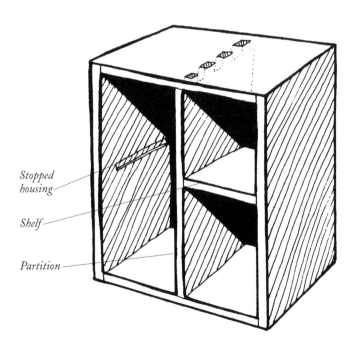

Stopped housing

Shelf

Partition

FIG. 187 PARTITIONS & SHELVES

CABINET

use a tapered and stopped dovetail housing. The tapered housing is easy to fit since it is not secure until pushed nearly all the way home, making it much easier to detect any tight spots.

Consider locating any partitions or shelves so that they coincide with any interior rails or muntins that might form part of a frame-and-panel back, and remember to reduce the depth of any such shelves or partitions by an amount equal to the thickness of any inset back.

When all the parts have been prepared and all the joints test-fitted dry, plane all surfaces clean and then assemble the case in the following order: first, glue together the vertical partition and the sides to the bottom piece, then glue and assemble the top piece, next glue and fit the shelves, and finally attach any back you may have made.

PANEL FRAMEWORK

THE OUTSIDE MEASUREMENTS OF THE DOOR FOR THIS PARTICULAR cabinet are the same as the outside measurements of the carcase itself. The door may consist of one or more panels, but no matter how many panels are incorporated into the design, the outer framework is always made the same way. The addition of extra panels merely entails the cutting of extra mortises in the outside framing members. The sides of the door panel are known as stiles, and the top and bottom pieces connecting them are called rails. Chapter 17 has much to say about the design of frame-and-paneling, but for this first exercise keep the design as simple as possible, attempting no more than four panels at most, as illustrated in FIG. 191, but preferably limiting yourself to one.

However many framing members there may be, cut them all to length, remembering to leave enough for tenons on the rails, and a little extra at the ends of the stiles so that they may be trimmed evenly to length after the frame is assembled, and then groove all interior edges into which the paneling will fit. Ideally, the panel groove will be as wide as the thickness of the tenons, which should be approximately a third of the thickness of the wood being used. Remember also that the mortises and tenons should align with the grooves.

HAUNCHED TENONS

THE RAILS ARE TENONED INTO THE STILES WITH BLIND TENONS. Because the insides of the framing members are grooved to receive the panel itself, the tenons must be made with a haunch to fill the extreme top and bottom of the grooves in the stiles.

A second very important point to remember when making this kind of framework is that when the groove is made on the inside of the rail, part

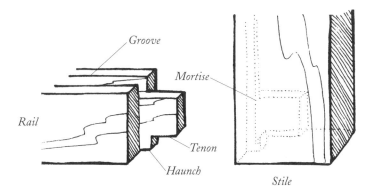

FIG. 188 HAUNCHED TENONS

of any tenon already made is also necessarily removed. Although some people like to cut the tenons firſt, this potential problem can be avoided if the rails are firſt grooved and then tenoned. The mortises are then laid out directly from the finished tenons.

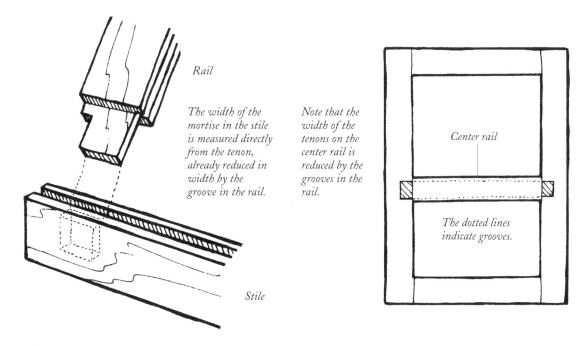

Rail

The width of the mortise in the stile is measured directly from the tenon, already reduced in width by the groove in the rail.

Note that the width of the tenons on the center rail is reduced by the grooves in the rail.

Stile

Center rail

The dotted lines indicate grooves.

FIG. 189 MORTISE LAYOUT   FIG. 190 CENTER-RAIL TENONS

Similarly, if there are to be two panels in the frame, then each side of the center rail's tenon will be reduced by the depth of a panel groove, and the corresponding mortise muſt be reduced commensurately.

If there are four or more panels, the same principle holds good for the the muntins (intermediate uprights) and the cutting of their mortises.

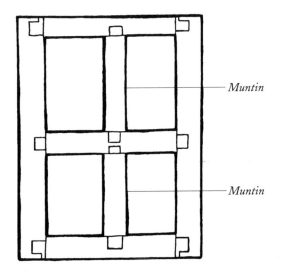

Muntin

Muntin

FIG. 191 TENON WIDTH OF FRAMING MEMBERS

It is generally easiest to cut the stiles first. Make them a little longer than the finished size so that there is 1 in. or so extra (known as a 'horn') at either end. This extra length makes it less likely that the ends will split out when and however the mortises are excavated, and is also useful when disassembling a dry test-fit. The extra length may be cut off and trimmed down to the rail with a block plane after the frame is finally glued.

Complete all layout and marking of the tenons first. Clamp opposite parts together in the vise, and square the required lines right across both pieces. This is both quicker and more accurate than marking one piece at a time. Remember that the tenon should be as thick as the groove, since its haunch must fit in the groove, and cut in the same plane. Both should be about one third the thickness of the wood being joined. If you mortise by hand, choose a mortise chisel that most nearly equals this measurement. For example, if you are working with ¾ in.-thick wood, you would ideally use a ¼ in. mortise chisel to make ¼ in. mortises in ¼ in. grooves. The mortises can be marked out directly from the completed tenons, and should be the same thickness as the grooves. This should all be apparent from studying FIGS. 188 and 189.

FOX-WEDGING

IN THE BEST CONSTRUCTION THE ENDS OF THE MORTISE ARE undercut a little so that wedges, inserted in the tenon and driven home as the tenon is inserted into the mortise, cause the tenon to spread and so become incapable of being removed. This kind of dovetailed mortise-and-tenon joint is known as a fox-wedged joint.

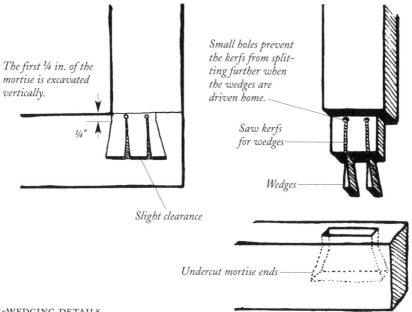

The first ¼ in. of the mortise is excavated vertically.

¼"

Slight clearance

Small holes prevent the kerfs from splitting further when the wedges are driven home.

Saw kerfs for wedges

Wedges

Undercut mortise ends

FIG. 192 FOX-WEDGING DETAILS

There are several points to bear in mind when making fox-wedged joints. Firstly, do not start undercutting the ends from the top of the mortise. By leaving ¼ in. or so of the mortise straight, the tenon will be held in the correct position when being clamped home. Secondly, take care not to cut the wedges too thick, too thin, or too long — or the faults illustrated in FIG. 193 will occur. Thirdly, bore a small hole at the end of each kerf made to receive a wedge in the tenon to prevent the possibility of the wedge causing the kerf to split farther back into the workpiece.

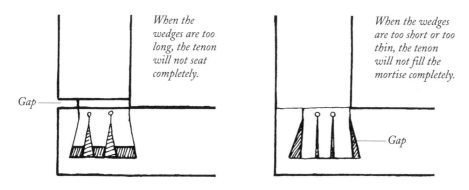

When the wedges are too long, the tenon will not seat completely.

Gap

When the wedges are too short or too thin, the tenon will not fill the mortise completely.

Gap

FIG. 193 FAULTY FOX-WEDGING

CABINET

When laying out tenons in narrow stock it is best to use a mortise gauge rather than a regular marking gauge, since the mortise gauge has two pins instead of one. Set these to the required thickness of the tenon, taking the measurement either from the mortise chisel or the groove, and then set the stock the required distance from the groove on the face of the wood, so that both sides of the tenon are accurately marked at once.

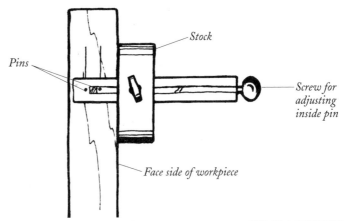

FIG. 194 MORTISE GAUGE

PANELING

THE SUCCESS OF FRAME-AND-PANEL WORK DEPENDS ON HOW well the panels fit: neither too tight nor too loose. The paneling must also be free to slide in the grooves holding it. This means that it must be made slightly smaller than a perfect fit, and never glued or otherwise fixed in place, except perhaps at its center. The grooves, while preventing the panel from warping or twisting, allow it to expand or contract without splitting or tearing apart.

If the panel is made of stock thicker than the grooves, then the edges of the panel must be reduced in order that they may fit in the grooves. This

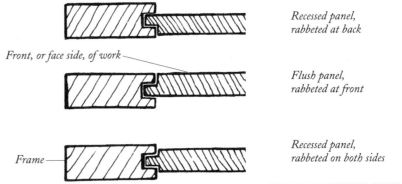

FIG. 195 RABBETED PANELS

may be achieved either by rabbeting the front, back, or both edges of the panel, or by tapering the edges, a process known as feathering.

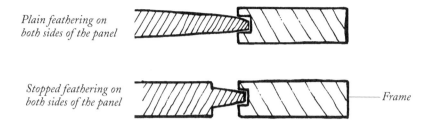

Plain feathering on both sides of the panel

Stopped feathering on both sides of the panel — Frame

FIG. 196 FEATHERED PANELS

Rabbets may be made as described in chapter 2. Feathering is similar to the process of making a raised panel as described in chapter 3. Here the process is simply repeated on both sides, care being taken to ensure that the edge of the panel is cut away equally on both sides — although it is of course possible to make a panel that is flat on one side if so desired.

Remember that a panel does not have to consist of a single board. Making panels from several pieces joined together with plain glued edge joints is a useful way of using up narrow scrap pieces.

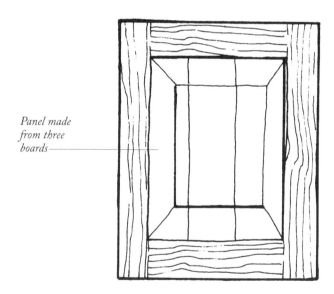

Panel made from three boards —

FIG. 197 COMPOSITE PANEL

It is, indeed, sometimes possible to make a virtue out of necessity by using differently figured or colored pieces to construct panels to form interesting designs.

FIG. 198 FIGURED PANEL

When all the paneling has been made and test-fitted to satisfaction, assemble the complete door as follows: If you have made a single-paneled door, first fix two rails into a stile, slide in the panel between them, and then fix the remaining stile. The joints may be simply glued and clamped, or pinned, or even draw-bored, this last being the strongest method. If there is more than one panel, as in FIG. 191, start by assembling the muntins to the rails, slide in the panels, and then fix the stiles. If you glue the joints, be careful not to get glue in the grooves where the panels will fit, for these should remain free to slide should they expand or contract.

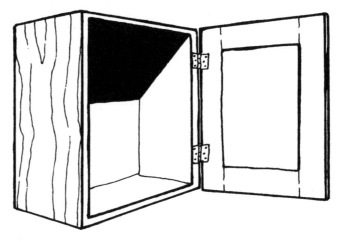

FIG. 199 HINGES

The door, when assembled, is hung on the carcase with plain butt hinges, rabbeted into the back of the stile from which you want the door to open, and into the front edge of the corresponding side of the cabinet.

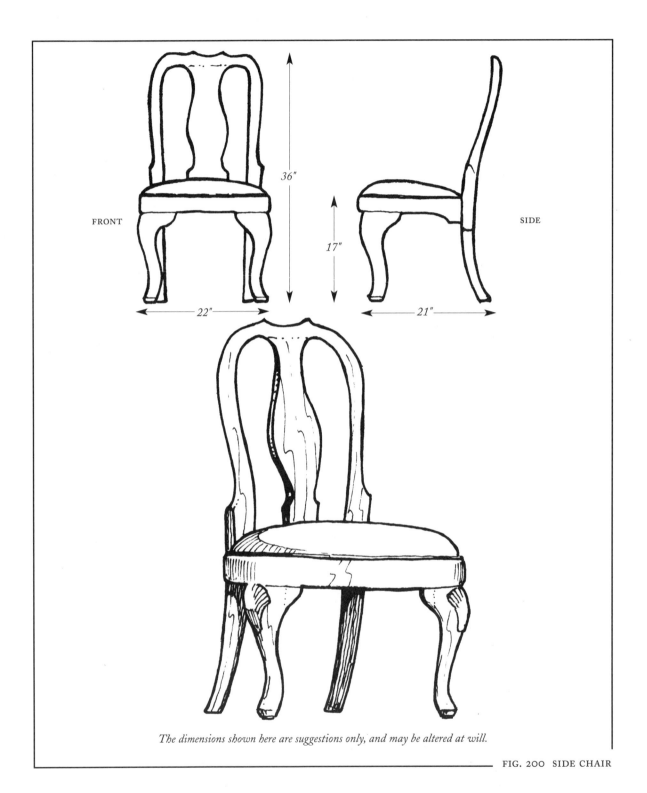

FRONT

SIDE

36"

17"

22"

21"

The dimensions shown here are suggestions only, and may be altered at will.

FIG. 200 SIDE CHAIR

9

SIDE CHAIR

Cabriole Legs • Templates • Spokeshaving • Splats •
Rail Joints • Ears & Corner Blocks • Feet

CHAIRS ARE WITHOUT DOUBT ONE OF THE MORE DIFFICULT PIECES OF FURNITURE TO MAKE, NOT ONLY BECAUSE THEY HAVE TO WITHSTAND MORE STRESSES THAN MOST OTHER pieces but also because they frequently contain many curved parts. The side chair with cabriole legs described here is therefore at the same time both an excellent introduction to the construction of non-rectilinear furniture as well as to furniture with special strength requirements.

The term 'cabriole' comes from a word meaning to leap, and it is because of the resemblance of this type of chair leg to the leg of a leaping animal that it is used to describe a form common throughout much of the 18th century.

The woods most used during this period were walnut and mahogany, and it is hard to dispute their suitability, though you may well experiment with other hardwoods. Remember that one of the advantages of hardwoods is that because of their greater strength they may be worked to finer proportions than softwoods.

The very best way to understand any piece of furniture, to grasp its form and function, and its design and construction, is to make a copy. So choose a simple model from the countless examples of this style of chair readily observable in homes, museums, antiques stores, as well as in a wealth of books, and use this chapter, which describes general principles, to learn how the relevant techniques are worked and may be applied to various designs.

The structure of most chairs of this type may be divided into three parts: the cabriole front legs; the back, which consists of the back support and back legs, joined by rails and a splat; and the seat, which is formed by the rails connecting the legs, and in which rests the upholstered seat itself. Of necessity these three parts are discussed separately and consecutively, but remember that in practice many operations may need to be performed in a different order. For instance, the front rail must be tenoned into the legs before the legs are cut to shape — which is, however, the first thing discussed here.

CABRIOLE LEGS

THE BEAUTY OF THE CABRIOLE LEG IS TO BE FOUND IN ITS proportions. Whatever strikes you as pleasing, elegant, and beautiful is what you should endeavor to emulate. That opinions can vary is shown by the fact that the shapes of cabriole legs can vary noticeably, depending on the period in which they were built.

Few people have a good enough eye to be able to draw the most felicitous shape completely by hand. Professional designers commonly rely on various proportional systems, ratios, and other paradigms to help them achieve graceful shapes. This aspect of furnituremaking, commonly referred to as 'the art and mystery of the craft', was one of the most important parts of the 18th century cabinetmaker's training. Chapters 17 and 19 contain detailed information on this process, but the following pointers will help you to form a good-looking cabriole leg: Keep the knee high and you will avoid making the leg appear bandy. Excessive shaping tends to create the same effect, so keep all lines as smooth and as flowing as possible. Taper the entire leg from knee to ankle, but note that the extent of this taper is often slight. Feel free to experiment, but finally do not hesitate to trace a curve that pleases you from a photgraph of an appropriate example.

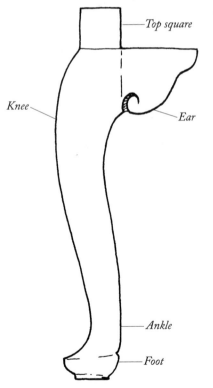

Top square

Knee

Ear

Ankle

Foot

FIG. 201 CABRIOLE LEG

The leg is typically cut from a 3 in. by 3 in. square of wood, although sometimes the design may be got from a slightly smaller piece. The design is drawn on two adjacent faces of the square and cut out with a bow saw or on a bandsaw as explained below.

TEMPLATES

SINCE THE FRONT LEGS SHOULD BE IDENTICAL, IT IS ADVISABLE to work up the shape you require on a template, and use the template to trace the design onto the squared stock.

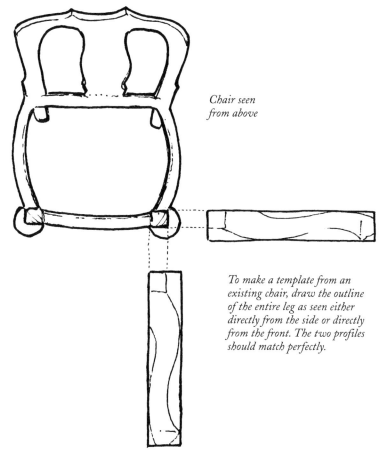

Chair seen from above

To make a template from an existing chair, draw the outline of the entire leg as seen either directly from the side or directly from the front. The two profiles should match perfectly.

FIG. 202 TEMPLATES

Either a thin piece of plywood or some other reasonably stiff but thin material is ideal for use as a template. Make your drawing on the template as carefully as possible, and aim for smooth curves. Note the relationship of the front of the foot to the front of the knee, and that of the hollow behind the knee to the size of the top square, and so on. When you have the outline drawn on the template to your satisfaction, cut it out, and then trace around the template on two adjacent faces of the square blank so that the knees are facing each other. If the grain of your square is at all pronounced it will look best if you orient the square as shown in FIG. 203.

Be sure to leave the square top part long enough, and lay out both legs at the same time to further guarantee that they match one another.

Orient a blank with diagonal end grain (to avoid having markedly different grain figure on adjacent sides) so that the side grain follows the curves of the leg as nearly as possible.

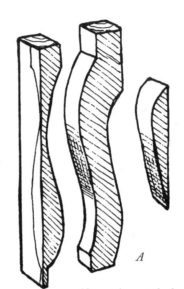

A

B

After cutting out the front profile, as at A, temporarily reattach the waste pieces, and then saw out the side profile to produce B.

FIG. 203 LEG LAYOUT

FIG. 204 SAWING BOTH PROFILES

Note that the ears (FIG. 201) are made from separate pieces, and are fitted after the rails are attached. Although they may be included on the template in order to aid the drawing of the whole leg, they cannot be cut from the same square of wood as the leg.

The next step is to cut out the design from the square. This is most easily done on a bandsaw, but lacking a bandsaw, a bow saw offers a much cheaper if somewhat slower alternative. Note that when the first profile is cut, the lines for the second profile are necessarily removed with the waste. Therefore, in order to cut the second side, you must now replace the waste pieces you have just removed, temporarily fixing them back where they came from with double-sided tape, small clamps, or even small nails. The small waste piece cut from behind the knee is not marked and does not contain any template lines, but is often very useful as the blank is held or manipulated while being cut, since it can provide a little extra support.

SPOKESHAVING

NOW THAT YOU HAVE A ROUGH BUT REGULARLY CURVED BLANK, you may continue the shaping and smoothing with a spokeshave. This will require turning the future leg this way and that, and the simplest way to secure the workpiece while shaping it is to clamp the top square of the leg in the jaws of a wooden handscrew and then clamp the handscrew in the bench vise, as shown below.

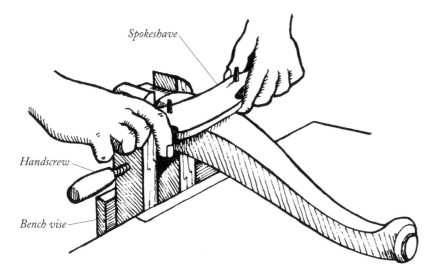

Spokeshave

Handscrew

Bench vise

FIG. 205 SHAPING WITH SPOKESHAVE

As you use the spokeshave, try to follow the grain as much as possible. Keep the shave's cutting edge as sharp as can be, and set the iron to take as fine a shaving as possible. Even if you have been able to utilize the grain direction of the square to best effect when laying out the leg, it is still likely that you will be obliged to turn the wood from end to end as you work, in order to avoid working against the grain.

The arrows indicate the direction in which the spokeshave should be used.

FIG. 206 CUTTING DIRECTION

Maintain a good overall view of the work as it progresses, and do not concentrate on only one area at a time. It is better to take a little from one side, and then a little from the other, gradually producing the desired shape from the whole piece.

As you work, take note of the differing cross-sections of the leg. At the ankle the leg is circular, whereas at the knee the leg is nearly square, with just the corners rounded. As soon as you have achieved the overall correct shape, use a file to adjust any flat or irregular spots. Finally, finish with a scraper and sandpaper. Needless to say, patience is the greatest virtue at this stage. Take an extra hour if need be, for the chair, if properly made, will last a long time, and as time passes you will regret ever more having stopped just a little too soon.

The next part to be discussed is the chair back. Although there are as many variations for backs as there are for legs, the basic construction invariably consists of two uprights and two rails. The uprights typically curve both backwards and inwards, and are joined by two rails, usually with mortise-and-tenon joints, but in cheaper construction dowels are sometimes used.

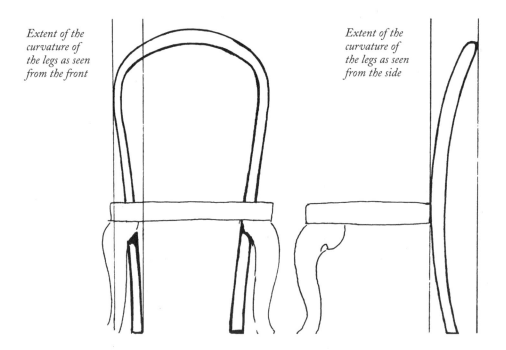

Extent of the curvature of the legs as seen from the front

Extent of the curvature of the legs as seen from the side

FIG. 207 CURVATURE OF BACK

The compound curvature of the back legs is worked in the same way as is that of the cabriole legs, being similarly set out and cut. When cutting and finishing these pieces, follow the same principles outlined earlier. Work the two legs together to minimize any differences that might occur if working one at a time.

Although the top rail may be designed to form a continuous line with the sides, it is usually mortised into the sides from above.

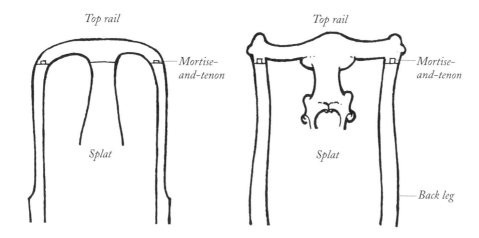

FIG. 208 TOP RAIL

In some designs this top rail may be made from a straight piece, but many examples exist where the top rail curves in two directions. If this is the case, then it too must be laid out using templates, as were the legs. But note that it is much easier to make mortises and tenons in square stock than in curved stock, so cut these joints after you have laid out the rail but before cutting it to shape.

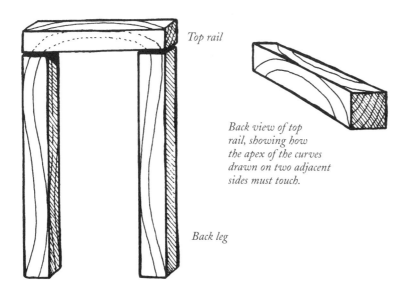

Back view of top rail, showing how the apex of the curves drawn on two adjacent sides must touch.

FIG. 209 BACK LEGS AND TOP RAIL LAYOUT

SIDE CHAIR

For the same reason, at the same time as the mortises for the tenons of the back legs are cut in the top rail, lay out and cut the mortise for the splat, which should similarly have been laid out but not cut to shape.

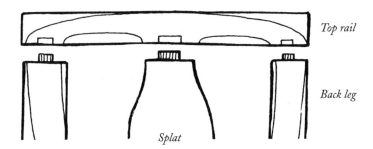

FIG. 210 SPLAT MORTISE IN TOP RAIL

SPLATS

THE SPLAT IS USUALLY MADE FROM STOCK CONSIDERABLY thinner than the legs. Early splats for these chairs were usually solid, with edges shaped to a simple vase-like profile. As the 18th century progressed the designs became more complicated, often involving fretted designs carved to give the effect of intertwining and overlapping strips. Keep your first splat simple, and concentrate more on neat joinery.

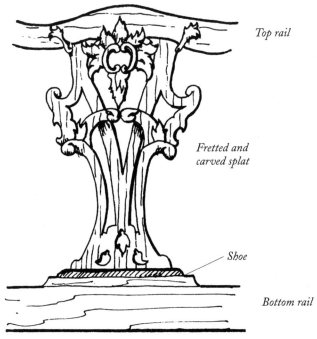

FIG. 211 SPLAT

The rear seat rail is tenoned into the back legs. It also receives the foot of the splat. The place where the splat enters the seat rail is therefore called the shoe. In the early 18th century this shoe consisted almost invariably of one or two separate pieces fixed to the top of the rail. Later on, however, it became increasingly common to make the shoe and the rail out of one piece of wood. So look carefully at the model you are copying to see which variety you have before you. But note that it is probably easiest to make the rail and the shoe out of one piece, thereby avoiding the problem of having to join the splat to the rail.

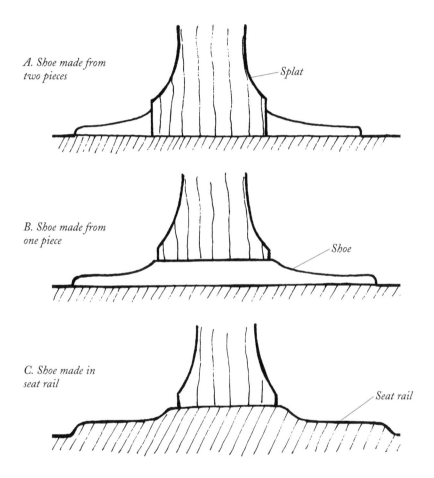

FIG. 212 SPLAT SHOES

Nevertheless, while you should feel free to adapt a design — for after all, it is precisely through adaptation that many new designs have evolved — try not to end up with a hotchpotch of unrelated features. The great majority of successful designs are usually surprisingly integrated and interdependent in their parts.

RAIL JOINTS

REGARDLESS OF WHETHER THE SIDE AND FRONT RAILS ARE curved or straight they will typically join the legs at an angle other than 90°, since the front rail is invariably wider than the back rail. Therefore, although the mortise-and-tenon is to be marked out in the same way as if it were a right-angled joint, you must use the adjustable bevel in conjunction with the trysquare when laying out the tenon. Unless the grain dictates otherwise, it is usually best to cut the tenon square to the rail and have all the angularity in the mortise.

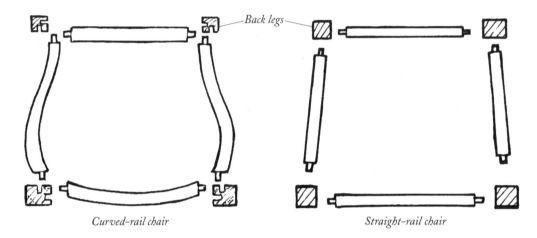

Back legs

Curved-rail chair

Straight-rail chair

FIG. 213   PLAN VIEW OF SEAT RAILS

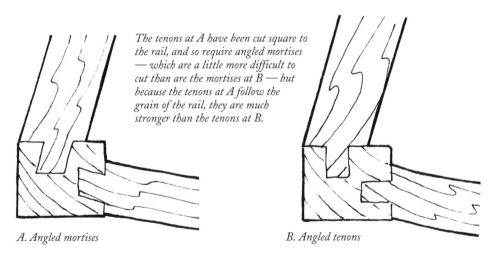

The tenons at A have been cut square to the rail, and so require angled mortises — which are a little more difficult to cut than are the mortises at B — but because the tenons at A follow the grain of the rail, they are much stronger than the tenons at B.

A. Angled mortises

B. Angled tenons

FIG. 214   ANGULARITY IN MORTISE

An additional technique for producing a stronger joint is to miter the ends of the tenons of adjacent rails. This allows them to be longer and so increases their gluing surface.

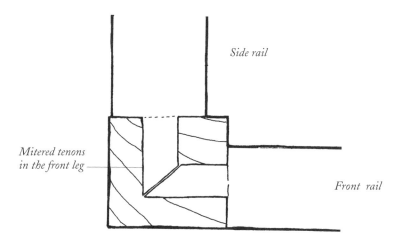

Side rail

Front rail

Mitered tenons in the front leg

FIG. 215 MITERED TENONS

Lengthened and mitered or not, the tenons of the rails should be pinned through from the outside of the leg for maximum strength.

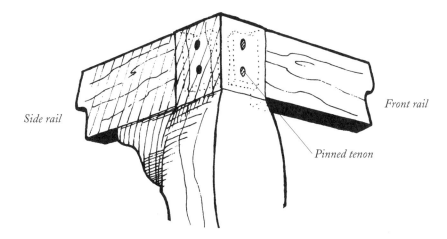

Side rail

Front rail

Pinned tenon

FIG. 216 PINNED TENONS

Yet another way to increase the length of the tenons, and so strengthen the joint even further, is to shift the alignment of the tenons from the middle of the rail towards the outside. There is, of course, a limit to the extent that this may be done without weakening the side of the mortise, but with care an appreciable increase in tenon length can be obtained, as shown below.

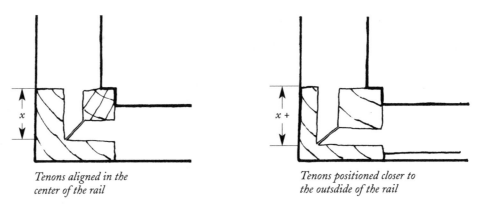

Tenons aligned in the center of the rail

Tenons positioned closer to the outsdide of the rail

FIG. 217 POSITION OF TENONS

However you form the tenons, the rails must be rabbeted to receive the drop-in upholstered seat *before* joining them to the legs. Usually only the front and side rails are thus rabbeted. The depth and extent of the rabbet naturally varies with the size of the seat to be inserted.

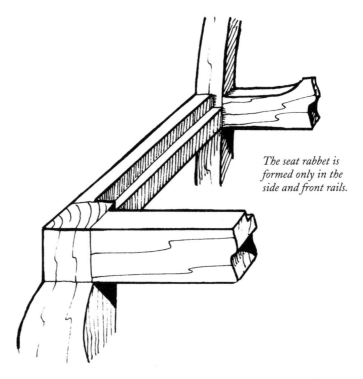

The seat rabbet is formed only in the side and front rails.

FIG. 218 SEAT RABBET

On the other hand, since any moulding worked in the outside top edge of the rails is usually continued around the outside top edges of the leg, it is generally more convenient to work this *after* the legs and rails are assembled.

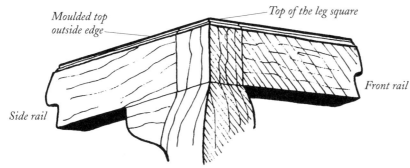

FIG. 219 RAIL MOULDING

One of the most noticeable characteristics of these chairs is their lack of stretchers or rungs connecting the legs. The ability of the legs to withstand the stresses and strains to which chairs are commonly subjected without the aid of such stretchers and rungs is made possible not only by the strength of the mortise-and-tenons as just described in conjunction with the sturdy width of the rails, but also by the use of ears and corner blocks.

EARS & CORNER BLOCKS

EARS ARE USUALLY MADE SO THAT THEY CONTINUE THE CURVE of the cabriole leg up to the bottom edge of the side rails. They are made

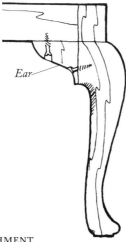

FIG. 220 EAR ATTACHMENT

from separate pieces, cut to match the legs, and glued in place. When the glue has set, much extra strength may be gained by screwing through the ear into the leg and the rail, as shown in FIG. 220.

By fixing the ears first, a larger surface is obtained for affixing corner blocks (see FIG. 133, chapter 5). When you make corner blocks, take care that they are no higher than the bottom edge of the rabbet on the inside of the rails, or the upholstered seat will not fit.

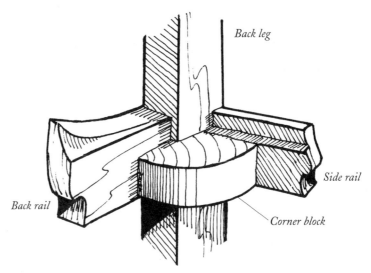

Back leg

Side rail

Back rail

Corner block

FIG. 221 CORNER BLOCK AT BACK LEG

Like the ears, the corner blocks may be glued and then screwed for additional strength, although it is not necessary to plug the screw holes afterwards, as it is in the ears.

FEET

PARTICULAR ATTENTION SHOULD BE PAID TO THE FEET OF THE cabriole legs (see FIG. 222). Sometimes these consist of a simple rounded end, known as a pad foot, but often they are made quite literally in the form of a carved foot, usually animal. Some pieces used a lion's paw, others a goat's hoof. Many more are a form of ball-and-claw foot, the particular design of which may be associated with particular makers, as illustrated in chapter 19. Aim for something simple the first time. It will be a sufficiently great achievement to have built an elegant and well-constructed chair with the simplest of lines.

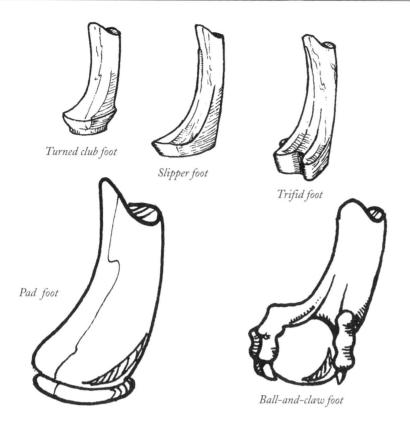

Turned club foot

Slipper foot

Trifid foot

Pad foot

Ball-and-claw foot

FIG. 222 FEET VARIETIES

So far as the drop-in seat is concerned, you may easily make a simple mortised-and-tenoned frame to fit in the seat rabbet, leaving enough room for the upholstery fabric, but the upholstery itself may be best left to an upholsterer.

A variety of finishes may be suitable for such a chair, but one of the easiest and most appropriate is a brushed varnish.

SIDE CHAIR

PART TWO

JOINTS & TECHNIQUES

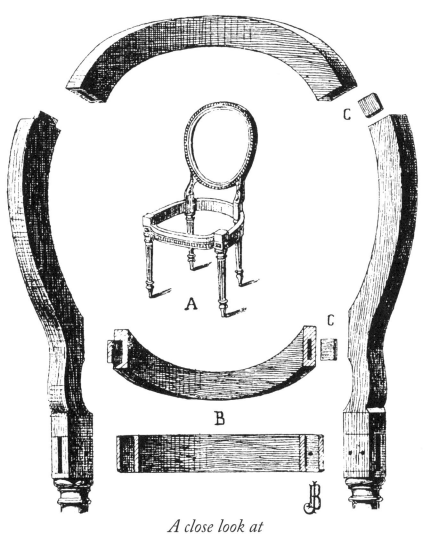

A close look at
furnituremaking details

Mitered Mortise-and-tenon Joints
from *Furnituremaking* by J. Boison, 1922

A. Stool with splayed legs.
B. Slanted mortise-and-tenon.
C. Moulded frame.
D. Mitered open mortise-and-tenon (used when the frame is painted or gilded).
E. Mitered blind mortise-and-tenon (used when the frame is to remain natural).

10

MITERS

Moulded Miters • Tall Miters • Splined Miters •
Biscuit-joined Miters • Mitered Rabbet • Mitered Lock Joints •
Stopped Miters • Large Miters

A WOODWORKING JOINT USUALLY IMPLIES A CONSTRUCTION WHEREBY TWO PIECES OF WOOD ARE HELD TOGETHER BY BEING SHAPED SO THAT ONE PIECE FITS INTO OR GRASPS the other. Dovetail joints and mortise-and-tenon joints are particularly good examples. In fact, a joint may be far simpler and consist of nothing more than the permanent juxtaposition of two pieces. Glued butt joints, whether of solid stock or thin sheets of veneer, are good examples. Theoretically, all joints might be made this way, but considerations of strength and appearance have resulted in a much greater variety of forms. Knowing which joint is appropriate for any given situation is part of good woodworking.

So when and why are miters, which would seem to be examples of the simple juxtaposition class, needed? The answer has much to do with appearance, and to a lesser extent with structural considerations. Firstly, unless used purposely for effect, visible end grain is generally less desirable than face or side grain. Mitering provides a way to avoid visible end grain when pieces meet at an angle. Secondly, since all wood shrinks or expands with changes in ambient moisture content, and since this movement occurs at a different rate along the grain than it does across the grain, two pieces that are not joined in the same plane may eventually become uneven. Mitering provides a way to lessen this effect.

A mitered joint should not be considered a necessarily weaker joint than a mechanically interlocking joint, nor easier to form. Indeed, its very simplicity can make perfection frustratingly difficult to achieve, but since in many cases it is indisputably the best joint for the job, it is important to know how to make some of the main varieties. The following examples illustrate only the basic classes of miters and the kinds of applications they are best suited for, but trying them should make you feel more secure about tackling one of woodworking's more demanding classes of joints.

Note that there are many ways, some easier than others, to make miters. The method you choose depends on the kind of miter being made and the tools at your disposal. While the methods described here may be best suited to the particular projects described, you should feel free to 'mix and match'. General layout procedures and clamping techniques are similar for most varieties, but use the cutting instructions as suggestions only.

MOULDED MITERS

MITERING IS ONE OF THE BEST WAYS TO JOIN PIECES WITH moulded profiles. This includes relatively small workpieces such as applied mouldings on solid stock, edgings to flat surfaces such as tables and counter tops, and facings such as cock beading around drawers and drawer openings. Not only is end grain avoided, but in addition the profile is made continuous.

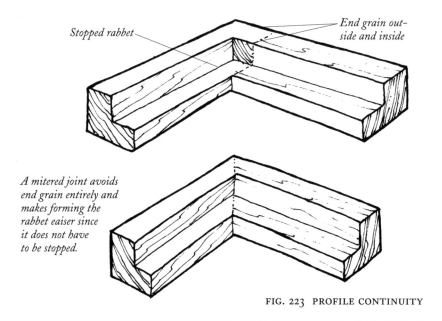

Stopped rabbet

End grain out-
side and inside

A mitered joint avoids
end grain entirely and
makes forming the
rabbet eaiser since
it does not have
to be stopped.

FIG. 223 PROFILE CONTINUITY

A picture fame is the perfect example, since even plain picture frames invariably possess a rabbet on the inside of the frame to receive whatever is to be framed. Much work is saved if the corners are mitered, since this allows the rabbet to turn the corner unobstructedly. From a structural standpoint a miter is superior to a right-angled butt or lap joint because the miter guarantees that any dimensional change in the two joined pieces will occur equally in both pieces, leaving the face profiles and the glass rabbets aligned in the two pieces. Such alignment is useful, especially in wide profiles, but note, however, that a mitered joint will open at the inside if it dries and open at the outside if it becomes wetter.

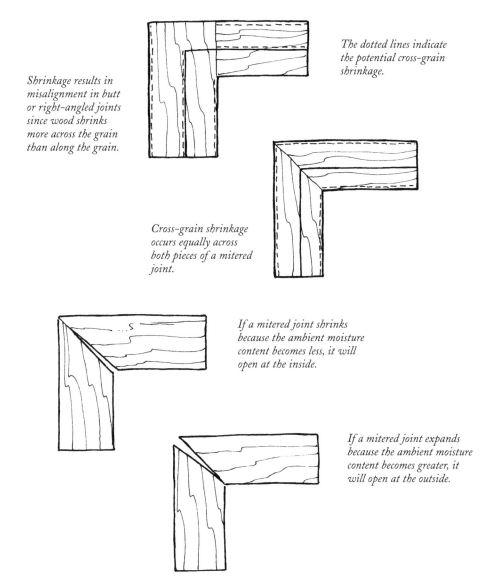

Shrinkage results in misalignment in butt or right-angled joints since wood shrinks more across the grain than along the grain.

The dotted lines indicate the potential cross-grain shrinkage.

Cross-grain shrinkage occurs equally across both pieces of a mitered joint.

If a mitered joint shrinks because the ambient moisture content becomes less, it will open at the inside.

If a mitered joint expands because the ambient moisture content becomes greater, it will open at the outside.

FIG. 224 MOISTURE CONTENT CHANGES

MITERS

A medium-sized picture frame, or any similarly dimensioned stock that might form part of something other than a picture frame, can be mitered easily and accurately using handtools. Picture frames vary enormously in shape, size, and profile, but what is most important for all is as perfect a joint as possible, since the joint is so visible. The first point to bear in mind is that no matter how two pieces (of the same width) to be mitered may meet, their overall angle of meeting must be exactly halved in order to form a perfect miter joint. For right-angled joints this means a miter of 45°. For pieces joining at angles greater or smaller than 90° care must be taken to bisect the angle exactly. This is true even when mitering certain curved sections, and is the reason why the line of miter in these cases is itself necessarily curved (see FIG. 333, chapter 15).

You may work this angle out from a full-sized or scaled drawing using a compass and protractor, or you may use a sliding bevel to take the exact overall angle and with care divide it. There is, however, a very useful tool called an angle divider which can be used to produce the required bisection mechanically without recourse to figures or calculations. If you adjust the angle divider to duplicate the overall angle, you can then use it like a double-sided sliding bevel to lay out the required miter.

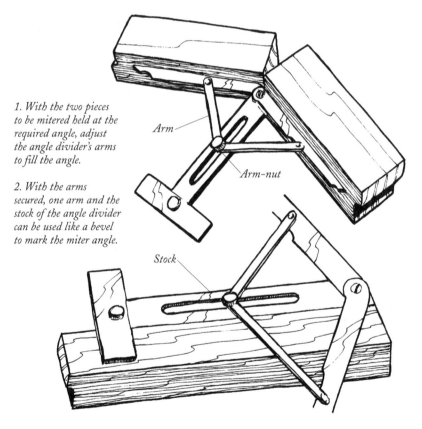

1. With the two pieces to be mitered held at the required angle, adjust the angle divider's arms to fill the angle.

2. With the arms secured, one arm and the stock of the angle divider can be used like a bevel to mark the miter angle.

Arm

Arm-nut

Stock

FIG. 225 ANGLE DIVIDER

The second point to bear in mind when laying out miters is that it is usually best to take all measurements consistently from one side of the miter or the other to avoid inadvertently cutting pieces to the wrong length. Furthermore, remember to allow a little extra for any trimming that may be contemplated when sawing to the layout line.

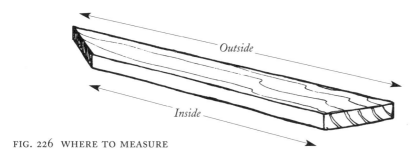

Outside

Inside

FIG. 226 WHERE TO MEASURE

For carpentry work that will be subsequently painted, cutting a miter with a fine handsaw is usually sufficient, but for cabinet work, miters that are cut by hand should also be trimmed with a plane to ensure a smooth joint, free of the ragged edges left by a saw. In any event, to minimize the effect of the rag caused by the saw, always work *into* the miter by sawing from the outside, no matter whether you are cutting an internal or external miter.

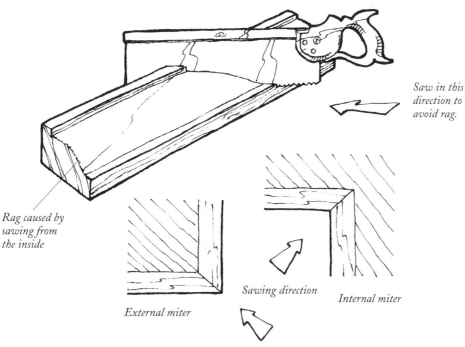

Saw in this direction to avoid rag.

Rag caused by sawing from the inside

External miter

Sawing direction

Internal miter

FIG. 227 AVOIDING RAG

MITERS

Using handtools does not necessarily mean working freehand. Both sawing and trimming are best done with guides. For small miters, use a small saw such as a dovetail saw; for larger miters you may need a regular backsaw, but use both with some kind of miter box. Factory-made metal miter boxes are typically provided with guides for the saw and clamps for the workpiece, both adjustable to the required angle, and if the workpiece is neither too large nor too small these can be virtually foolproof devices. A shop-made wooden miter box is easy to construct, and may be designed for use with your smallest or your largest handsaw.

The chief difficulty when using a miter box, especially when observing the injunction to saw into the miter, has to do with presenting an already moulded or other than square-sectioned workpiece such as a length of crown moulding to the saw at the correct angle. The best results will be achieved if you can fix the workpiece in the miter box at the correct angle, either by providing a back support or by tacking a small stop to the floor or wall of the wooden miter box.

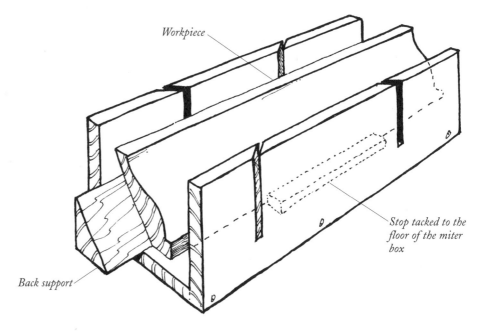

Workpiece

Stop tacked to the floor of the miter box

Back support

FIG. 228 SUPPORTING THE WORKPIECE

Trimming should certainly never be attempted freehand, since a miter shooting-board is very easy to make and virtually guarantees that any square-sided plane will leave a finished surface to the miter at exactly the right angle, even if the sawing has been done less than perfectly. Different stops should be made for the shooting-board so that both internal and external miters can be accommodated, since you should always plane *into* the stop to avoid the danger of splitting the end of the miter.

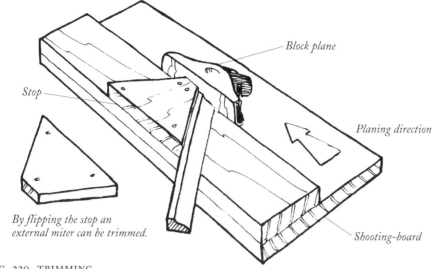

Block plane

Stop

Planing direction

By flipping the stop an external miter can be trimmed.

Shooting-board

FIG. 229 TRIMMING

The professional framemaker is typically equipped with a large miter trimmer, which works like a guillotine. A little like a one-sided miter box, the trimmer has two blades fitted at opposing 45° angles that are lowered onto the work to trim off a very thin slice, leaving a perfect angle.

If the mitered piece is attached directly to a larger frame or carcase, the miter itself may need no fixing. But picture frames are required to be self-supporting. Glue alone is rarely sufficient, since end grain will not glue to end grain securely. Small miters may be tacked, stapled, or held together with special picture-frame fasteners hammered in from the back. Heavier frames may have triangular supports glued and tacked to the back.

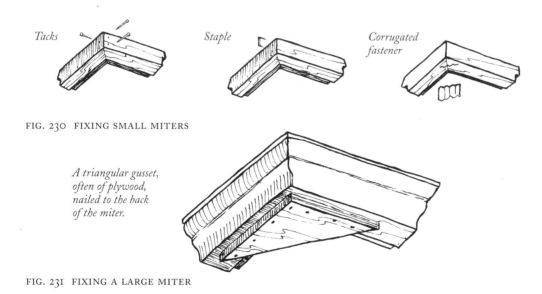

Tacks

Staple

Corrugated fastener

FIG. 230 FIXING SMALL MITERS

A triangular gusset, often of plywood, nailed to the back of the miter.

FIG. 231 FIXING A LARGE MITER

MITERS

Finally, there is the matter of assembly and clamping. Individual corner clamps designed to hold two pieces together may be used in groups to hold an entire four-sided frame securely for fixing, gluing, or clamping. Success requires that all four pieces be held in the same plane. Make sure that each piece seats into the clamp all the way to the bottom, and that each clamp rests evenly on the same flat surface. Lacking corner clamps, you may use regular clamps to hold the pieces to blocks tacked to a work surface, or employ a band clamp or a shop-made rope or string tourniquet wrapped around the perimeter of the frame, providing angled corner blocks for protection if necessary. Using pipe or bar clamps is risky, since the individual members might bow and cause the miter to open.

TALL MITERS

THE SECOND CLASS OF MITERS IS REPRESENTED BY THOSE varieties used for joining small but wide sections, such as might be found in boxes, carcase sides, plinths, or pediments. These are all cases where end grain might be particularly objectionable, and where a continuous surface that shows a continuing grain pattern is preferable. The difficulty here is to keep the miter, which is often too tall to be cut in a miter box, perfectly straight. Laying out the actual miter angle may be accomplished as before, but with additional care being taken to ensure an accurate and square line across the width. While a large square such as a framing square or an appropriately sized trysquare may be useful, it is essential to start the miter layout from an accurate baseline.

There are several varieties of corner miters, including plain miters held together by splines or dowels, miters used in combination with rabbets, tongues, and grooves, and even dovetails (this last includes the infamous

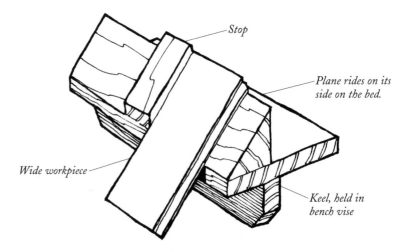

Stop

Plane rides on its side on the bed.

Wide workpiece

Keel, held in bench vise

FIG. 232 DONKEY'S EAR MITER SHOOTING-BOARD

secret mitered dovetail that used to be a staple of apprentices' examinations, see FIG. 294, chapter 13) that are suitable for this type of work. The simpler kinds may be cut easily on the tablesaw, using the miter fence to support the work while tilting the sawblade to the required angle. If the blade used is sufficiently fine-toothed and supported by a stiffener it should leave an adequately smooth surface, but if trimming is necessary a special kind of shooting-board for tall miters, with the curious name 'donkey's ear miter shooting-board', is needed.

Cutting a simple miter on the tablesaw requires little more than accurate setting of the blade angle and perfect squareness of the miter fence. If the box is to be rectangular, opposite sides will be equal; if the box is square, all four sides will be equal. To ensure that identical sides are cut to the same length, clamp a stop block to the outboard end of the miter guide fence or its extension.

SPLINED MITERS

A SPLINED MITER JOINT IS PREPARED FIRST AS A PLAIN MITER joint, each miter face then being grooved to accept the spline by being turned over and passed across the sawblade, which is set to half the previous height. If the same stop blocks are used as before, the spline grooves will all be consistently relative, but take care to position them equally within the width of the actual miter. Making splines that match the thickness of the saw kerf will obviate the necessity of multiple passes to cut the spline groove.

BISCUIT-JOINED MITERS

AN ALTERNATIVE TO USING SPLINES, USEFUL WHEN YOU DO not want the end of the spline to show, is to join the miters with biscuits. Most biscuit jointers have fences that can be adjusted for beveled slotting. If your biscuit jointer only has a square fence, clamp the mitered workpiece so it overhangs the bench, and run the fence against the outer edge of the miter, providing more support if necessary by clamping an additional mitered side on top of the piece being slotted. The important thing about this procedure, apart from using biscuits of an appropriate size, is to align the slots on both sides of the joint.

MITERED RABBET

A THIRD VARIETY OF BOX MITER, WHICH IS ALSO EASILY MADE on the tablesaw, is a mitered rabbet. This is made by cutting a rabbet in the first piece and then mitering the very end of the rabbet. The second piece is now rabbeted so as to leave a tongue the thickness of which is equal to the width of the mitered section on the first piece. This tongue is then also mitered. Each piece thus requires only three passes across the tablesaw blade to complete the joint. To strengthen this joint even further you may add dowels to the rabbet, as shown in FIG. 233.

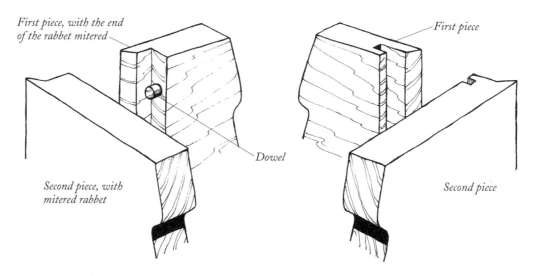

First piece, with the end of the rabbet mitered

Second piece, with mitered rabbet

Dowel

First piece

Second piece

FIG. 233 MITERED RABBET

FIG. 234 MITERED LOCK JOINT

MITERED LOCK JOINTS

A MITERED LOCK OR MITERED KEY JOINT IS ESSENTIALLY THE SAME joint with the addition of a tongue formed in the rabbeted piece that 'locks' or 'keys' into a groove in the second piece. One of the advantages of this form of miter is ease of assembly, since it holds itself together and requires only minimum clamping after gluing.

The process is illustrated in FIG. 235: Start by cutting the groove in the second piece, as shown at *1*. Now remove a rabbeted section at the end of this piece to leave the short square that will be mitered. Lay out this cut on the end of the workpiece, and use the miter guide to bring it to the sawblade; a block clamped to the saw fence and moved against the end of the workpiece will guarantee an exact cut, as at *2*. Clamp the first piece to a tenoning guide and, using a dado headset, cut a dado that will leave a tongue on the inside of the piece that equals the thickness of the groove cut in the second piece, and a lap equal in thickness to the square left on the outside of the second piece, as at *3*. Now lay this piece flat on the table and cut the tongue to length, as at *4*. Finally, set the sawblade to 45°, and trim the end of the lap on the first piece, and the end of the square on the second piece, taking care not to shorten either, as at *5* and *6*.

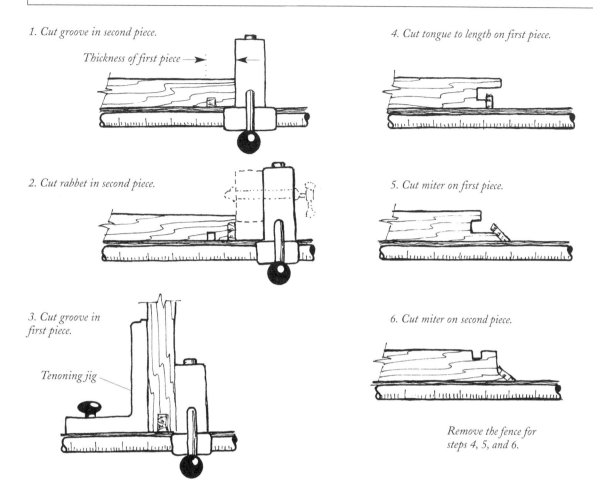

1. Cut groove in second piece.

Thickness of first piece →

2. Cut rabbet in second piece.

3. Cut groove in first piece.

Tenoning jig

4. Cut tongue to length on first piece.

5. Cut miter on first piece.

6. Cut miter on second piece.

Remove the fence for steps 4, 5, and 6.

FIG. 235 MAKING A MITERED LOCK JOINT

STOPPED MITERS

MITERS USED IN COMBINATION WITH OTHER JOINTS, SUCH AS dovetails, lap joints, and half-housed joints, are known as stopped miters, since, like the locked miter shown above, they are but one part of the complete joint.

When lapped joints are moulded, like the muntins in a multi-paned glazed door, the miter provides an efficient way to preserve the smooth continuity of the moulding without complicating the main body of the joint. The alternative is either to cope the moulded section or, as was earlier more common, laboriously carve the profile in the adjacent section to form the so-called mason's miter, which is technically no miter at all.

Better-quality framing, whether designed to include paneling, meant to be glazed, intended as face-framing, or forming part of carcase work, is usually constructed with mortise-and-tenon joinery, although cheaper

MITERS

work often makes use of dowels or biscuits. If any of the mortise-and-tenon forms include integral moulding, as opposed to moulding that is separately applied after the framing is complete, the profile and any associated rabbeting is formed first, prior to the mortise-and-tenoning, along the entire length of the various members.

The next step is to cut back the moulded section down to the level of the bottom of the profile, and as far back as the end of the mortise on one piece and as far back as the depth of the tenon on the other, as shown below. Now mark out and cut the two halves of the joint as for a regular mortise-and-tenon joint, but before fitting them together clamp a miter guide to the side of the moulded section and pare away the waste to form a miter with a chisel held flat against the guide. Note that it is sometimes easier to hold the whole assembly on the vise, since there is then no clamp to interfere with the chiseling.

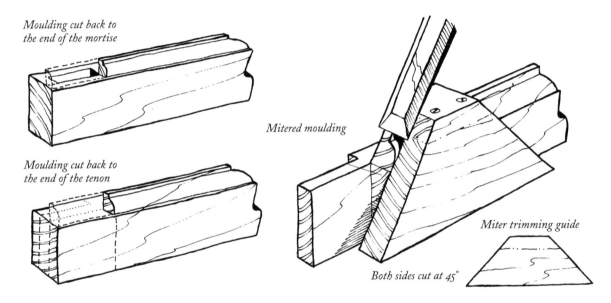

Moulding cut back to the end of the mortise

Moulding cut back to the end of the tenon

Mitered moulding

Miter trimming guide

Both sides cut at 45°

FIG. 236 MOULDED MORTISE-AND-TENON

FIG. 237 TRIMMING MITERED MOULDING

Dovetailed carcase sides whose edges form the face of a cabinet are sometimes finished with a miter at the end, since this looks better than the apparent butt joint that the dovetailing would produce. One trick commonly used in the final fitting of this joint may be borne in mind as an emergency method of saving other poorly cut miters. The joint is assembled as well as can be, and a fine dovetail saw is then used to cut a kerf at the precise spot where the miter should (and may indeed already partly) join. If the error has been one of slightly overcutting the joint, this procedure will not only bring the two sides together but also leave a perfectly positioned miter.

LARGE MITERS

THE LAST CLASS INVOLVES LARGE MITERS FORMED IN SOLID stock. These can vary greatly in design, proportion, and purpose, but they all share in common a large surface area that may be difficult to cut on the tablesaw. When the nature of the joint or the workpiece makes it difficult to bring the work to the saw, consider using a radial-arm saw or the now more common chopsaw, and bringing the saw to the fixed workpiece.

The radial-arm saw, with its blade tilted to 45°, may also be used to cut wide miters more conveniently than moving a large workpiece across a tablesaw's table. Keeping the blade vertical, however, can give you a some-what greater depth of cut, and with some radial-arm saws may also offer greater accuracy. To cut miters this way, make an auxiliary table fitted with two mutually perpendicular fences set at 45° to the back fence. This will permit perfectly mating miters to be cut on the radial-arm saw when the saw's arm is locked in the standard crosscutting position.

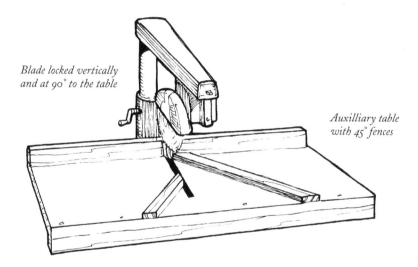

Blade locked vertically and at 90° to the table

Auxilliary table with 45° fences

FIG. 238 RADIAL-ARM SAW MITER JIG

For stock that is too large to be cut by a single pass of either a radial-arm sawblade or a tablesaw blade, clamp a guide block to the workpiece, and use a handsaw held closely against the guide block to make the remainder of the cut.

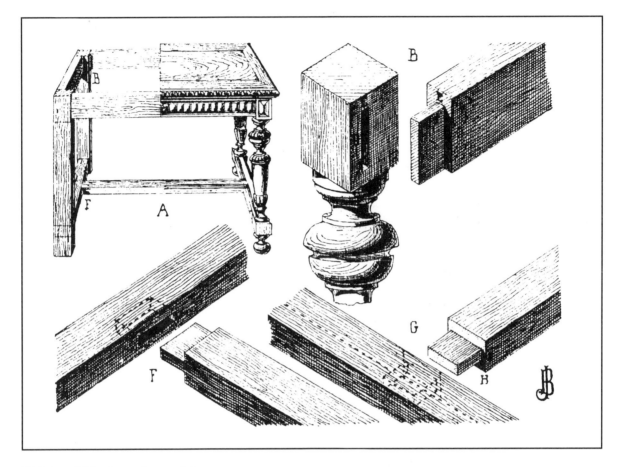

Varieties of Mortise-and-tenon Joints
from *Furnituremaking* by J. Boison, 1922

A. Construction of a Louis XIII table.
B. Leg and apron assembly.
C. Mortise face.
D. Tenon cheek.
E. Shoulder depth at the top of the joint.
F. Central stretcher joined to leg stretchers with a two-shouldered blind tenon.
G. Central stretcher joined to leg stretchers with a four-shouldered blind tenon.
H. Small side shoulders concealing the mortise.

11

MORTISE & TENON

I. VARIETIES & USES

Framing Varieties • Haunches & Franks • Heavy Varieties •
Wedging • Draw-boring • Carcase Varieties • Leg Joints •
Tenoned Clamp • Joints for Curved & Angled Work

THE MORTISE-AND-TENON JOINT IS ONE OF THE MOST COMMON JOINTS IN THE WOODWORKER'S REPERTORY, SINCE IT CAN BE USED FOR A WIDE VARIETY OF PURPOSES. Although the basic definition of this joint might be 'a way to join two pieces of wood together at right angles', it is far from adequate when you realize that more than two pieces of wood can be brought together in the same joint, and that a 90° joining angle is not essential. This chapter describes many of the commonest varieties and their particular functions; the next chapter focuses on how to design a successful joint and explains basic construction techniques.

The simplest form consists of a single piece of wood let into a pocket, called the mortise, cut into the side or face of another piece of wood. In FIG. 239, overleaf, the mortise is exactly the same size as the piece being let into it. The part that fits into the mortise is called the tenon, but in this example there is nothing to differentiate the tenon from the rest of the piece of which it forms a part, since both are the same size.

This form of the joint lacks the feature, common to all other forms of the joint, known as a 'shoulder'. A shoulder is formed by reducing the

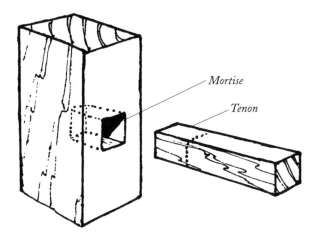

FIG. 239 SIMPLEST FORM OF MORTISE-AND-TENON JOINT

dimension of the actual tenon in relation to the piece from which it is cut. As shown in FIG. 240, a rectangular tenon may have one, two, three, or even four shoulders. When it is realized that the mortise may be cut with the grain or across the grain, that there may be other features such as haunches and franks, and that for different purposes tenon shoulders may exist in different combinations and be at different heights and of unequal widths, the large number of ways in which this joint may be made becomes very apparent.

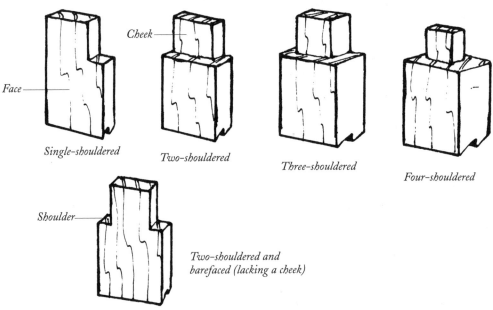

FIG. 240 SHOULDER COMBINATIONS

Shouldering the tenon not only lends much strength to the joint by providing extra bearing surfaces, but also allows two pieces of wood of equal dimensions to be joined. Any mortise must necessarily be smaller than the piece it is cut in or it cannot exist. The form illustrated in FIG. 239 can therefore only be made when a smaller piece is joined to a larger piece, as, for example, when joining small slat-like pieces to the headboard of a bed or the back of a bench. Although it is the simplest form, it is actually quite difficult to make well, since the mortise must be absolutely perfect in all respects, or gaps around the tenon will be apparent and the tenon will not enter to the precise depth required.

A mortise-and-tenon joint with a tenon that has at least one shoulder is a safer proposition, since the shoulder acts as a depth stop and automatically ensures that the tenoned piece retains its required length. If the mortise is too shallow it is a simple matter to deepen it; if it is too deep, the shoulder will prevent the tenon from entering too far.

As well as making it possible to join pieces of the same dimensions and ensuring the correct depth for the tenon, shoulders also accomplish something else that is very useful: they hide any imperfections at the mouth of the mortise. It is all too easy to damage the edges of the mortise when levering out the waste or paring away the sides, but this need never become a visible blemish if hidden under a shoulder. This advantage is gained at a price, however, since it requires that the shoulders themselves be cut with care. The moment there is more than one shoulder around a tenon it becomes critical to cut every shoulder at exactly the right height, or one will seat properly at the expense of gaps around the others.

Although there are few absolute rules about which joints may be used when and where, and while woodworkers are constantly discovering and inventing new variations for different applications, the easiest way to categorize and describe this large family is according to the kind of work for which the different varieties are used.

FRAMING VARIETIES

PERHAPS THE LARGEST OF THESE CATEGORIES CONTAINS THOSE joints used in frame-and-panel work, a variety of construction that is much used for paneled doors, wall paneling, case furniture, and many other articles. Many of the forms of this class of mortise-and-tenon joint are a result of the way in which the paneling is held within its framing, and they range from the simplest to some of the most complicated.

The simplest form, which is illustrated overleaf in FIG. 241, is that consisting of a right-angled, two-shouldered tenon such as might be used to join a rail to the middle of a stile, or a muntin to the middle of a rail*.

* In general, the terms 'stile' and 'muntin' refer to vertical framing members, and the term 'rail' refers to horizontal members.

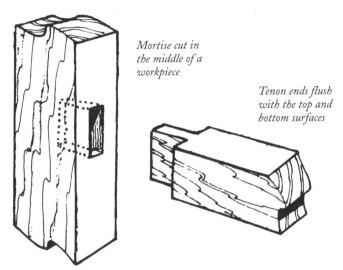

Mortise cut in the middle of a workpiece

Tenon ends flush with the top and bottom surfaces

FIG. 241 TWO-SHOULDERED TENON

If a two-shouldered tenon enters at the end of a workpiece, as may be necessary where a top or bottom rail joins a stile, the result is an open mortise, which is generally not strong enough for framework. In this case, a three-shouldered tenon is used which allows the end of the mortise to be set back some distance from the end of the workpiece.

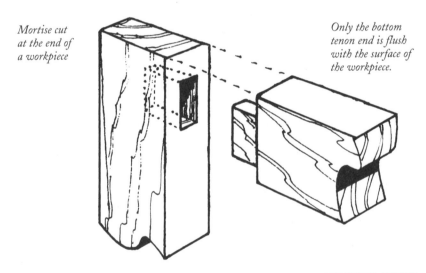

Mortise cut at the end of a workpiece

Only the bottom tenon end is flush with the surface of the workpiece.

FIG. 242 THREE-SHOULDERED TENON

HAUNCHES & FRANKS

CONSIDERABLY BETTER THAN A SIMPLE THREE-SHOULDERED tenon is a two-shouldered tenon made with a haunch. The haunch helps greatly in preventing any twisting in the framework, and also helps to guarantee that the mortise is located correctly.

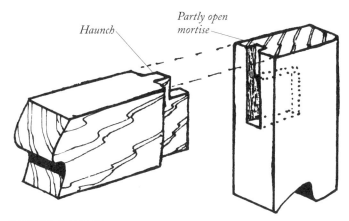

FIG. 243 HAUNCHED TENON

Achieving virtually the same effect, but presenting a better appearance, is the secret-haunched two-shouldered tenon. This joint may be used where the outside edge of the framing will be visible, and where a simple line between the two members is preferable to the extra detail of a groove cut in the end grain of one piece, as seen in FIG. 248.

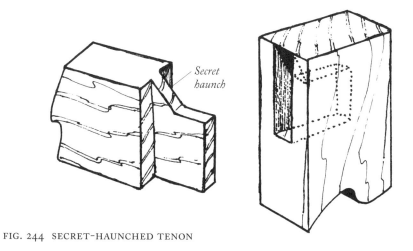

FIG. 244 SECRET-HAUNCHED TENON

MORTISE & TENON 1

All the above types presume a form of frame-and-paneling where the panels are held in place by subsequently planted (attached) strips or sections of beading or moulding. More common is framing that is either rabbeted or grooved to receive the paneling. This, of course, complicates

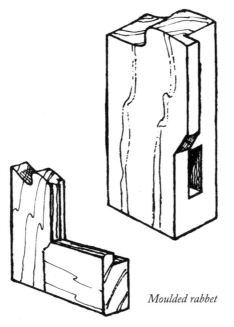

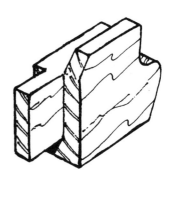

The side wall of the rabbet, especially when this part is moulded, is mitered in line with the shoulder of the tenon and the end of the mortise.

Moulded rabbet

FIG. 245 THREE-SHOULDERED TENON WITH MITERED RABBET

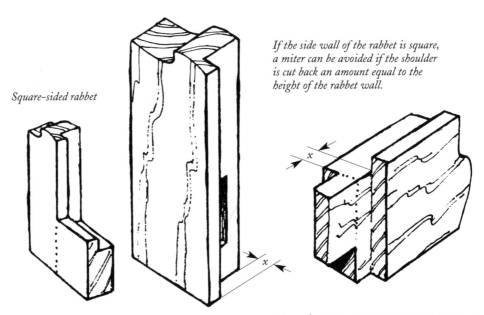

Square-sided rabbet

If the side wall of the rabbet is square, a miter can be avoided if the shoulder is cut back an amount equal to the height of the rabbet wall.

FIG. 246 UNEQUAL-SHOULDERED TENON

the form of the joint. In the case of rabbeted framing, if the side wall of the rabbet is mitered at the corner where it meets the side wall of the rabbet in the mating piece, a simple three-shouldered or haunched tenon may be employed, as in FIG. 245.

A simpler form of square-edged (unmoulded) rabbeted framing without a mitered corner requires a slightly more complicated tenon: one with unequal shoulders (FIG. 246), needed since a shorter shoulder is necessary on one side to accommodate the rabbet cut in the mating piece.

As mentioned before, tenons made with haunches make a better joint than ones without this feature, but there is a curious reverse exception to this rule. Together with several other idiosyncratic features, the mortise-and-tenon joint used for the framework of window sash is made not with a haunch, but with a frank. A frank is a recess designed to accommodate the central part of the moulding. The moulding forms part of the rabbet in which the glass is set, and the mortise is cut exactly to coincide with this moulding. The part beyond the mortise, towards the end of the piece, is left intact and is known as the spur. It is this spur which fits into the recess known as the frank cut below the tenon.

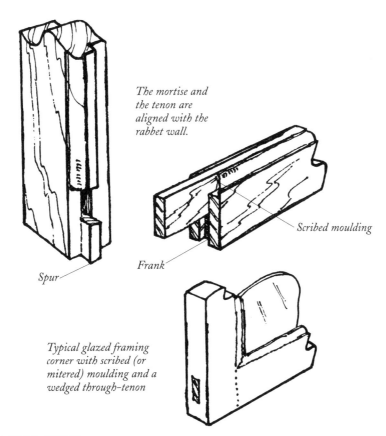

The mortise and the tenon are aligned with the rabbet wall.

Scribed moulding

Spur

Frank

Typical glazed framing corner with scribed (or mitered) moulding and a wedged through-tenon

FIG. 247 FRANKED TENON

One very common form of framing that always requires a haunched tenon is grooved framing. Since it is much easier to form a groove in the edge of a piece by running it clear through from end to end, rather than ſtopping it — and this is true whether the groove is made with a plane, a router, or on the tablesaw — any tenons designed to fit mortises cut in the groove (the usual location) muſt necessarily be provided with a haunch to fill that part of the groove left beyond the mortise, as shown below.

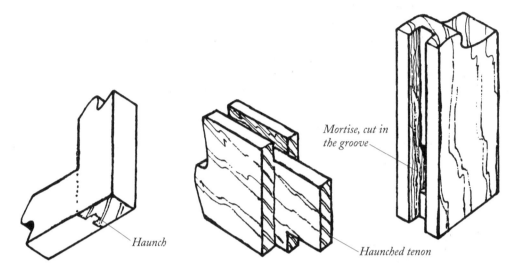

Haunch

Mortise, cut in the groove

Haunched tenon

FIG. 248 HAUNCHED TENON

HEAVY VARIETIES

THE JOINTS DESCRIBED ABOVE ARE FINE FOR MODERATE WORK, but where large pieces are involved, such as big and heavy doors, extra ſtrength may be required. This can be achieved in various ways, such as by twinning or doubling the tenons. If the ſtock is thick, twin tenons (FIG. 249) can be used, since this doubles the surfaces that may be glued, and at the same time requires that less wood be removed from the piece containing the mortise. The ſtrength of a mortise-and-tenon joint is largely determined by the proportions of the tenon and the mortise in relation to the thickness of the ſtock being used, but nevertheless the joint will be ſtronger as more surface area is created for gluing.

Double tenons (FIG. 250) are of more use where especially wide rails are joined to ſtiles. Since the two pieces are perpendicular to each other, the wide tenon runs the risk of splitting as its cross grain shrinks and expands to a different extent than does the long grain of the mortise. By making a double tenon this risk is reduced, and a more ſtable joint is produced.

A third approach to extra-large ſtock is to use a single tenon of no more than moderate width accompanied by separate slips or tongues fitted into the resulting extra-wide shoulders, as in FIG. 251. The (glued) tongues help prevent excessive movement between the two pieces, which is especially important if the framework is to be veneered, for any movement of this kind can be telegraphed through the veneer with unsightly results.

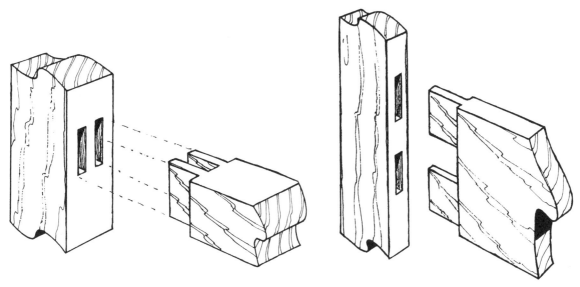

FIG. 249 TWIN TENONS

FIG. 250 DOUBLE TENONS

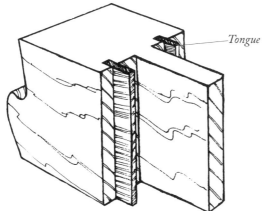

Tongue

FIG. 251 TONGUED TENON

Almost all the above varieties can be made either blind or through. 'Blind' implies that the tenon stops within the wood; 'through' indicates that the tenon goes all the way through to the other side. Although a through joint requires careful cutting, it is generally stronger, since it is bigger, but sometimes a blind joint is preferable on esthetic grounds. Of course, even if the end of the tenon cannot be seen, a joint should still be made as well fitting as possible in order to enjoy maximum strength.

MORTISE & TENON 1

WEDGING

WEDGING PROVIDES A MECHANICAL GUARANTEE THAT THE joint will not come apart. Although wedging a through mortise-and-tenon joint is straightforward, there are variations possible here, too (see FIG. 257). The usual procedure is to widen the far end of the mortise to accommodate the wedges, which may be inserted either at the ends of the tenon or, better, in slits cut within the tenon (see FIG. 252).

Blind mortise-and-tenon joints may also be wedged, this process being known as fox-wedging (FIG. 253). This is useful when strength is required but when there are reasons to avoid a through joint. Extra care must be taken with this kind of joint, however, for a loose fox-wedged mortise-and-tenon is almost worse than useless, and drastic measures will be necessary should it have to be disassembled.

The only cure for a loose fox-wedged tenon is to saw between the shoulders of the tenon and the face of the mortise down to the wedge slits, remove the remains of the severed, ill-fitting tenon by boring and chiseling if necessary, and install a new, loose tenon, mortised into both pieces, enlarging or filling the original mortise with fresh wood to make a good fit. This new tenon is called a 'loose tenon', but is loose only in the

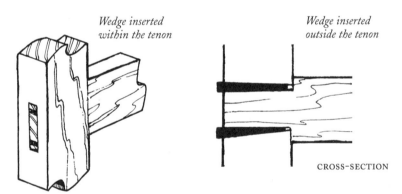

Wedge inserted within the tenon

Wedge inserted outside the tenon

CROSS-SECTION

FIG. 252 WEDGED THROUGH MORTISE-AND-TENON

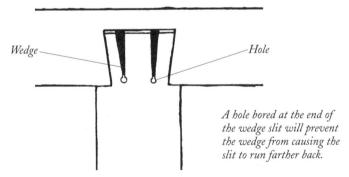

Wedge

Hole

A hole bored at the end of the wedge slit will prevent the wedge from causing the slit to run farther back.

FIG. 253 FOX-WEDGED MORTISE-AND-TENON

sense that it is not formed at the end of either of the pieces to be joined. It is fitted and glued securely in place into fresh mortises cut in the matching ends. Note that this method is not only useful as a repair, for making a mortise-and-tenon joint with a loose tenon can also be a legitimate method of dealing with particular design problems. Indeed, it is the essence of modern plate joinery, which employs 'loose' biscuits as tenons.

DRAW-BORING

PROVIDED THE JOINT IS WELL CUT AND THE TENON FITS SNUGLY within the mortise, gluing is usually sufficient to secure the joint. There is, however, another method which may be used where extra security is desired, and which has the additional advantage of drawing the joint tightly together. In small work this should not be necessary, although it does partly eliminate the need for clamps when gluing up. It is mainly of use with mortise-and-tenon joints that connect heavy framing members in buildings and other large constructions. The method is called draw-boring, and consists of inserting a pin, or wooden peg known as a trenail, through slightly offset holes in the tenon and the mortise. The drawing together of the two pieces is accomplished by having bored the hole for the pin in the tenon slightly closer to the bottom of the mortise than are the holes bored in the sides of the mortise itself.

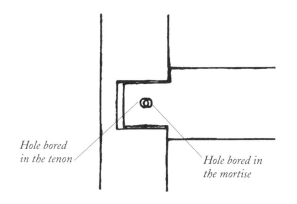

Hole bored
in the tenon

Hole bored in
the mortise

1. Bore a hole through the empty mortise.

2. Insert the tenon and mark it with an awl inserted through the hole in the mortise.

3. Remove the tenon and bore the same diameter hole in it, but somewhat closer to the shoulder.

4. Drive in a pin.

FIG. 254 DRAW-BORE CROSS-SECTION

CARCASE VARIETIES

MORTISE-AND-TENON JOINTS ARE ALSO USED EXTENSIVELY IN assembling carcase work — the containing framework, solid or open, that forms the main body of any particular piece, such as the outside of a chest or cabinet, the framework of a bed, or the shell of a chest of drawers.

Rails and uprights needed to support drawers within a carcase are frequently secured with a simple, two-shouldered mortise-and-tenon, but where the member being fitted is wide enough, double tenons offer greater resistance to twisting.

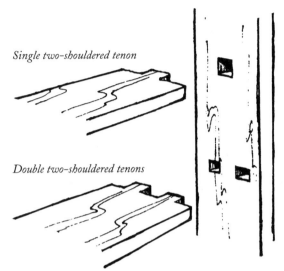

Single two-shouldered tenon

Double two-shouldered tenons

FIG. 255 TWO-SHOULDERED RAIL JOINTS

In cheap construction, wide partitions, if they are jointed at all, may be simply housed in a dado, but in the best-quality work they are secured with a whole row of tenons formed in the ends of the partition, which process is sometimes referred to as pinning — not to be confused with the use of pins in draw-boring.

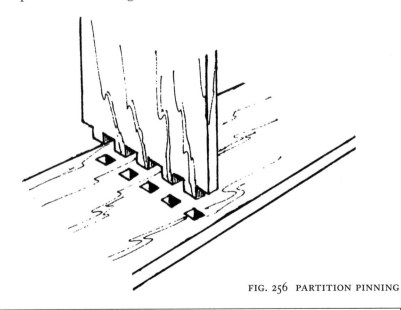

FIG. 256 PARTITION PINNING

Such carcase joints may be blind or, if possible, since it is a stronger method, through and then wedged. Since joints used this way frequently occur in such a position that the tenons enter the mortises across the grain, the wedges should not be inserted in such a way that they might split the mortise, but should be used so that they are always at right angles to the grain of the mortise. An alternative method, which can also take account of the grain direction of the tenon itself, is to insert the wedges diagonally, as at *A* in FIG. 257.

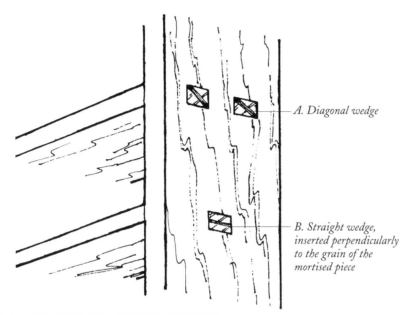

A. Diagonal wedge

B. Straight wedge, inserted perpendicularly to the grain of the mortised piece

FIG. 257 STRAIGHT AND DIAGONAL WEDGING

A large cousin of this kind of joint is the tusk tenon. This joint is secured by a wedge inserted perpendicularly through that portion of the tenon which protrudes through the far side of the mortise. The simplest form is shown below. This is a useful joint for furniture which must be disassembled, and is frequently found securing the bottom rail of trestle tables to the trestles.

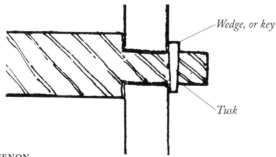

Wedge, or key

Tusk

FIG. 258 TUSK TENON

A more substantial version, and one that also carries some weight — necessary when joining joists, stair treads, or other supporting pieces of any size — is the stepped tusk tenon shown below.

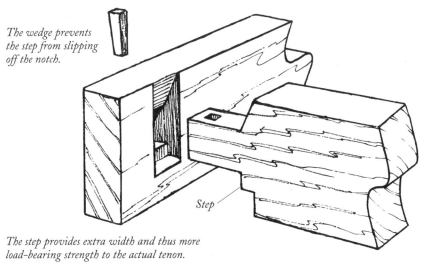

The wedge prevents the step from slipping off the notch.

Step

The step provides extra width and thus more load-bearing strength to the actual tenon.

FIG. 259 STEPPED TUSK TENON

LEG JOINTS

THE THIRD MAJOR GROUP OF MORTISE-AND-TENONS IS THAT used for connecting rails, aprons, skirts, and even stretchers to legs of all kinds. One of the characteristics of this kind of joint is that two pieces often have to be joined to the same leg at the same place. When this occurs at a corner, the mortises are usually cut in the center of the leg's thickness, and, to gain maximum length and thereby the greatest possible gluing surface for the tenons, their ends are usually mitered, as shown below. An improvement over this method is to offset the tenons, as much as is consistent with not weakening the sides of the mortise, towards the outside corners of the legs, thereby gaining extra length, as illustrated in

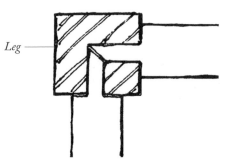

Leg

FIG. 260 MITERED TENONS, CENTERED

FIG. 261. Yet another method is to overlap the ends of the tenons so that part of each extends the full depth of the mortise, as in FIG. 262.

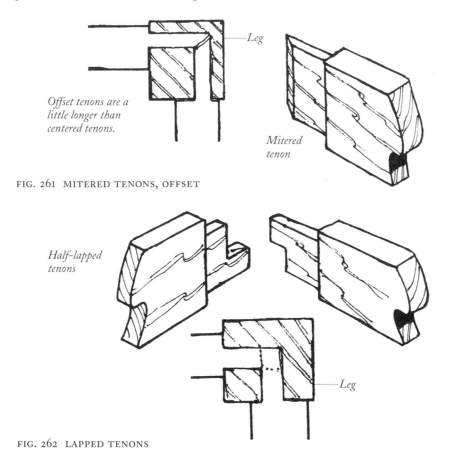

Offset tenons are a little longer than centered tenons.

Leg

Mitered tenon

FIG. 261 MITERED TENONS, OFFSET

Half-lapped tenons

Leg

FIG. 262 LAPPED TENONS

A further complication frequently encountered when assembling chairs is that their rails do not always meet legs at 90°. Sometimes the legs are cut so that each rail meets the leg squarely, as in FIG. 263, but more often it is the tenons which are cut at an angle, as in FIG. 264.

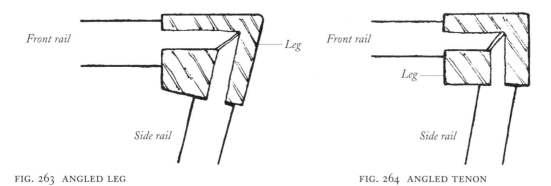

Front rail

Leg

Side rail

FIG. 263 ANGLED LEG

Front rail

Leg

Side rail

FIG. 264 ANGLED TENON

MORTISE & TENON 1

Legs are not only needed at corners. When they occur in the middle of a length — such as when needed to support a long table — one of two things may happen. Either the apron or rail is continuous and the leg is mortised into it, as in FIG. 265, the bridle section of the joint being necessary to preserve consistency with the way corner legs appear, or the apron or rail consists of two parts, each mortised with an overlapping miter into the leg as shown in FIG. 266.

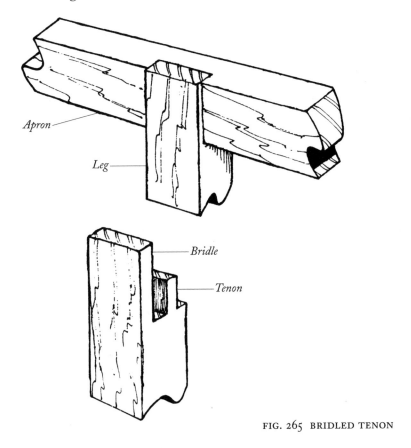

Apron

Leg

Bridle

Tenon

FIG. 265 BRIDLED TENON

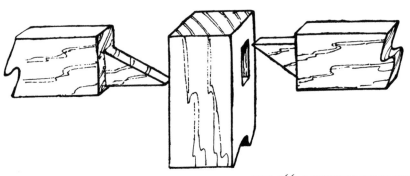

FIG. 266 LAPPED MITERED TENONS

TENONED CLAMP

THE TOOL KNOWN AS A CLAMP IN AMERICA IS CALLED A CRAMP in Britain. The word 'clamp' is, however, used in Britain but for something different, namely a cleat or strengthening band, and this is the meaning of the term 'tenoned clamp'. To avoid showing end grain and to prevent a wide board from cupping or warping, a piece is joined across the end of a board or a panel composed of several boards. The best method of attaching this clamp is with a form of mortise-and-tenon joint, shown below, designed to impart flatness without running an excessive risk of unequal shrinking which might cause cracks. The relatively short widths of the individual tenons help avoid this danger — but the method is not foolproof, and this is one case where we should be very grateful for the introduction of modern plywoods and composition boards.

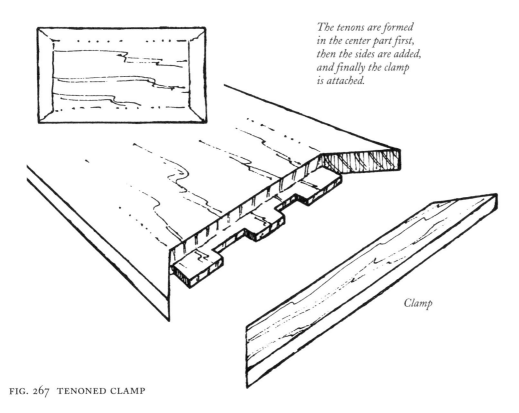

The tenons are formed in the center part first, then the sides are added, and finally the clamp is attached.

Clamp

FIG. 267 TENONED CLAMP

JOINTS FOR CURVED & ANGLED WORK

CURVED AND ANGLED WORK CREATES A UNIQUE SET OF PROBLEMS that demand different varieties of all the common joints. So far as the mortise-and-tenon family of joints goes, many of these problems can be solved by forming different shoulders. A simple example is provided by

MORTISE & TENON 1

the need to join a section of curved framing to a rectilinear stile, as in FIG. 268. If the standard joint is made, the bottom of the curved member runs the risk of being broken because the grain is so short. Two common solutions, shown in FIG. 269, demonstrate how easily the basic mortise-and-tenon may be adapted simply by adjusting the shoulders of the joint.

BAD

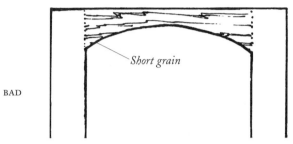

Short grain

FIG. 268 CURVED RAIL WITH VULNERABLE CORNERS

GOOD

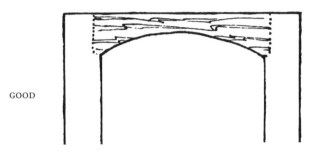

Offset, square-shouldered tenons

BEST

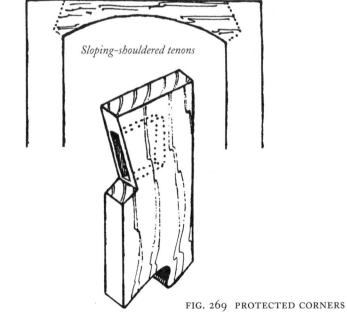

Sloping-shouldered tenons

FIG. 269 PROTECTED CORNERS

The thirty or so examples of mortise-and-tenon joints just described comprise no more than the basic types, of which endless variations are possible according to the need and the particular situation, a feature from one being combined with a feature from another almost limitlessly.

There is, however, yet another level of sophistication possible. The practice of airtight casemaking is all but dead, but the techniques involved in joining together two or three relatively thin members so that the smallest tolerances possible are created, require a highly specialized group of mortise-and-tenon joints that include refinements such as dovetailed tenons, loose tenons, and keyed mortise ways. It is interesting to note that much Chinese furniture from as long ago as the 12th century made use of similar sophisticated mortise-and-tenon joinery.

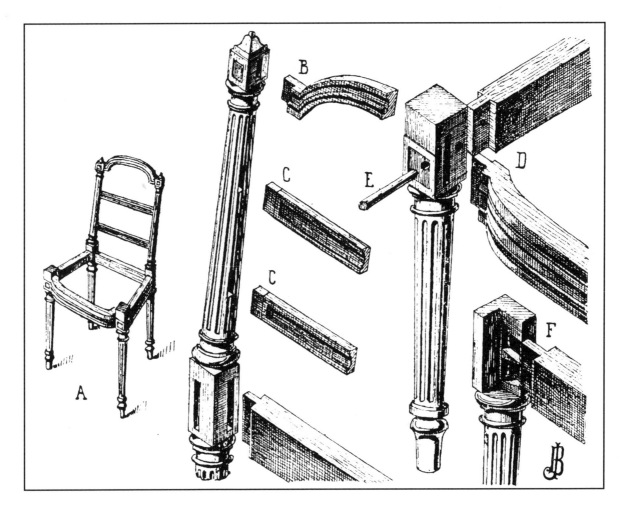

Pinned & Foxed Tenons
from *Furnituremaking* by J. Boison, 1922

A. Louis XVI chair.
B. Top rail joined with blind tenons.
C. Intermediate rails joined with shoulderless tenons.
D. Front and side seat rails disassembled.
E. Pin.
F. Rear seat rail, disassembled and cut away to show fox wedging with no pin.

12

MORTISE & TENON

II. DESIGN & CONSTRUCTION

Coherence • Layout Tools • Width • Length • Depth •
Cutting Order • Tenoning • Mortising

IN THE PREVIOUS CHAPTER WE SAW HOW A BASICALLY SIMPLE JOINT CAN BE TRANSLATED INTO A SEEMINGLY ENDLESS NUMBER OF VARIETIES, EACH TAILOR-MADE FOR A SPECIFIC purpose. From shoulderless tenons, straightforwardly fitted into mortises cut into larger mating pieces, to complex-angled, stepped-and-mitered tenoned members fitted into equally complex mortises, the family of mortise-and-tenon joints runs the gamut from one of the most basic joints in the woodworker's repertory to one of the more virtuoso feats of the joiner's art.

We also saw not only how the actual form of the joint varies to suit the specific application in which it plays a part, but also how its proportions and the way in which it needs to be made can be dictated by the type of construction in which it is involved, whether that be, for example, frame-and-panel work, sashmaking, or curved and angled work.

To a lesser, but equally important extent, the actual method by which these joints are manufactured also plays a part in determining their final form. This chapter looks at various ways of constructing the joint and examines how best to make the required forms.

Given the right handtools, and unaided by any form of power such as air, water, or electricity, even the most sophisticated joinery is eminently possible, as innumerable great pieces of the 18th and 19th centuries demonstrate. This supposes, however, that the handtools are of the best quality and that their operators are skilled in their use. Today, however, it is largely only exhibition purists in educational settings such as museum villages who depend entirely on traditional handtools; everyone else, to a greater or lesser extent, takes advantage of contemporary technology. Even the smallest shop is likely to contain at least an electric drill, and indirectly reaps the benefits of technology by using commercially obtained lumber. Most professional shops, even if only single-person operations, usually contain at least two or three stationary machines such as a bandsaw, a tablesaw, or a jointer-planer. So while some forms of the mortise-and-tenon joint may indeed still be best made entirely with the use of handtools, for most people the process will involve a synthesis of handtools and powertools depending on the work involved and the equipment to hand. But in both cases, whether you make mortise-and-tenon joints with traditional handtools, using tenon saws and mortise chisels, or employ powertools such as routers or tablesaws equipped with tenoning jigs, or stand-alone mortising machines, only continued care and practice will produce perfect results.

While some techniques, such as those involving routers, are totally new, most methods derive from traditional, tried and true hand techniques. Understanding how these were originally performed will usually make the power-assisted method easier to grasp and result in a better-made joint. For this reason this chapter concentrates mainly on the basic hand techniques that can be used for most forms of the joint.

COHERENCE

BEFORE BEGINNING TO DISCUSS THE VARIOUS TOOLS AND techniques of using them, the principle of tool coherence deserves to be mentioned. Coherence means that for best and easiest results all the tools you use for a particular operation should be matched. For example, if you are making a mortise-and-tenon joint in a section of framing that is to be grooved to receive the paneling, not only will the work proceed faster, but there will also be less room for error if the plane iron, router bit, or shaper bit that is used to cut the groove is the same size as the mortise chisel, mortising bit, or whatever else may be used to cut the mortise, since the mortise is almost invariably cut in line with the groove. It is, of course, perfectly possible to cut a mortise that is a different width than the groove it is located in, but this complicates matters just as much as attempting to excavate a mortise with a tool that is not the same width as the required mortise.

LAYOUT TOOLS

NO MATTER WHAT FORM OF THE JOINT MAY BE INVOLVED, SOME layout is usually required before any cutting or machining is done. It is true that one of the advantages of using machines is that this kind of work is often limited to the first piece, and that once measurements have been accurately taken, any fences and guides securely positioned, and perhaps special jigs made, all subsequent parts can be made without repeatedly having to measure and mark every facet of the required joint, but there will always be some initial measuring and marking required. The tools needed for these jobs are largely the same as they have always been: the marking gauge, the mortise gauge, the bevel, and the trysquare.

For the most accurate layout, the pins on marking and mortise gauges should be sharpened on one side only rather than to a conical or V-shaped profile, and used so that the beveled edge is always to the waste side of whatever is being marked.

A mortise gauge, despite its name, is actually more useful for laying out tenons than mortises, since if the mortise is excavated with a tool that matches the required width only one side of the mortise need be marked. Marking both sides (using a mortise gauge) simply introduces opportunities for error: the pins might not have been set exactly the right distance apart, or if the beveled side of the pins is to the outside of the mortise and the marks are made deeply, the exact width may be lost.

Nevertheless, if there is a lot of mortising to be done on a particular job, it can help to use a mortise gauge whose pins have been sharpened to points rather than to a flat-sided knife edge, to mark the locations of both the mortises and the tenons, provided it is used very lightly.

The pins must also be exactly the same height. If one pin is higher than the other the gauge will be lopsided when marking, and this will throw off the distance from the tool's fence at which the points are set. To make this easier, the pins should extend from the stem no more than ⅛ in. (see FIG. 270 overleaf). Good-quality gauges allow for the adjustment and replacement of these pins, but even if they are fixed do not shrink from filing them down; pins that are ½ in. long are a liability if you are after easy accuracy every time.

A further point to bear in mind is that the stock should be firmly adjustable on the stem. If it wobbles at all, as it tends to in old, worn tools, it will be extremely difficult to mark consistently accurate lines. Similarly, thumbscrew-adjusted gauges often develop slop on the inside pin. Make sure that when the points are set they can stay set. Avoid mortise gauges whose pins are set with thumbscrews that may work loose or get in the way. There are many types available*, but the best are the old-style ebony gauges with screws set in the ends of the stem (see FIG. 271 overleaf).

* For an in-depth discussion of marking gauges, see *Traditional Woodworking Handtools,* chapter 7.

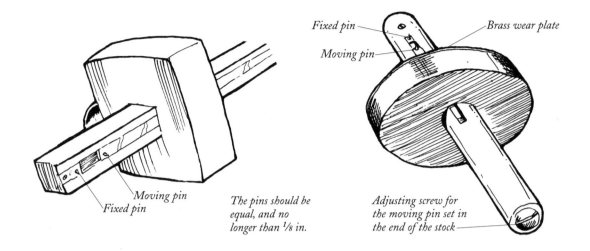

Fixed pin — Brass wear plate

Moving pin —

Moving pin

Fixed pin

*The pins should be
equal, and no
longer than ⅛ in.*

*Adjusting screw for
the moving pin set in
the end of the stock*

FIG. 270 COMMON MORTISE GAUGE

FIG. 271 BEST MORTISE GAUGE

The same requirements hold true for the simpler marking gauge: a short pin, sharpened on one side only; a firmly adjustable stock that can be fixed at a perfect right angle; and a wear plate set in the face of the stock to maintain this relationship.

A cutting gauge, which is fitted with a small knife instead of round points like the marking gauge, is also useful on occasions, but you must remember that the knife will necessarily leave a line that is V-shaped. The deeper you press, the wider the 'V' left by the tool. Therefore it is even more important that one side of the 'V' be vertical, the bevel forming the cutting edge being ground on one side only, and that the knife should be inserted in the stem so that the beveled side faces the waste side of the line being scribed.

WIDTH

THE IDEAL PROPORTIONS OF TENON TO MORTISE ARE GENERALLY the same for all varieties of the joint, except in a few special cases, and reflect the basic principle that the strongest joint is that which assuming the two pieces being joined are approximately the same thickness requires the removal of the least amount of wood from each of the two pieces. A thicker tenon, while stronger, means a mortise with narrower and thus weaker walls; similarly, a mortise with thicker walls, while stronger, means a thinner and thus weaker tenon. Thus in frame-and-panel work, where the tenons are formed on the rails, the actual tenon will equal about a third of the stile's thickness (see FIG. 272). The exact measurement should be a function of the tools available to cut the mortise. Of course, if the rail

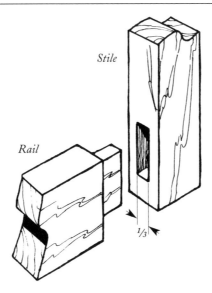

FIG. 272 WIDTH OF TENON

is much thinner than the stile, the tenon may not be able to be as thick as one third of the stile's thickness. But the point to remember is that the strength of the joint will be greatest when the mortise most nearly approaches this ideal: one third the width of the stile.

It does not matter so much what proportion of the rail the tenon occupies. This is not to say that side shoulders do not add strength, but that whereas almost any thickness will work for the tenon, a mortise which is too thick necessarily implies weak walls. At the same time, beware of forming a tenon that is too thin relative to the piece in which it is cut, especially if there is insufficient long grain running through the tenon into the rest of the member. There is, however, an upper limit to the practical width of a tenon, at which point it is easier to form twin tenons.

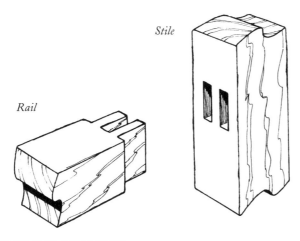

FIG. 273 TWIN TENONS IN THICK WORK

MORTISE & TENON 2

Having sufficient long grain running through the tenon is especially important when making tenons that are angled, as is often the case when making tenoned chair rails. If the material you are working with has less than ideal grain, as below, consider loose tenons or plate joinery.

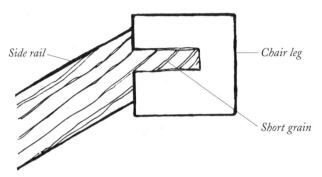

Side rail   *Chair leg*

Short grain

FIG. 274 CROSS-SECTION OF ANGLED TENON

LENGTH

MORTISE-AND-TENON JOINTS MAY BE MADE EITHER WITH THROUGH tenons or blind tenons. The former, as the name implies, go all the way through the mortised piece, and are generally stronger, while the latter finish within the piece being mortised. There are good reasons for both.

Through mortise-and-tenon joints, if they are laid out correctly and are executed with care, can be easier and faster to cut than blind joints, since there is no need to excavate the bottom of the mortise to exactly the right depth. It is also easier to wedge such joints, as well as to disassemble them later, if need be. However, although such wedging can be decorative, the appearance of end grain is generally undesirable in a lot of furniture work, so through tenons are usually reserved for millwork, such as doors and windows that are designed to be painted.

How long blind tenons should be is usually a question of what tools you use to make the mortise. Although longer tenons have more gluing surface, and hence more strength, you do not want to risk breaking through the bottom of the mortise. Neither do you want to create a mortise that is impossibly difficult to excavate. It is easier to excavate a deep mortise with router bits and boring machinery than it is with chisels, but even with boring tools it is possible to attempt a mortise deeper than is safe. The guide to the correct length should be the safe operating limit of whatever you use to make the mortise.

If the tenon is being used merely to locate the workpiece then the merest depth may be sufficient. This kind of blind tenon is known as a stub tenon. For much practical work, blind tenons 1 in. or 1½ in. long will be found to be sufficient and within the range of most tools.

DEPTH

BY DEPTH IS MEANT THE MEASUREMENT FROM THE TOP OF THE tenon to the bottom, or the surface length of the mortise. The rule of thumb here is once again to use thirds: one third is reserved for the distance from the top of the tenon to the top of the stile and two thirds for the tenon.

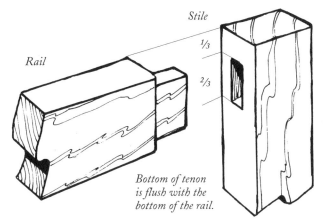

Stile

Rail

¹/₃

²/₃

Bottom of tenon is flush with the bottom of the rail.

FIG. 275 DEPTH OF TENON

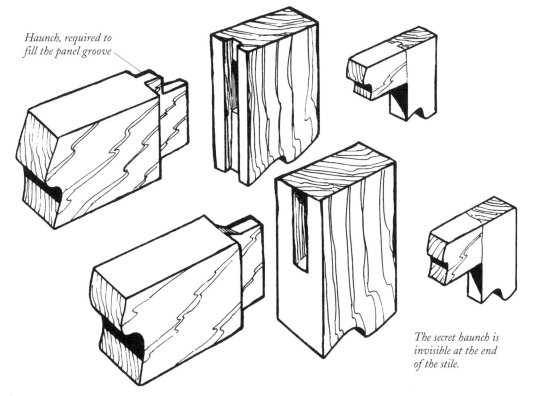

Haunch, required to fill the panel groove

The secret haunch is invisible at the end of the stile.

FIG. 276 HAUNCHED TENONS

MORTISE & TENON 2

Of course, the tenon does not always enter a mortise as in FIG. 275; the requirements of the piece may dictate other shoulders or even no shoulders, but where possible this is ideal — with a couple of provisos: First, in much work a haunch is an extremely good idea as it goes a long way to prevent possible twisting and racking. It is, in any case, almost always necessary in frame-and-panel work, since the groove for the paneling is invariably run through the length of the piece and must be filled on the other side of the tenon at the corner of a frame (see FIG. 276 above). Even if there is no groove, the provision of a secret haunch is still a good idea so far as preventing twisting is concerned.

Second, if the tenon will be very deep, problems involving cross-grain expansion and contraction are possible. To avoid these, very deep tenons should be made double, in thirds, as in FIG. 277.

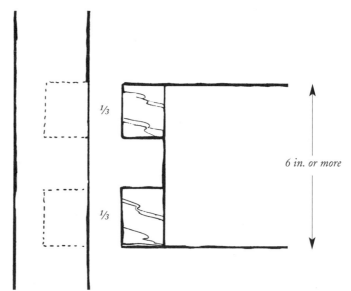

FIG. 277 DOUBLE TENONS

CUTTING ORDER

AS WITH DOVETAILS (SEE CHAPTER THIRTEEN), THE PERENNIAL argument is which part of the joint should be cut first. It all depends on the particular form of the joint. If both parts are correctly marked, then it should make no difference. But sometimes it is more practical to mark one part of the joint, the mortise or the tenon, directly from the other part. Many people prefer to make the tenon first, then mark and make the mortise to match. This is a good method to use when making framing, since it is easy to lay the tenoned rails across the stiles and from them mark the locations of the matching mortises, especially since stiles that have mortises cut at their ends are always more safely handled if extra wood is left beyond the mortises and is only trimmed or sawed off after the mortise has been excavated. This extra wood, which acts as insurance against the end splitting open when deep mortises are being excavated, especially in softwoods, is known as the horn. Such overlong stiles make it difficult to locate the mortises by simply measuring from the end, since it can become confusing trying to allow for the horn.

On the other hand, if the mortise dimensions are absolute, as when, for example, they must be located exactly within a panel groove, it can be safer to make the mortises first and then make the tenons to match.

No matter which part you make first, however, it is safer to make all measurements, and all adjustments to any fences or guides on tools used to cut both mortise and tenon, from the same side — usually the face side — of the work. Unless the mortise and tenon are exactly centered in the material, you do not want to run the risk of misaligning mating pieces as a result of cutting either the mortise or the tenon on the wrong side.

TENONING

IT IS IMPORTANT TO CUT THE TENON TO THE CORRECT THICKNESS. If it is too thin the joint will be loose, and if it is too thick it may split the mortise. Although sloppy sawing can be somewhat compensated for — in the former case by gluing extra thickness onto the tenon and in the latter by careful paring away — it is much more difficult to correct a poorly cut shoulder without compromising the required overall length. For this reason, mark and cut the shoulders first, taking care to provide an exact guide for the first passes of the saw by scoring around the perfectly marked shoulders with a chisel held so that it makes a groove deep enough to guide the saw teeth. The side of the groove that marks the shoulder should, of course, be vertical.

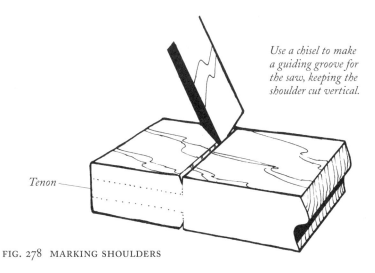

Use a chisel to make a guiding groove for the saw, keeping the shoulder cut vertical.

Tenon

FIG. 278 MARKING SHOULDERS

Having cut the shoulders carefully to the exact depth on as many sides as they are to be formed, secure the piece in the vise and saw down the cheeks, first with the piece tilted towards you, as at *1* in FIG. 279, and then with the piece tilted away from you, as at *2*. Sawing this way allows you to keep all the lines you are attempting to saw to visible all the time.

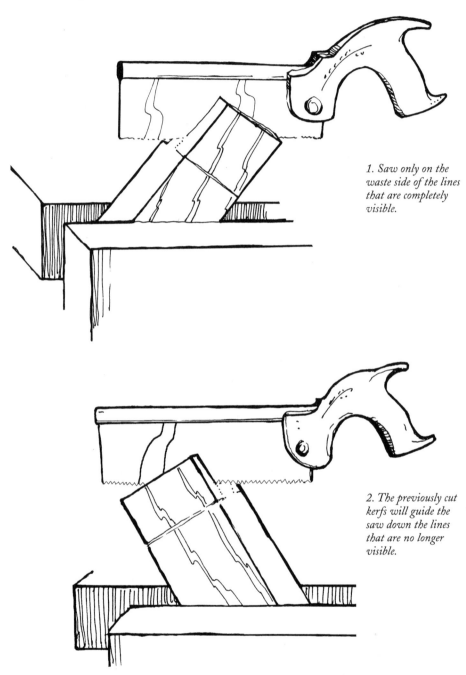

1. Saw only on the waste side of the lines that are completely visible.

2. The previously cut kerfs will guide the saw down the lines that are no longer visible.

FIG. 279 SAWING THE CHEEKS

Assuming your marks are exact and your saw sharp, practice will make perfect. Some of the things that can go wrong and that you should be on guard against are shown below.

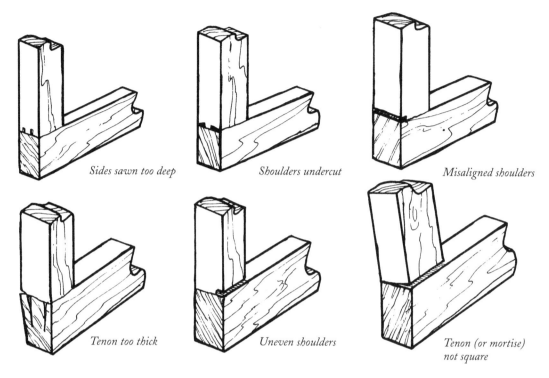

Sides sawn too deep

Shoulders undercut

Misaligned shoulders

Tenon too thick

Uneven shoulders

Tenon (or mortise) not square

FIG. 280 TENONING MISTAKES

After the sides and shoulders have been cut it may be necessary to clean out the corners with a sharp chisel, and sometimes adjust the thickness with a very finely sharpened shoulder plane. Low-angled, square-sided,

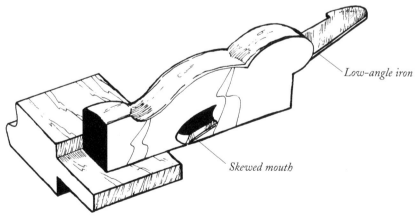

Low-angle iron

Skewed mouth

FIG. 281 SHOULDER PLANE

MORTISE & TENON 2

and often provided with an adjustable mouth, this plane is named for precisely this operation, but it is far from easy to use. In the hands of a skilled operator it can perfect a nice fit with ease, but it is precisely the beginner who is likely to have most recourse to it. It must be very sharp, the iron must be perfectly aligned with the sole, and care must be taken not to split out the wood by planing all the way across cross grain. To help avoid this last fault, many old shoulder planes were often made with skewed irons, and these are well worth looking for. It is best to try to cut the tenon well enough to avoid the need for a shoulder plane, but if it is necessary and one is not to hand, a paring chisel can be substituted, the wider the better.

Of course, this is sometimes a two-part operation. The tenon is cut, then used to mark the mortise, and only then tried, and adjusted if necessary, for fit. Before doing this, however, chamfer the ends of the tenon slightly to allow it to enter the mortise easily.

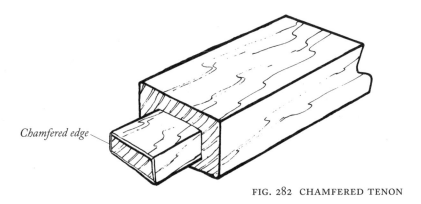

Chamfered edge

FIG. 282 CHAMFERED TENON

MORTISING

THE REASON MANY PEOPLE GIVE FOR PREFERRING TO CUT mortises by machine is that it is easier to cut them exactly perpendicular. In fact, it can require just as much care to set up the boring machine, or whatever powertool is used to mortise, as it does to excavate mortises by hand. Put the other way round, it is no harder to cut a properly perpendicular mortise by hand than it is to use some other method, provided you know how.

There are three different types of mortise chisel: sash, lock, and registered. All share two things in common: they are proportionately longer than paring chisels or firmer chisels (the common bench chisels), and their blade's section is more nearly square, which means their sides are proportionately thicker and, most importantly, straight and parallel.

It is this straight-sidedness which defines a mortise chisel, for it means that no matter how deeply the chisel enters the work, the width of the mortise remains constant, which is precisely the attribute required of a well-cut mortise. This is, of course, the reason why it makes most sense to design the mortise so that it can be cut with a mortise chisel of the required width. Mortises wider than the tool used to excavate them are possible but no longer automatically perfect.

The extra length usually possessed by the mortise chisel not only enables it to penetrate more deeply, but also makes it easier — providing you stand directly in line behind the chisel when working — to see that the chisel is being entered perfectly vertically.

The largest mortise chisel, known as a registered mortise chisel, has an oval handle, unlike the round handle of most contemporary chisels. This makes it possible to feel that the chisel is being presented to the work at the same angle while your eye is on the verticality of the blade. Also, should the blade become twisted when deep inside the mortise, the oval, tanged handle affords more control over the blade, unlike the handle of a sash chisel which might simply rotate within its socket.

Using a mortise chisel to chop (excavate) the mortise is a fast and efficient way to form relatively small joints. Used properly it guarantees a straight-sided, correctly dimensioned mortise. But for especially wide mortises you can save a lot of work by first boring away as much of the mortise as possible and then cleaning up the sides with a paring chisel. Unless you are using some kind of jig, however, this introduces more room for error, as it is harder to bore perfectly vertically freehand than it is to wield the mortise chisel. If you are less than completely confident about your ability to bore straight, choose a bit that is narrower than the mortise to avoid the risk of encroaching upon the sides.

In both cases, position a small clamp on the outside of the mortise to prevent accidentally splitting out the sides should anything be driven in less than perfectly perpendicularly.

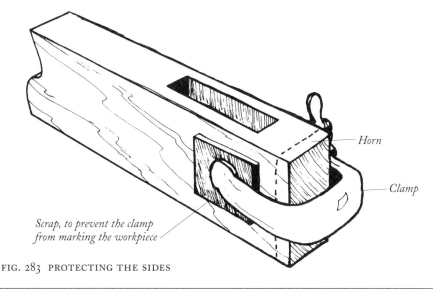

Horn

Clamp

Scrap, to prevent the clamp from marking the workpiece

FIG. 283 PROTECTING THE SIDES

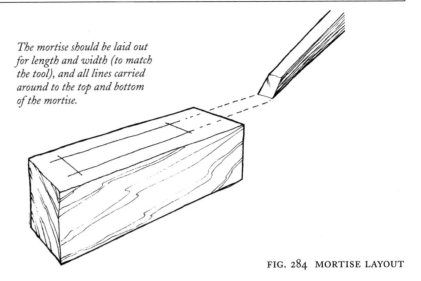

The mortise should be laid out for length and width (to match the tool), and all lines carried around to the top and bottom of the mortise.

FIG. 284 MORTISE LAYOUT

Through mortises should be excavated by working in from both sides to avoid splitting out the far side. If they have been laid out exactly there should be little difficulty in meeting properly at the center of the work. But blind mortises present a different problem: excavating to the correct depth. While the tenon should fit as completely as possible, it is wise, particularly when working in large-pored wood such as white oak, or softwoods such as pine, to leave a small space for excess glue at the bottom of the mortise. A gap of about ⅟16 in. at the bottom of the joint should be sufficient for an average 1 in. mortise. Make it a habit to check, with the end of a wooden rule or even a marked dowel, the depth of every mortise before trying to assemble the joint.

The chief danger when working on the bottom of the mortise lies in damaging the top corners when levering out the waste. If the joint has been designed with shoulders at each end of the mortise the shoulders may hide any bruised wood, but it is better not to damage the wood in the first place. This is, of course, one problem that can be avoided if the mortise is made with a plunge router or a mortise bit in a drill press.

To avoid damage when working by hand, do not cut the mortise the full length until you have cut the full depth. Start excavating from the center and stop before the end layout line is reached. Then reverse the chisel and work in the opposite direction, again stopping short of the end layout line. Only when the full depth has been excavated should you approach the ends. Holding the back of the chisel against the end, pare down vertically, as shown in FIG. 285. This, of course, requires that the back of your mortise chisel be perfectly flat. If it has been even slightly rounded through inattentive sharpening, the curve will force the blade away from the vertical, as in FIG. 286. A few vertical cuts should form square, undamaged ends.

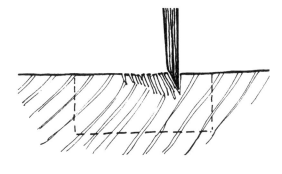

1. Work from the center towards either end.

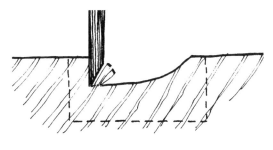

2. Reverse the chisel (or the work), and work towards the other end.

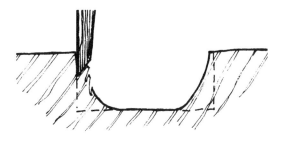

3. Cut the vertical ends.

FIG. 285 MORTISE EXCAVATION

A chisel with a rounded back cannot make a vertical cut.

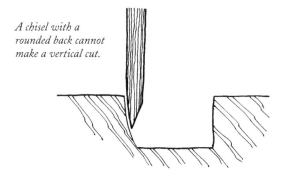

FIG. 286 EFFECT OF A ROUNDED MORTISE CHISEL

Lapped & Hidden Dovetails
from *Furnituremaking* by J. Boison, 1922

A.   Wall cabinet with marquetry and gilt bronzes, after Boulle, 17th century, Louvre Museum.
B. C.   Hidden dovetails joining the plinth to the center rail.
D. E.   Lapped dovetails joining the plinth to the side rail.
F. G.   Interior view of the hidden dovetails.

13

DOVETAILS

*Tails & Pins • Angles & Proportions • Through Dovetails •
Lapped Dovetails • Hidden Dovetails • Carcase Dovetails • Slot
Dovetails • Housed Dovetails • Decorative Dovetails*

DOVETAILS — THE WORD CONJURES UP THE VERY ACME OF FINE WOODWORKING, BUT IT CAN ALSO PRODUCE UNNECESSARY AWE IN BOTH BEGINNERS AND PEOPLE who have never tried to make this form of joint. It is true that making a dovetail joint is one of the harder parts of qualifying for the British trade examination known as 'City and Guilds', still regarded by many as the contemporary standard of professionalism, but what the examiners want is a handcut example of one of the more complicated forms of the joint, which does indeed constitute a real test of woodworking knowledge and skill. Most forms of the joint are not that difficult.

Apart from often being a very showy joint, the dovetail's main claim to fame is that it is one of the strongest ways to join pieces, most typically end-to-end and at right angles, although in airtight casemaking and much traditional Chinese joinery, there are many examples of three-part dovetails. Airtight casemaking, which was the trade of making display cases out of glass held in narrow wooden frames, may not be common today, but many of its techniques, together with those of traditional Chinese joinery, can be very useful for the contemporary furnituremaker.

Airtight casemaking and Chinese joinery apart, the dovetail joint is widely used for all kinds of top-quality work, including drawers, boxes, carcases, and cabinets of all sorts. Furthermore, there are now several ways to make this joint — previously the exclusive property of handworkers — using both portable and stationary powertools, thereby ensuring accuracy and facility even for those who have not had the benefit of a seven years' apprenticeship in a traditional cabinetmaker's shop.

TAILS & PINS

BEFORE EXPLORING THE EXTENDED FAMILY OF DOVETAIL JOINERY let us first take a look at some basic concepts. Probably the greatest initial confusion for beginners arises from trying to tell the two parts of the joint from one another. If you look at an assembled basic dovetail, such as the corner of a box made with standard through-dovetail construction (FIG. 287), one side will look like a series of more or less equal finger joints, depending on the spacing, while the other side will show a series of alternating dovetail shapes. Trying to decide which are the tails and which are the pins can be very confusing until you pull the joint apart, mentally or literally. The easiest way to keep things clear is to remember that the tail part of the joint, no matter what the spacing or proportions (except in a few specialized versions of the joint mentioned later), possesses a dovetail shape that can be seen as such from two different angles, whereas the pin only looks like a dovetail if viewed from one particular angle, namely, the end.

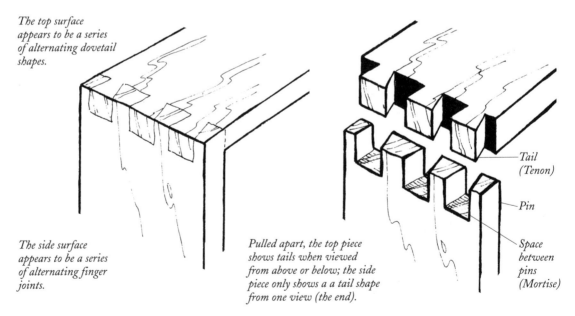

The top surface appears to be a series of alternating dovetail shapes.

The side surface appears to be a series of alternating finger joints.

Pulled apart, the top piece shows tails when viewed from above or below; the side piece only shows a a tail shape from one view (the end).

Tail (Tenon)

Pin

Space between pins (Mortise)

FIG. 287 THROUGH DOVETAIL

Put another way, the tails are technically tenons, while the mating pieces — the slots cut to receive these tenons — are technically mortises, whose sides are the pins. What can also create confusion is the fact that the mortised part — the part containing the pins — is traditionally referred to by means of the pieces that are left — namely, the pins — after the mortises have been cut out. Since the ends of the pins also appear dovetail-shaped, confusion is easy unless you remember the previous rule that the tails look like dovetails when viewed from either side. The pins, of course, are narrower on one side than on the other.

Another thing that sometimes creates confusion for the beginner is that when dovetailing pieces such as drawers and boxes, traditional usage refers to the the inside as the face side, and the bottom edge as the face edge. This derives from the way in which dovetails are laid out and made by hand, and is at odds with normal usage, which would suggest that the outside of a drawer would be referred to as the face side and the top edge of the drawer as the face edge.

ANGLES & PROPORTIONS

FUNDAMENTAL TO THE DOVETAIL'S EXISTENCE IS THE FACT THAT it has considerable mechanical strength due to the way its shape provides absolute resistance to all strain in one direction and significant resistance in the other. Experience has shown that for this shape to be most effective, the angle at which the sides of the tails are cut must be neither too steep nor too slight. The usual angles are most clearly shown overleaf in FIG. 288 in terms of side-to-base ratios. Note that for softwoods, such as pine, the angle may be somewhat greater than when cutting the joint in hardwoods. If too great an angle is attempted with certain hardwoods the short grain at the corners of the tails is liable to break off; this must be balanced against the fact that the greater the angle, the greater is the resistance. Do not feel rigidly bound by these angles, but remember that the proportions shown are good practical guidelines.

The other essential element in the dovetail joint's effectiveness is its spacing, or the relative proportions of tails to pins. For greatest strength the spaces between the pins should be equal to the width of the pins. However, since making dovetails is relatively time-consuming, for most purposes sufficient strength will be obtained, and the work required will be halved, if the tails equal approximately twice the width of the pins.

Another approach to a well-proportioned joint is to aim to make the widest part of the pins roughly equal to half the thickness of the wood in which they are being cut.

Having said this it must be pointed out that since the decorative aspect of dovetails is often one of the most important reasons for using them, considerable variation in proportions exists. When designing your own

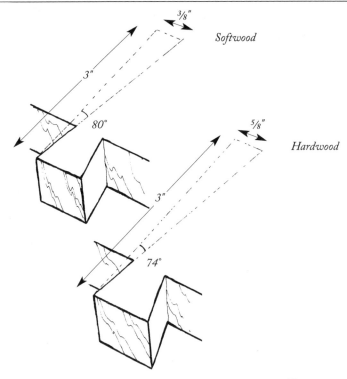

FIG. 288 TAIL ANGLES

pieces feel free to do the same, and allow esthetic concerns to play a part in the way you set out the joint, but bear in mind the underlying structural requirements as explained above.

Exactly how far it is safe to stretch the structural requirements varies from one kind of dovetail joint to another, and from one application and species of material to another. The following discussion of the varieties of the joint that are at your disposal will include remarks on their structural appropriateness and individual requirements. Try to understand what is essential but do not be afraid to experiment. Many apparently ironclad rules and traditional procedures are merely the result of continuing blind acceptance of what was originally little more than someone's whim, and on examination may often be found to be susceptible to change. For example, it used to be considered best if as much joinery as possible could be hidden, since it was the overall form and design that was important. But with the growing interest in craft procedures there has been an increasing tendency to value joinery techniques as design elements in their own right, and expose as much as possible, frequently drawing attention to such details by juxtaposing contrasting woods. Sometimes this is justifiable on structural as well as esthetic grounds, such as using light-colored but hard-wearing maple for drawer sides dramatically dove-tailed into darker drawer fronts whose material might not be quite so appropriate for use in the secondary parts of a piece. In any event, the well-cut dovetail is eminently suited to such visual effects, although there are varieties designed precisely to be completely invisible.

THROUGH DOVETAILS

THE FIRST MAJOR CLASS OF DOVETAILS COMPRISES THOSE USED in the construction of box-like structures big and small, such as drawers, boxes, and chests. Dovetails used in this way can in turn be divided into three main groups: through dovetails, lapped dovetails, and hidden or secret dovetails.

If there is no objection to end grain showing on both sides of the joint, then the through dovetail is the most straightforward and easiest of all to make. Bearing in mind the remarks concerning strength, angle of tail, and proportion of tail to pin, you may design the joint as you want, with as many dovetails as you think look best along the given length of the piece to be joined. In much traditional joinery the distance from the beginning of one tail to the next often equals the thickness of the material in which the joint is made plus 1/16 in., the pins being thereby automatically very narrow at their narrow end. Such work is usually perceived as having been made with very narrow pins, and people are wont to remark that narrow pins are the hallmark of good joinery, but in truth it is the other way round: these proportions are arrived at by setting out the tails as just described.

Only at the ends is there a structural consideration that must be borne in mind. Unless there is a good reason to the contrary, the ends of the joint should consist of pins, not tails. Furthermore, it is best to make these pins to a fixed proportion, as shown below. If you look closely you will see

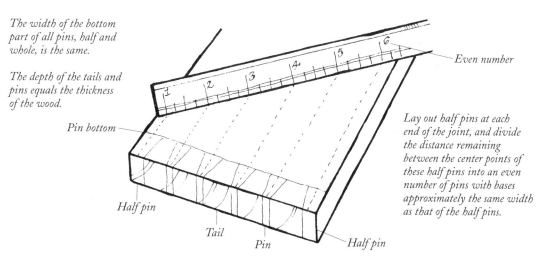

The width of the bottom part of all pins, half and whole, is the same.

The depth of the tails and pins equals the thickness of the wood.

Pin bottom

Even number

Half pin

Tail

Pin

Half pin

Lay out half pins at each end of the joint, and divide the distance remaining between the center points of these half pins into an even number of pins with bases approximately the same width as that of the half pins.

FIG. 289 PROPORTIONS

DOVETAILS

that, in fact, the end pins are half pins, although their width at their widest part, which is on the face side of the piece (the face side being the inside, as mentioned above), is approximately the same as that of a single full pin.

There are two reasons for setting out the end pins in this way: first, the joint is stronger if the ends are formed by pins rather than tails, and second, this presents the easiest way to set out any given number of tails equally spaced between them. All that it is necessary is to draw a line through the center of each half pin and divide the remaining space by the number of tails wanted, as shown above in FIG. 289.

The through dovetail is the ideal joint for the back corners of drawers, and also an ideal joint for the corners of any container or case where end grain is unobjectionable on both sides of the joint. Although when using a shaper, an electric router, or a dovetail jig it is important to set out and cut the joint with precision, with practice it is possible to cut workman-like through dovetails by hand almost entirely by eye. It is not difficult, and indeed not overly critical, to cut the approximate 80° angle of the tail by eye, especially if the piece is held in the vise so that the saw may be worked vertically, as shown below. By cutting two sides at once, assuming you are making a four-sided box, the work is halved and a degree of symmetry is obtained even if each individual tail has a slightly different angle. But well-prepared material, whose ends have been planed perfectly square and perfectly true, is essential. This will permit exact setting out and will facilitate a well-fitting joint. All you need to do is to scribe a line equal to the thickness of the material around the ends of the pieces to be joined,

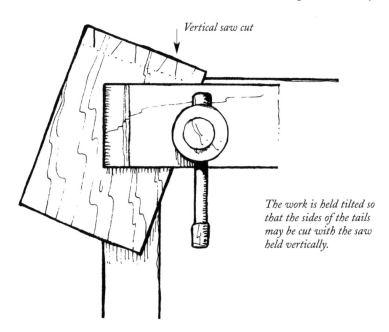

Vertical saw cut

The work is held tilted so that the sides of the tails may be cut with the saw held vertically.

FIG. 290 CUTTING THE TAILS

and then cut the tails by eye — providing you are confident enough about your ability to space the tails acceptably. Some people advocate cutting the pins first, but it is usually easier to use the tails to mark the pins than vice-versa. In fact, by marking the pins directly from the tails, you can guarantee a better fit than might be obtained if you were to rely on a measured layout. You also reduce the amount of actual layout necessary with all the attendant opportunities for error.

When laying out and cutting dovetails the following tips may prove useful:

- Instead of fumbling with trysquare and adjustable bevel, use a dove-tail marker to lay out the angles of the tails.
- When marking the pins directly from the tails, use a sharp scratch awl or pointed penknife rather than a pencil.
- Until you become practised, take the precaution of shading the waste areas before you start to cut anything.
- Be especially careful always to cut on the waste side of the lines.
- Be very careful not to cut below the level of the scribed lines defining the bottom of the pins and tails.

Since this joint, more than many others, looks sloppy unless cut with great accuracy, and since there are so many cuts to it, your first attempts may not be perfect. Rather than giving up on dovetails because of this, try joining a couple of sides, with perhaps no more than two dovetails to a 6 in. width, entirely by eye. Aim not for perfect accuracy, but for speed and basically correct proportions. The ability to do this will make you readier to use this powerful joint for many odd jobs, such as knocking

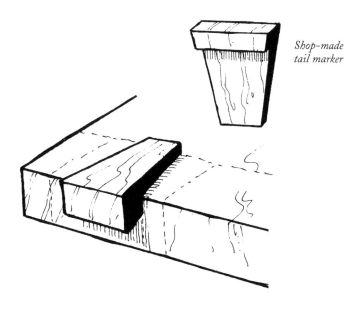

Shop-made tail marker

FIG. 291 TAIL LAYOUT

together a scrap box or two. It will also give you a better appreciation of the mechanics involved, and allow you to concentrate more on careful cutting when you do need to make the joint as perfectly as possible for a finished piece of fine furniture.

This approach is a good idea in general, and a excellent way to become familiar with new joinery techniques. You will discover which parts are truly critical and which parts are not complete disasters even if bodged a bit. You will learn things such as how softwood may be compressed a little in some areas to present a perfect fit, and exactly what the limits are of certain hardwoods. Best of all you will come to regard the dovetail as an all-round, everyday kind of joint, useful for a lot of things as well as more precious pieces.

LAPPED DOVETAILS

LAPPED DOVETAILS ARE USEFUL FOR CABINET OR DRAWER construction where it is desirable to conceal the ends of the tails (see FIG. 292). Two things to consider are the amount of lap to leave — it will depend on the species of material, but remember that the longer the tail the stronger the joint — and the fact that when using this joint for large carcase construction it will help resist any tendency of the ends to twist if the tails are spaced more closely at the ends. At the same time, the tails in the center may be more widely spaced to reduce the amount of work necessary.

Dovetails are often the joint of preference when making carcases to be veneered, and it is important to remember that although these particular dovetails will not be seen, and may consequently be cut somewhat less than perfectly, the joined surfaces must be absolutely flat, for with time any unevenness may telegraph through.

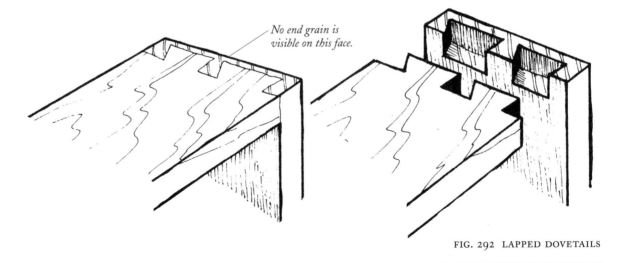

No end grain is visible on this face.

FIG. 292 LAPPED DOVETAILS

HIDDEN DOVETAILS

DOVETAILS MAY BE HIDDEN, THEREBY LEAVING ONLY A THIN LINE of end grain visible, by means of a projecting lap left on either the tail ends or the pin ends, as shown below. If you decide to leave the extra lap on the pin ends, note that it is much easier to cut these first, and then mark the tails from them rather than the other way round.

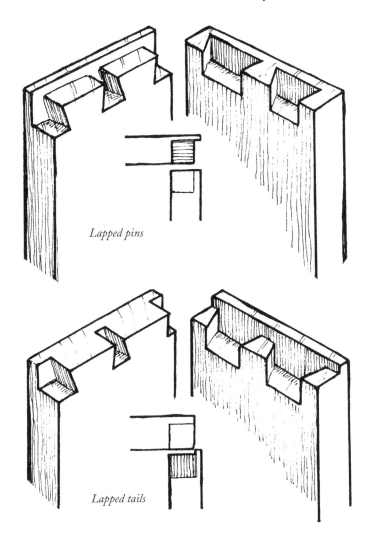

Lapped pins

Lapped tails

FIG. 293 DOUBLE-LAPPED DOVETAILS

The ultimate form of hidden dovetail, which when assembled gives the appearance of nothing more than a simple miter, is the so-called secret mitered dovetail. This is the monster referred to at the beginning of the chapter, and which takes a lot of practice to perfect since there are so many chances for spoiling a perfect fit. It also requires a certain zen-like strength of character to make, since when well done this difficult joint can give the impression that in fact you opted for no joint at all. You will, however, have the satisfaction of knowing that time will demonstrate the superior integrity of the procedure as this joint remains secure while simple miters may separate. Its uses are chiefly in fine work where visible joinery would work counter to the desired effect, such as at the corners of plinths, hoods, and certain carcases.

Although well-fitting pins and tails are essential to the joint's strength, without which there is very little point in attempting it in the first place, the visible success of the joint lies in how well the mitered sections are made. These are most easily formed by hand, providing a really well tuned low-angle shoulder plane is available, and used in conjunction with a guide block, pre-cut to a perfect 45° angle, as shown below. Note that this is another instance where it is easier to cut the pins before the tails, in order that the former may be used to mark the latter.

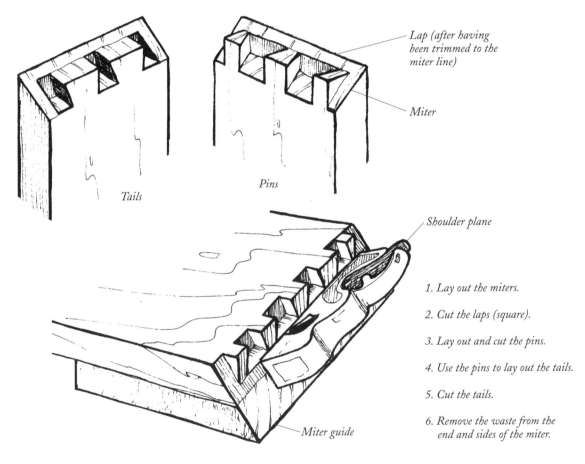

Lap (after having been trimmed to the miter line)

Miter

Tails

Pins

Shoulder plane

Miter guide

1. Lay out the miters.

2. Cut the laps (square).

3. Lay out and cut the pins.

4. Use the pins to lay out the tails.

5. Cut the tails.

6. Remove the waste from the end and sides of the miter.

FIG. 294 SECRET MITERED DOVETAIL

CARCASE DOVETAILS

THE SECOND MAJOR CLASS OF DOVETAILS CONSISTS OF THOSE joints used — usually singly or in pairs and at most in threes — in the framework of various carcases for drawers, table substructures, desks, sideboards, and other pieces of casework.

The most typical form of this joint is known as the carcase dovetail, and is used for joining the sides of a carcase to a horizontal framing member such as might constitute the top of a drawer opening. It is a kind of lapped dovetail with a pair of uneven tails.

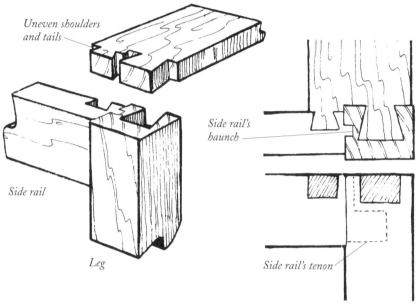

FIG. 295 CARCASE DOVETAILS

What usually makes this joint a little tricky is the necessity for making the tails different lengths and sizes according to the individual nature of the piece involved. It is not enough merely to cut the joint so that it connects the top of the post and adjoining panel or side, but care must also be taken that any mortises, grooves, or other joinery details connected with the carcase are not compromised by the dovetail itself. This can require some extra forethought when making the basic framing to which it is to be connected. For example, the rail that connects to the post shown in FIG. 295 must be made with a mortise haunched deeply enough to accommodate the dovetail. As usually made, the tail might cut into the rail's tenon or its haunch. You must also bear in mind the fact that not all rails meet all posts the same way; some are flush and some may be more or less rabbeted. This can involve cutting shoulders of various depths in the inside dovetail.

SLOT DOVETAILS

A SECOND FORM OF FRAMING DOVETAIL IS THE SIMPLE SLOT dovetail shown in FIG. 296. What makes this joint distinctive is that the tail is often cut in the width, rather than in the thickness, of the wood. Extremely useful as a right-angled way of connecting framing members, it may also be made barefaced, as in FIG. 297. The simpler variety is quicker and often perfectly adequate structurally. The stopped variety shown in FIG. 298 is especially useful for stretchers under tables where a visible dovetail might be objectionable. If stopped above as shown, rather than below, a transverse pin fixed into the tail provides good extra security, especially if the stretcher may be expected to have feet resting on it. Likewise, although a barefaced slot dovetail might be strong enough from a structural point of view, making the joint with two sloping sides produces two shoulders and avoids the possibility of an unsightly gap on the shoulderless side.

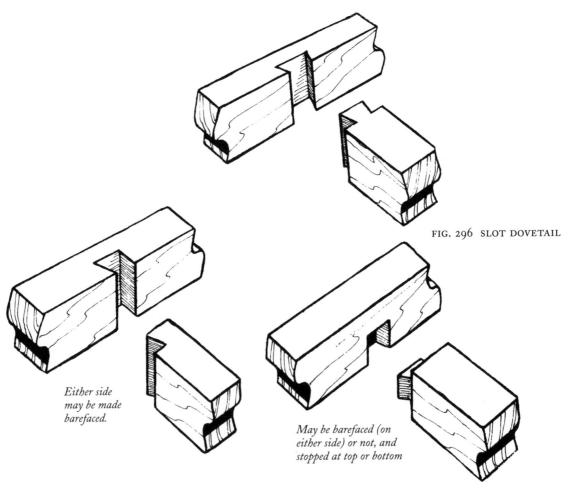

FIG. 296 SLOT DOVETAIL

Either side may be made barefaced.

May be barefaced (on either side) or not, and stopped at top or bottom

FIG. 297 BAREFACED SLOT DOVETAIL

FIG. 298 STOPPED BAREFACED SLOT DOVETAIL

HOUSED DOVETAILS

WHEN SLOT DOVETAILS ARE CUT ACROSS THE WIDTH OF A BOARD
they become a very useful means of joining partitions and shelving in
carcases. Not only does this joint, often referred to as a housed dovetail,
provide a way of joining shelves to cupboard sides, for example, without
the necessity of completely penetrating the sides with either fasteners or
through tenons, it also offers the advantage of preventing the sides from
bowing or cupping as they might if the shelves were merely housed.

In its simplest form the dovetail is taken across the entire width of the
board, as shown below. The horizontal partitions in many 18th century
chests and cabinets are joined this way. Sometimes the joint is barefaced
and sometimes shouldered (FIG. 300), but all three varieties are somewhat
awkward because the mortise for the tail must be cut very accurately or it
will be very difficult to slide the dovetail home across the width of the
board, and furthermore it is not always desirable to have the front of the
dovetail showing. The easy way to avoid both these problems is to make
a tapered housed dovetail. This form not only hides the potentially imperfect end of the dovetail, but, more usefully, makes the joint much easier to
assemble, since everything slides together easily until the last moment —

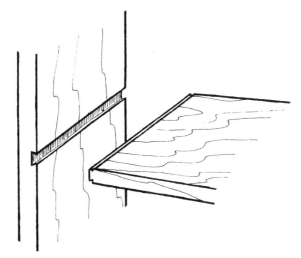

FIG. 299 HOUSED DOVETAIL

FIG. 300 HOUSING VARIETIES

DOVETAILS

when the dovetail finally makes sudden contact with the tapered sides of the mortise. The way to set out this joint is shown in FIG. 301. An even simpler form wherein only the end of the dovetailed part is actually dovetailed is shown in FIG. 302.

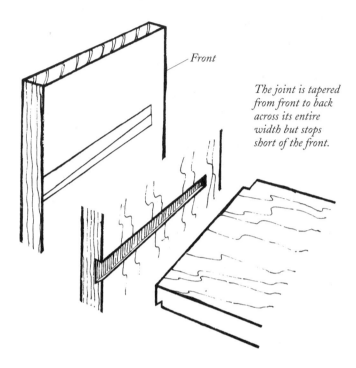

Front

The joint is tapered from front to back across its entire width but stops short of the front.

FIG. 301 TAPERED HOUSED DOVETAIL

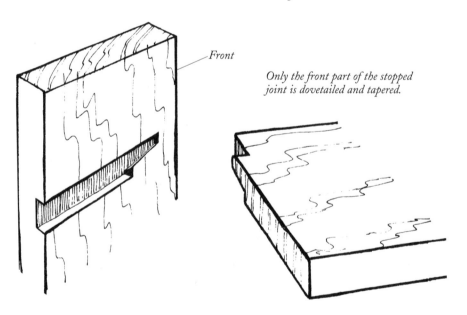

Front

Only the front part of the stopped joint is dovetailed and tapered.

FIG. 302 SHORT TAPERED HOUSED DOVETAIL

DECORATIVE DOVETAILS

THE THIRD MAJOR CLASS OF DOVETAILS OWES LITTLE TO structural demands and is unashamedly ostentatious. Taking advantage of the contrast between side grain and end grain, and the often even greater contrast possible with differently colored woods, the distinctive shape of a dovetail can become a decorative design element in its own right. For this to be perfectly successful it is important to make sure that the joint is carefully cut with no untoward and unsightly gaps anywhere apparent. Because of this, decorative dovetails such as the variety shown in FIG. 303 are peculiarly suited to production with the aid of various dovetail jigs designed for use with electric routers, especially those jigs capable of adjustable pin depths and variable spacing.

Another form of decorative dovetail is the lined dovetail (FIG. 304). This may be made in the normal fashion, after which the interstices of tail and pin are sawed out to receive slivers of contrasting material, further defining the characteristic shape.

A third variety, named for Bermuda, where it has been traditionally used in chest-on-frame construction, and which is also seen in much Spanish work, is a form of lapped dovetail. The dovetails shown overleaf in FIG. 305 are made by using templates to trace varying designs in the ends of the tails and matching shapes in the lapped portion of the pins.

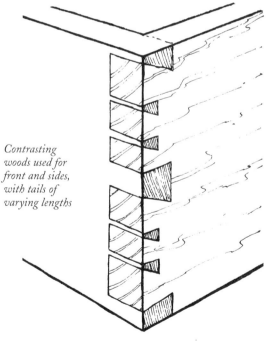

Contrasting woods used for front and sides, with tails of varying lengths

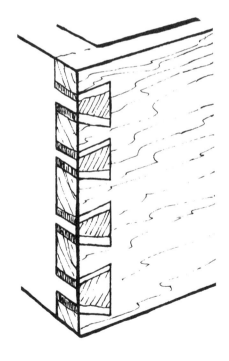

FIG. 303 DECORATIVE DOVETAILS

FIG. 304 LINED DOVETAILS

DOVETAILS

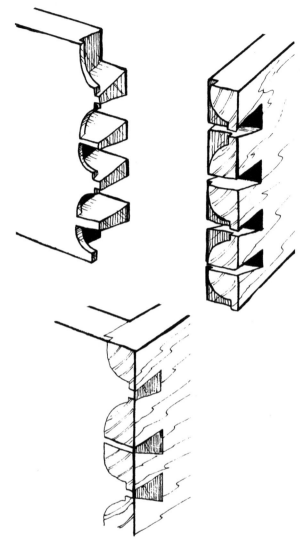

FIG. 305 BERMUDA DOVETAILS

Other variations of dovetails are legion, as are the methods of constructing them and the ingenious methods of incorporating them as design solutions into constructions requiring mitered edges or rabbets. Mention has been made of three-part dovetails; there are also end-to-end dovetails (FIG. 306), a legitimately useful way of joining two pieces end-to-end, but which are often regarded as trick 'puzzle' joints — their construction becomes obvious once you stop thinking that pins and tails must always be formed perpendicularly to the face of the work (the joint is formed and slid together diagonally) — as well as a whole field of

Tails are visible on all four sides, giving the illusion of four separate tails, but because they are cut diagonally there are in reality only two tails to this joint.

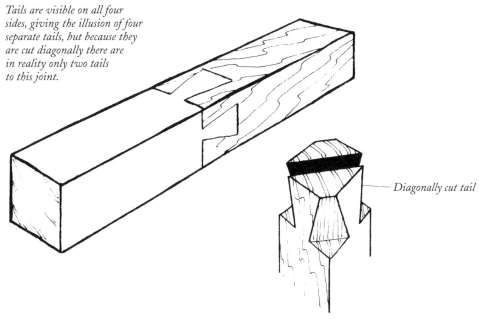

Diagonally cut tail

FIG. 306 END-TO-END DOVETAILS

splayed dovetails depending on compound angles, of which more is explained in the next chapter.

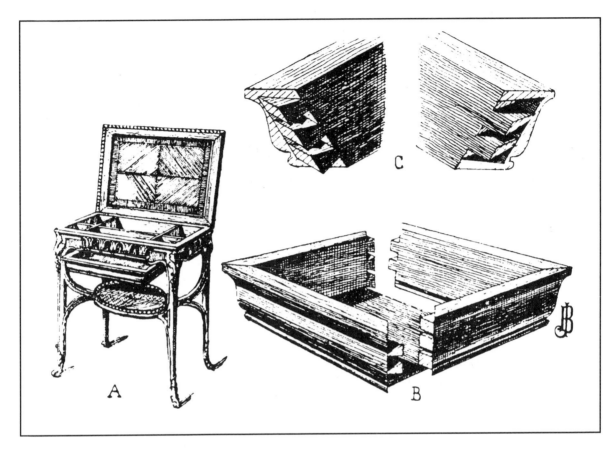

Splayed Dovetails
from *Furnituremaking* by J. Boison, 1922

A. Modern worktable, cabinetmaking wood and gilt bronzes, with a vide-poche drawer and an oval shelf below.
B. Vide-poche drawer made with hidden splayed dovetails.
C. Interior view of the hidden splayed dovetails.

14

SPLAYED JOINTS

Splayed Butt Joints • Housed Butt Joints •
The Elevation Method • Splayed Miter Joints •
Splayed Dovetails

A T FIRST SIGHT, LAYING OUT AND MARKING THE JOINTS FOR SOMETHING WITH SPLAYED SIDES MIGHT SEEM ONE OF THE MORE CONFUSING AND DAUNTING PROJECTS THAT you could ever imagine. Although the actual cutting of these joints is not very difficult, figuring out the correct angles and trying to draw the right lines can quickly degenerate into a mind-numbing exercise in frustration. The problem is that whichever way you look at something with splayed sides you are always seeing something on a slope, so that it is impossible to take a direct measurement from a plan or an elevation view.

There are shortcuts, such as charts which give the angles at which the blades of tablesaws or radial-arm saws and their miter gauges must be set to cut various compound miters, but making the effort to understand the geometry involved is far better in the long run. This will not only liberate you from a blind dependence on charts which are often annoyingly incomplete, sometimes inaccurate, and rarely to hand when you need them, but will also make possible a whole new level of joinery. Free from the tyranny of rectilinearity, you will be able to undertake projects far more sophisticated than you might previously have thought possible.

In any case, as most woodworkers discover sooner or later, there are many times when splayed joinery is unavoidable. Such instances range from the simple mitering of crown moulding for cornices (for since such moulding is designed to be applied at an angle, it is by its very nature splayed), to objects such as knife trays, hoppers, troughs, flower boxes, chests, and other elements in fine furniture made with sides that are beveled in two or more directions, such as elegant vide-poches (see the plate facing page 233). Furthermore, the underlying geometric principles involved in laying out these compound angles are often very useful to carpenters who have to frame roofs with hips and dormers.

Since the principle is similar for all these things, the knife tray shown below will illustrate the process of how to lay out simple butt joints, then how to lay out housed butt joints (the same process as laying out splayed keyed-corner joints), splayed or compound miter joints, and finally splayed dovetails, the which are sometimes called beveled dovetails.

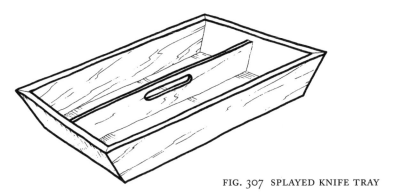

FIG. 307 SPLAYED KNIFE TRAY

SPLAYED BUTT JOINTS

NO ACTUAL MEASUREMENTS OR ANGLES ARE GIVEN IN THE FOLLOWING explanations, since the method works equally well for any measurement or set of angles you may choose. But once having decided on these, do make full-sized drawings using them.

Start by drawing a plan and elevation of the knife tray, as in FIG. 308. You will see that it is impossible to take off the correct angles from this drawing, since whichever way you look at it every part is sloping. What needs to be done is to imagine the ends and the sides laid flat, so that when looked at from above, as in a plan view, the true shape may be directly measured. Begin with the ends. Note that the height and angle of the top and bottom bevels can be taken off directly from the elevation, since this is a true cross-section of these parts. What you cannot see is the actual shape and true angles of the sides of the ends, since in the drawing these pieces are sloping towards you. What needs to be done is to lay these ends flat.

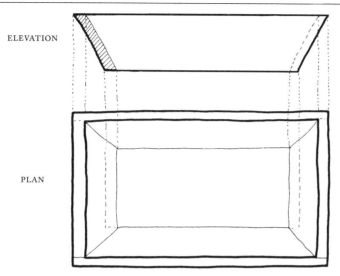

ELEVATION

PLAN

FIG. 308 PLAN & ELEVATION

By describing an arc, whose center is the bottom outside corner *(A)* and whose radius is the length of the side *AB*, that intersects with the continuation of the bottom of the tray at *C,* and then dropping perpendiculars from *C* and *A* so that they intersect with the continuation of the insides of the tray at *D* and *E*, and *F* and *G*, and finally connecting these points as shown, we can, in effect, lay the end flat so that it can be measured.

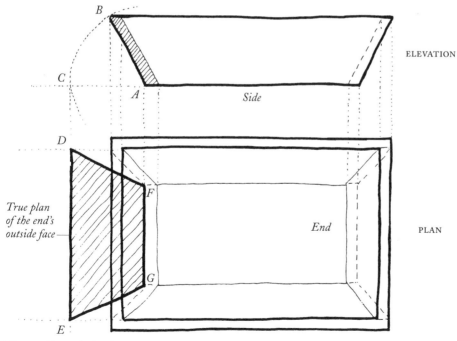

ELEVATION

Side

True plan of the end's outside face —

End

PLAN

FIG. 309 TRUE PLAN OF END

SPLAYED JOINTS

It is now possible to measure the true shape of the end directly from the shaded area of the drawing and transfer these measurements to the workpiece. But note, however, that we started with the end pieces already beveled on the top and bottom edges, and that therefore the shaded area represents the *outside* of the end. The same procedure could have been followed with equal success had we hinged the end piece from the bottom inside corner (*H*, in FIG. 310), but in this case we would have ended up with the plan of the *inside* surface of the end.

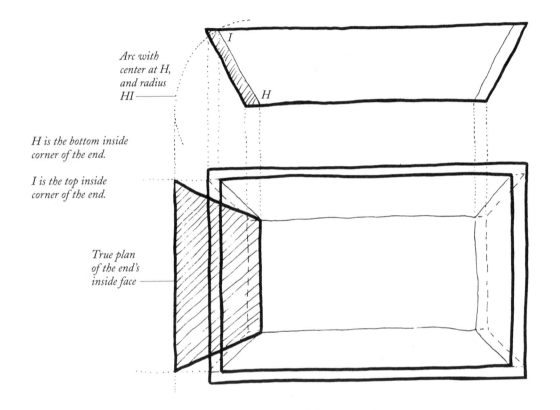

Arc with
center at H,
and radius
HI

H is the bottom inside
corner of the end.

I is the top inside
corner of the end.

True plan
of the end's
inside face

FIG. 310 TRUE PLAN OF INSIDE END

Most splayed knife boxes are constructed with the same amount of splay at the sides as at the ends. In which event, having discovered the correct angle of splay for the ends, you will at the same time also have discovered the correct angle of splay for the sides, and no further drawing will be necessary. But if these sides should be splayed differently from the ends, the procedure for finding the second true splayed shape remains the same as for finding the first true splayed shape: simply draw a new elevation showing the end, rather than the side, and repeat the process illustrated in FIG. 309.

HOUSED BUTT JOINTS

IT DOES NOT MATTER WHETHER THE SIDES ARE HOUSED IN THE ends, or the ends are housed in the sides; once you have drawn the true plan of either side or end, any housing is simply a matter of drawing parallel lines. FIG. 311 shows the same knife tray as in FIG. 308, but this time with the ends housed into the sides, rather than being simply butt-jointed. Having first drawn the elevation of the right-hand end, and from this having produced a true plan of the side, mark the groove for the housing by drawing parallel lines produced down from the side elevation, which contains a true section through the ends.

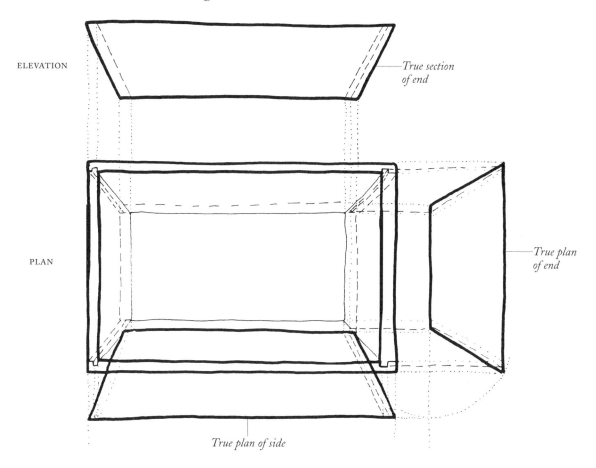

ELEVATION

True section
of end

PLAN

True plan
of end

True plan of side

FIG. 311 PLAN, & TRUE SIDE & END ELEVATIONS

Keyed corner joints of any variety are laid out in precisely the same way, for once you have produced a true plan of the sides and the ends, any amount of grooving or housing can be drawn directly onto the plans, and measurements taken directly from them.

SPLAYED JOINTS

THE ELEVATION METHOD

AN EVEN SIMPLER METHOD OF DETERMINING THE TRUE ANGLES of splayed sides that may be used when all the sides are splayed at the same angle is shown in FIG. 312. Start by drawing the elevation of one end (defined as a side that fits between two other sides), as at *1*. Note that the shaded parts represent true sections through the sides (beveled only at the bottom for the sake of clarity — this does not affect the method). Draw arcs whose centers *(A* and *C)* are the bottom inside corners of the end piece, and whose radii are the same as the insides of the side pieces *(AB* and *CD* at *2)*. Erect perpendiculars from *A* and *C* to intersect the arcs you have just drawn, and draw a line *(EF)* that runs through these two intersections, as at *3*. Finally, erect perpendiculars from the inside top corners of the sides, *(B* and *D),* and from the intersection of these perpendiculars and the line passing through the intersections of the

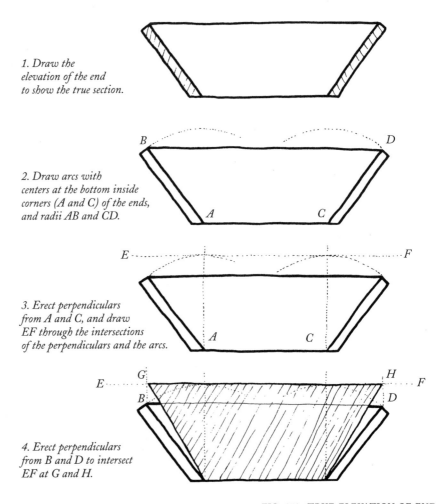

1. Draw the elevation of the end to show the true section.

2. Draw arcs with centers at the bottom inside corners (A and C) of the ends, and radii AB and CD.

3. Erect perpendiculars from A and C, and draw EF through the intersections of the perpendiculars and the arcs.

4. Erect perpendiculars from B and D to intersect EF at G and H.

FIG. 312 TRUE ELEVATION OF END

previous perpendiculars and arcs, draw lines back down to *A* and *C*. The shaded area thus defined at *4 (AGHC)* is the true elevation of the end, and the angles contained therein will be the same for all four sides.

SPLAYED MITER JOINTS

THE PROCEDURES DESCRIBED ABOVE WILL HELP YOU DETERMINE accurately the true shape of the ends and sides, as well as the true angles formed by the top and bottom edges with all the sides. But if the sides are to be mitered rather than butt-jointed, there is another angle to be measured: the angle of the miter, since a splayed miter is necessarily a compound miter and not a simple 45° miter.

The elevation and plan of one corner of our knife tray is shown with its equally splayed sides at FIG. 313. The normal way to determine the angle of any miter is to bisect the overall angle by drawing a line from the outside corner to the inside corner. This can usually be done directly from the plan. In the case of a splayed corner, however, the plan of the top edges is necessarily narrower than in reality, since we are looking at them from an angle. For clarity, the end is shown with its top edge cut square to its sides. This way, when seen from above, it appears thinner than it is and the lines in FIG. 314 representing the true thickness fall outside the other lines. If the top edge were beveled, so as to be horizontal, then this edge would be thicker than an square edge, and lines representing the true

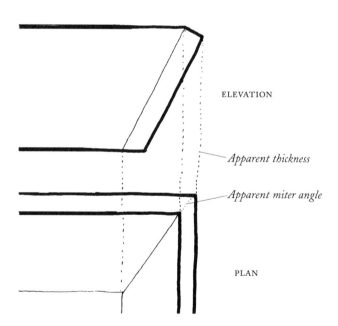

ELEVATION

Apparent thickness

Apparent miter angle

PLAN

FIG. 313 PLAN & ELEVATION OF MITERED TRAY

SPLAYED JOINTS

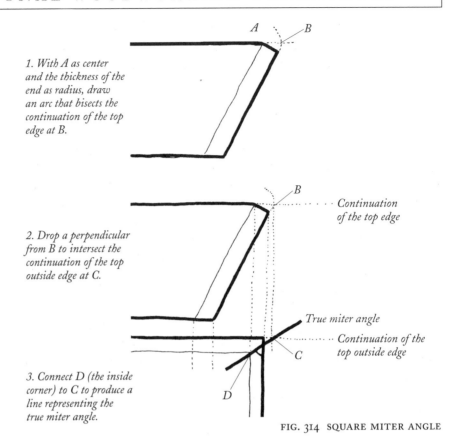

1. With A as center and the thickness of the end as radius, draw an arc that bisects the continuation of the top edge at B.

2. Drop a perpendicular from B to intersect the continuation of the top outside edge at C.

3. Connect D (the inside corner) to C to produce a line representing the true miter angle.

FIG. 314 SQUARE MITER ANGLE

thickness of the piece, although produced in exactly the same way, would not be so clearly shown as in the example.

To prove this, and at the same time obtain a true measurement of the actual thickness of the sides, draw an arc, whose center is at *A* and whose radius equals the thickness of the end, so that it cuts the continuation of the top edge at *B*, as shown above at *1* in FIG. 314. This operation will demonstrate the real thickness of the end.

Now drop a perpendicular from *B*, as at *2*, to cut the continuation of the top outside edge at *C*, as shown in the plan. A line drawn from point *C* to the inside corner *D* represents the actual miter angle. Set the bevel on the thickened lines and transfer this angle to both workpieces to be mitered.

Another method for obtaining the correct miter angle for splayed sides can be demonstrated from the elevation of a corner of a tray whose top edges are beveled so as to be horizontal, as in FIG. 315. From the outside top edge *C*, erect a vertical line (perpendicular to the base), as at *2*. Measure off the true thickness of the side (as represented by *AB* at *1*) on this line, and from this point, *D*, draw a line back to the inside top edge. The angle thus formed at *D* is the miter angle.

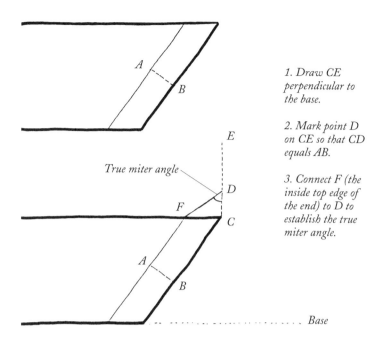

1. Draw CE perpendicular to the base.

2. Mark point D on CE so that CD equals AB.

3. Connect F (the inside top edge of the end) to D to establish the true miter angle.

FIG. 315 BEVELED MITER ANGLE

SPLAYED DOVETAILS

BEFORE ANY SPLAYED WORK DESIGNED TO BE DOVETAILED CAN BE set out, drawings must first be prepared as for butt joints. This will allow you to produce the correct angles and shapes of the various pieces, but you must then remember to allow for the extra length at the ends of those sides destined to be formed into the pins, since the pins necessarily engage the dovetails to the full thickness of the stuff being worked.

Furthermore, since both the bottom edges and the top edges of all the sides will eventually be planed flat, do not forget to allow for the extra width required to achieve this, as shown below.

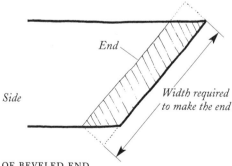

FIG. 316 TRUE WIDTH OF BEVELED END

SPLAYED JOINTS

Two ways of setting out through-dovetails in splayed work are shown in FIG. 317. Although the way illustrated at *A* perhaps looks better, the way shown at *B* is stronger, since when once the sides are fixed to the bottom, the two parts cannot be slid apart in the same plane.

A. Straight dovetails

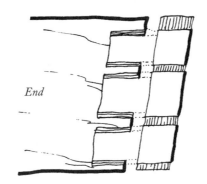
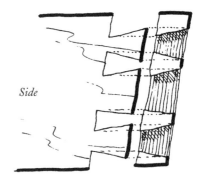

End

Side

B. Right-angled dovetails

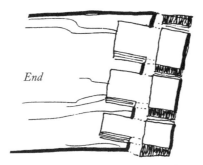
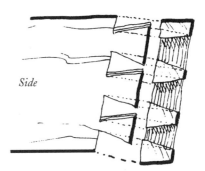

End

Side

FIG. 317 SPLAYED DOVETAILS

It is easier to use a bevel than a marking gauge to mark out the parts of the joint, and providing you do this with extreme care, the only difficulty that remains is in the cutting out of the joints. Wherever possible hold the wood in the vise so that all saw cuts can be made vertically, even though it will be found necessary to lower one end of the saw when approaching the bottom of the cuts. A pointed or skew chisel will be of great help when removing the waste between the pins and the tails.

When the joints have all been cut, the top and bottom edges of the sides may be planed to the correct bevel.

The last problem will occur with assembly. Since all four sides are sloping, using a mallet or clamps to bring the joint tight can be difficult.

Clamping, or even temporarily gluing, wedge-shaped blocks to the sides can make this task much easier.

Lapped dovetails are not very much more difficult, providing you take care in the layout, but for a real tour de force try your hand at a splayed version of a secret mitered dovetail joint (see FIG. 294, chapter 13). This joint was popular in the days when it was considered poor workmanship to leave exposed joinery. If cut and assembled well it cannot be distinguished from a plain miter joint, and no one will believe that you have really made such a difficult joint. Not only will it require the most labor and skill, but it will be a supreme test of your modesty in resisting ostentation.

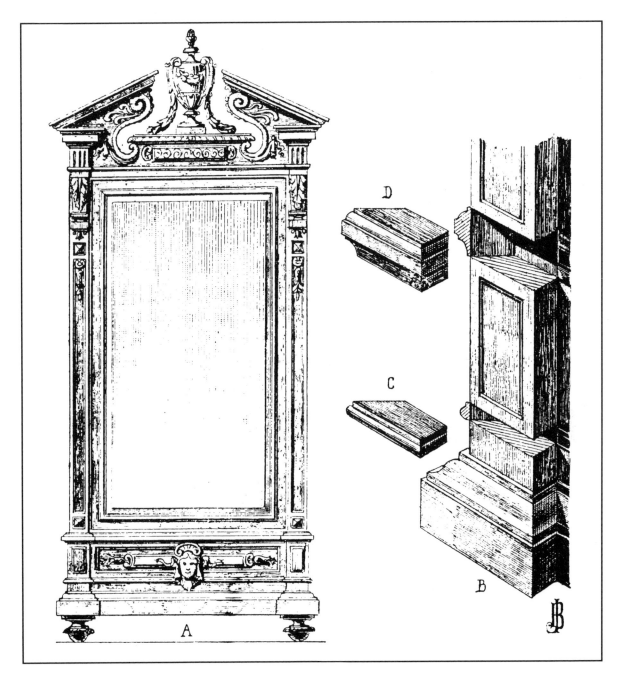

Wood Movement & Secondary Woods
from *Furnituremaking* by J. Boison, 1922

A. Armoire in cabinetmaking wood; designed by Eugène Prignot. Modern furniture, second half of the 19th century.
B. Plinth pilaster, notched to receive the horizontal moulded fillets C and D.
C. (and D.) Horizontal fillet with a proud moulded edge.

15

MOULDING

Historical Development • Fabrication with Powertools •
Handtool Methods • Installing Moulding

A T FIRST GLANCE MOULDING MIGHT APPEAR TO BE NO
MORE THAN ORNAMENTAL, AND AS SUCH AVAILABLE TO
BE USED FREELY AS THE FANCY TAKES YOU. WHILE SOME
mouldings are indeed purely fanciful, it is important to realize that not
only was much developed as a result of specific structural needs, but also
that since its use in different eras frequently became highly formalized
into related groupings of particular elements, random or freely chosen
combinations more often than not produce absurd results. It is therefore
essential to understand its development in order to use various mouldings
sensibly and appropriately.

HISTORICAL DEVELOPMENT

THE IMPULSE TO DECORATE IS OFTEN IRRESISTIBLE, AND THE
edges of woodwork have long been targets, such as the scalloped edges
found an much of the earliest American furniture. But long before this,
moulding as a form of edge treatment was a common feature for very

practical reasons. When frame-and-panel construction became common in the Middle Ages, together with the introduction of decoration for decoration's sake came the very practical use of simple chamfered edges along the top edge of the bottom parts of frames to help prevent dust buildup, in the same way that beveled edges were formed on exterior stonework to provide easy runoff for rain and snow. In the same way, other forms of edge treatment, such as moulded beads or chamfers, were used to provide protection to otherwise sharp corners, preventing damage both to the work and to passers-by.

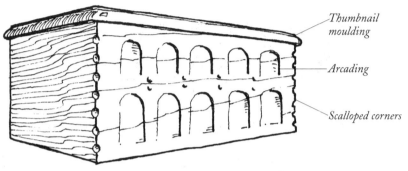

Thumbnail moulding

Arcading

Scalloped corners

FIG. 318 EARLY AMERICAN BOX

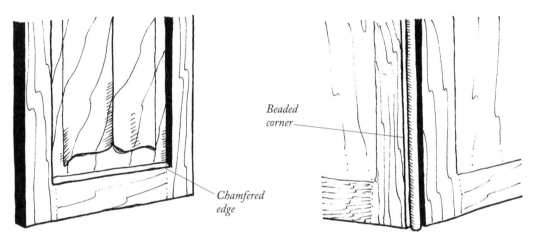

Beaded corner

Chamfered edge

FIG. 319 PARCHEMIN PANEL

FIG. 320 WALL PANELING

Moulding subsequently became much used as a method of making various added structural members more coherent with the overall design of a piece. For example, when a panel sits not in a groove cut in the edge of its frame but in a simple rabbet, it requires an added piece, nailed or glued to the frame, to keep it in place. This strip is invariably moulded, and thus becomes not only a structural piece but also an integral part of the overall design. Similarly, moulded pieces may be used to cover reveals and gaps between one section of woodwork and another. Closely related to this function is the use of moulding to ease the transition from one part of a structure to another, such as the use of crown moulding at the junction of wall and ceiling.

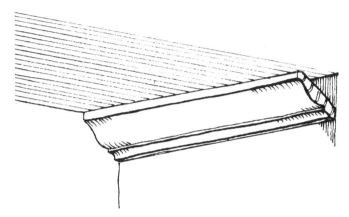

FIG. 321 CROWN MOULDING

Towards the end of the 18th century, mouldings used in this last way were increasingly grouped according to patterns derived from classical Greek and Roman architectural models. Indeed the dominant architectural forms of the time derived their basic proportions from the so-called *Five Orders of Architecture**, which represented varying proportional systems used in classical times. Since these proportions were interpreted from the mutual relationships of the various parts of columns and arches, all of which were replete with different sets of mouldings, new design incorporated not only the relevant proportions but also the particular mouldings that were appropriate for each Order. Therefore, combining mismatched mouldings with designs based on different proportional systems is not only inappropriate but more often than not also produces very unhappy results.

While deciding which mouldings to use for structural purposes may be largely pragmatic — since the shape and the proportion of the moulding must be largely governed by its function — deciding which mouldings are appropriate from a purely esthetic point of view requires a little study. Familiarity with actual examples of period furniture is the best way if you are involved with restoration or reproduction, or if you are designing something based on a period style, but a few generalizations may be made as follows: Most furniture built prior to the 18th century, in the period

* The term 'Five [sometimes 'Seven'] Orders of Architecture' derives from books by the Roman architect and theorist Vitruvius, and various Renaissance authors, most notably Palladio (see the Select Bibliography), which systematically analyze classical proportions.

247   **MOULDING**

often referred to as the 'Age of Oak' (see chapter 19), will be found to have mouldings ranging in nature from purely Gothic to shapes derived, often none too closely, from classical models (see FIG. 322).

With the emergence at the end of the 17th century and the beginning of the 18th century of the cabinetmaker as an artisan distinct from the carpenter and joiner, and together with the increasing use of veneers and the consequent emphasis on wood grain and color which took over from carving as the dominant form of decoration, the forms and proportions of mouldings became more refined (see FIG. 323). Examination of furniture from this period, referred to as the 'Walnut Period' (see chapter 19), is the best way to appreciate the difference.

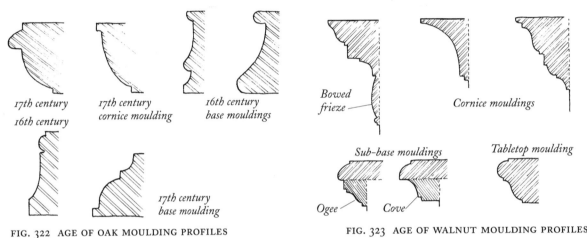

17th century

16th century

17th century cornice moulding

16th century base mouldings

Bowed frieze

Cornice mouldings

Sub-base mouldings

Tabletop moulding

17th century base moulding

Ogee   *Cove*

FIG. 322 AGE OF OAK MOULDING PROFILES

FIG. 323 AGE OF WALNUT MOULDING PROFILES

Subsequent styles, such as the various Georgian and Federal styles of the 18th and early 19th centuries, adhered much more closely to classical models (see FIG. 324). These may be studied in reprints of the classical models as published by Palladio, the 16th century Italian architect who served as the immediate inspiration for many 18th century cabinetmakers such as Chippendale and Hepplewhite.

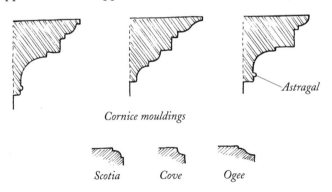

Astragal

Cornice mouldings

Scotia   *Cove*   *Ogee*

FIG. 324 MOULDINGS OF 18TH–19TH CENTURIES

It is generally the case that mouldings designed for architectural use are often considerably simplified when applied to furniture and interior woodwork. Nevertheless, certain broad observations may be made, such as that mouldings derived from Greek examples are based on an ellipse, whereas mouldings derived from Roman models are based on circles (see FIG. 325), and that convex and concave profiles are usually alternated in addition to becoming progressively larger or smaller, but only close study of the *Five Orders of Architecture* and their underlying proportions, together with direct observation of actual pieces, will serve to show what belongs with what if authenticity and esthetic logic are to be achieved.

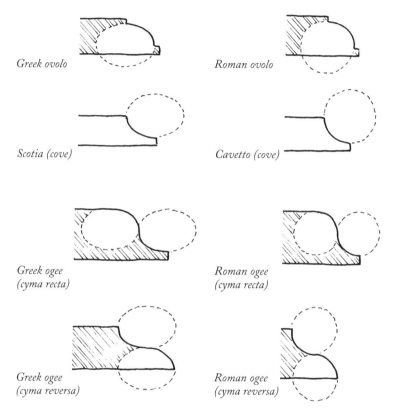

Greek ovolo   *Roman ovolo*

Scotia (cove)   *Cavetto (cove)*

Greek ogee   *Roman ogee*
(cyma recta)   *(cyma recta)*

Greek ogee   *Roman ogee*
(cyma reversa)   *(cyma reversa)*

FIG. 325 GREEK & ROMAN PROFILES

FABRICATION WITH POWERTOOLS

FOR MORE THAN A HUNDRED YEARS NOW MOST MOULDING that is required in quantity has been made by machine. Standardized commercial mouldings are supplied by millworks which manufacture them on specialty moulding machines whose sole job is to turn out thousands of feet of identical moulding (see FIG. 326 overleaf). For the occasional non-standard pattern, many large lumberyards have facilities

MOULDING

for custom-producing certain shapes, charging so much extra per foot, mainly to cover the cost of having the requisite cutters made.

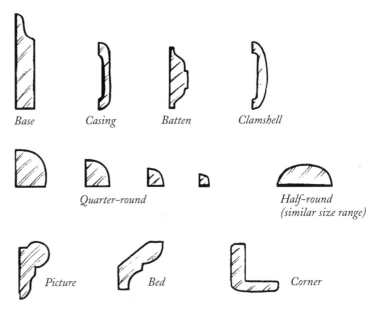

FIG. 326 COMMERCIAL MOULDINGS

A more recent development, spurred by laudable attempts to preserve natural resources, has been to produce non-wood moulding. But removed one step further from the traditional methods of production, these new products are often unfortunately even further removed from the original design-logic inherent in wooden mouldings, and as a result many are meanly designed, ill-informed, and poor imitations of the originals.

On the other hand, many small shops are now commonly equipped with shapers — or spindle moulders, as they are known in Britain — which, as well as making rabbets and other forms of edge joints, can also be used to produce moulded edges.

For the individual craftsperson making custom furniture, or those working in a small shop not equipped with a shaper, there are several alternative methods of producing a large variety of mouldings. These include various machine methods involving the use of tablesaws, radial-arm saws, and even drill presses, as well as other powertool methods using routers and electric drills. But the use of moulding planes (see FIG. 115, chapter 4) remains eminently viable, and indeed, in certain situations, such as creating mouldings with undercut profiles, these, and other hand-tools such as the scratch stock, may offer the only practical method.

If you are prepared to be limited by the relatively narrow range of commercially manufactured mouldings, and to be satisfied with the few species of wood in which they are supplied, it is doubtless economical to use millworks and lumberyards as your source of supply. Although this may be appropriate for much architectural woodwork, especially in certain contemporary styles using simplified profiles, it will rarely prove satisfactory to the more discriminating furnituremaker.

Providing the machines can be afforded in the first place, producing mouldings on shapers is unquestionably the most cost-efficient method of creating custom mouldings from whatever species of wood is required, although choices may be limited by your arsenal of cutters, and a certain amount of finishing work will still remain to be done in order to remove the marks left by the shaper cutters. Similarly, the use of a router, or even a router installed in a router table, while capable of producing large quantities in short order, is still limited by the selection of often expensive router bits at your disposal.

However, by combining the resources of routers and powersaws, as well as various handtools, you can enlarge your vocabulary of possible profiles almost infinitely. Far example, while routers can provide you with a wide range of relatively small mouldings (especially if successive passes are made with different depth and fence settings, as well as with different bits), larger mouldings, which may present problems beyond the capacity of the average router, can be approached with the help of the tablesaw. Although it can be used with special moulding-cutter attachments, the tablesaw is also very useful for producing large-profiled mouldings, of both straight and curved sections, using nothing more than a fine-toothed 10 in. blade.

There are two basic tablesaw techniques for producing mouldings. The first involves simple linear saw cuts at different depths into the stock until the desired profile is approached; finishing being accomplished with scrapers and sanding blocks.

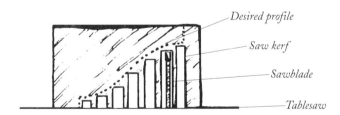

FIG. 327 TABLESAW MOULDING

The second requires the use of an angled fence, as shown overleaf in FIG. 328. While any straightedge clamped to the sawtable will work, using an easily made adjustable fence will prove more efficient. The greater the angle at which the fence is set to the blade, the more nearly will the profile cut approach a circle. Furthermore, if the blade is tilted, one side of the profile can be made steeper than the other. Of course, different diameter

MOULDING

blades will produce profiles with greater or smaller diameters as well. The secret to mastering this technique is not to attempt too much at once. Adjust the fence and the blade's angle until the required profile, which should be drawn on the end of the stock, is matched, and then lower the blade to take only a very shallow cut, increasing its height with successive passes. To work as safely as possible, proceed in such a manner that you leave the maximum bearing surface for subsequent cuts, and watch your speed. If you feed the wood too fast, the work might ride up or put undue strain on the blade or motor, and if you feed the work too slowly, you might burn the wood.

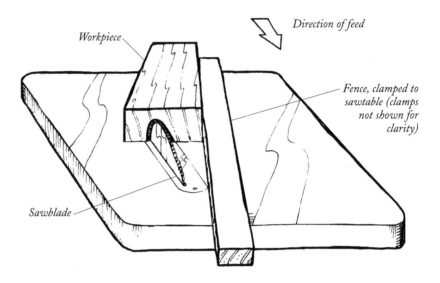

FIG. 328 COVE CUTTING ON THE TABLESAW

HANDTOOL METHODS

BY COMBINING TECHNIQUES SUCH AS THE TABLESAW METHOD and the use of a router equipped with the commonly available cove, chamfer, and round-over bits, a large variety of mouldings can be made easily without recourse to lumberyard stocks. With the added use of select wooden moulding planes or even a couple of sizes of the common hollow and round planes, almost any old moulding can be matched or new shapes devised. The guiding principle remains now as it always was, even in the days before powertools: work from the general to the particular. This means if you are attempting to make a wide, complicated moulding, take off as much wood as you can at first with the simplest, fastest method available — such as removing a wide chamfer or creating a large rabbet with the tablesaw — and then refine the shape with more complicated methods involving routers, moulding planes, or even carving tools.

The most common moulded shapes, found in designs of all periods from the classical to the most modern, are built on a simple chamfer, a rounded edge, and a hollowed edge. Developed further into rounded and hollow edges derived from circles or ovals, these basic shapes, used alone or in combination, account for the majority of moulding profiles. An excellent example of such a combination, and one that serves well for a discussion of creating and installing moulding, is the crown moulding (see FIG. 321 and FIG. 336). Although this may have derived originally from classical cornices, today it finds use not only in architectural woodwork but also on much furniture.

There are many varieties of crown moulding ranging from simplified shapes available at lumberyards to ornate curved examples used on fine furniture. When making your own, decide on the profile, and work from the large to the small, removing as much wood as you can with the simplest, fastest methods. An alternative approach is to use the built-up method: successive layers, each with a simple but differently shaped edge, combined until the required profile is obtained. In this way each section may be reduced to a basic square, rabbet, slope, or curve, simply made using router bits, the tablesaw, handplanes, scratch stocks, or even shaped sanding blocks.

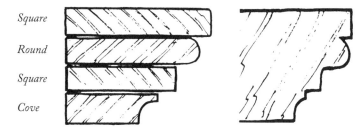

Square
Round
Square
Cove

FIG. 329 BUILT-UP MOULDING

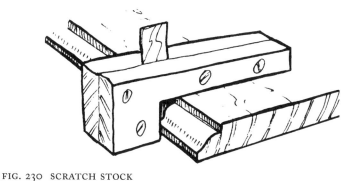

FIG. 230 SCRATCH STOCK

A scratch stock, which is nothing more than a piece of scrap steel filed to the required profile, held between two pieces of wood screwed tightly together to hold the blade, and shaped so as also to provide a fence, is also a wonderful way to refine the last stages of an otherwise built-up or roughed-out moulding. It may be used equally well on straight and curved sections, and, furthermore, is a remarkably efficient way of making shallow and narrow grooves for stringing and other inlay work.

INSTALLING MOULDING

HAVING PRODUCED THE REQUIRED MOULDING, WHETHER FOR architectural use or furnituremaking, installation presents two problems: the first has to do with the attachment process, and the second has to do with how the moulding is joined: butt-jointed, coped, or mitered.

Successful attachment depends on remembering that all wood moves, and that cross grain fixed to long grain invites trouble unless allowances are made. Moulding used for holding panels in place is usually glued and nailed to the surrounding frame, and there is rarely any conflict with opposing grain direction. At the corners the moulding is usually mitered, and this miter is kept tight by the pieces having being cut slightly over-length and then sprung into place. Moulding which is used as edging around tabletops, at the junction of tops and aprons, or as retaining moulding for the upper parts of two-part cabinets, is similarly most usually attached long grain to long grain. But where this is not possible, and it is necessary to fix a piece of long-grain moulding across the grain of another piece, allow for the inevitable movement differential between the two pieces by whatever method seems most appropriate. This might be pinning and gluing the moulding at the ends, if the dimensions are small, and using only small pins that are pliable enough to give a little in the center of its length. For stouter pieces of moulding, slot-screwing from the base into the moulding might be better. This involves making the hole in the base a little elongated and placing a washer under the head of the screw so that it can move sideways should the base change size in relation to the moulding. Very large moulding that must be affixed across the grain is sometimes made cross grain itself by being first joined to provide the required length and then shaped. Conversely, straight-grained moulding can be veneered with small pieces of cross-grained material, all of which are so narrow in width as to minimize any shrinkage.

How moulding is joined, length to length, is more complicated and depends on when the join occurs. Any unbroken length is best made from a single piece of moulding, leaving the joints between different pieces of moulding to corners and changes in direction. This is not always possible, however, and sometimes two pieces must meet somewhere in the overall length. Where this is unavoidable, as in the middle of a wall which is to receive crown moulding, for example, try to take advantage, wherever possible, of any architectural feature that might distract from the joint.

Where none presents itself, at least avoid joining close to a corner, since this simply gives the impression that the long piece was inadvertently cut too short!

If it is possible to cut both pieces slightly overlength, a simple butt joint may be made, since springing the two pieces together will ensure that the joint remains closed. This can be difficult, however, and may even introduce the danger that the spring may be absorbed not by the butt joint but at the ends, which can cause the joint there to fit less than perfectly. Consequently, it is better to cut the butt joint at an angle creating a sort of in-line miter. Should the pieces exhibit any tendency to shrink, the mitered ends will simply slide over one another rather than pull directly apart, exposing a gap.

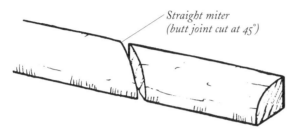

Straight miter (butt joint cut at 45°)

FIG. 331 IN-LINE MITER JOINT

Joining moulding at corners or angle changes requires either mitering or coping (often referred to as scribing). Coping, while possessing the great advantage of providing a joint that will not open up should the two pieces so joined shrink, is limited to certain profiles — those which slope only inwards — and cannot be used at all for external joints.

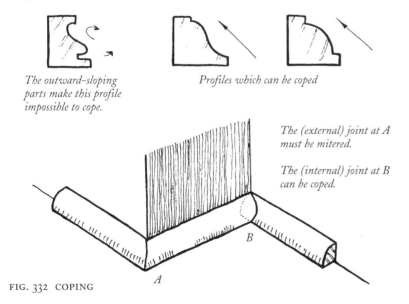

The outward-sloping parts make this profile impossible to cope.

Profiles which can be coped

The (external) joint at A must be mitered.

The (internal) joint at B can be coped.

B

A

FIG. 332 COPING

MOULDING

Mitering, which is fairly straightforward when joining simple profiles, can present some difficulties with more complicated shapes, especially when corners at angles other than 90° are encountered. The basic rule is that the angle of the miter must perfectly bisect the overall angle of the corner. With a 90° corner this results in a 45° miter. With corners of angles other than 90° bisection is necessary as follows: With the corner as center, describe circles cutting both sides; then using these points as centers, describe two more circles, and from the point where they intersect draw a line back to the corner. This line will be found to bisect the corner perfectly, and thus provide you with the angle of the miter.

A difficulty arises when a curved section of moulding meets a straight section. If the profiles of both sections are equal the miter will be a curved line. To prove this, and at the same time demonstrate how to establish the necessary curved line of the miter, follow the steps in FIG. 333. A straight miter may be obtained only if the relative sizes of the two sections of moulding are appropriately altered, but this is rarely practical. It should also be noted that similarly profiled sections of curved moulding will produce curved miters when curves of different diameters meet, as well as when curves of similar diameters meet in opposite directions, but when two equal curves meet in the same direction the miter will be straight.

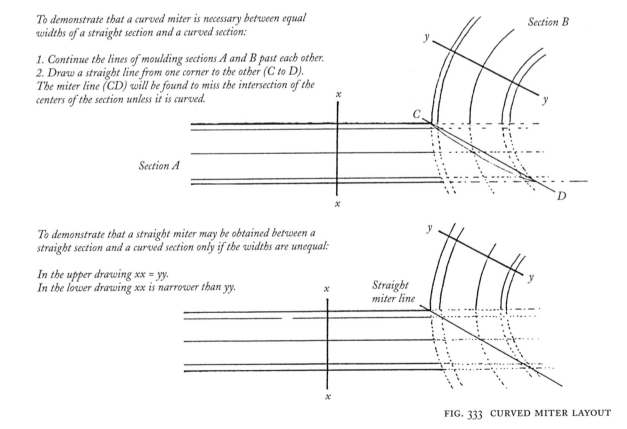

To demonstrate that a curved miter is necessary between equal widths of a straight section and a curved section:

1. Continue the lines of moulding sections A and B past each other.
2. Draw a straight line from one corner to the other (C to D). The miter line (CD) will be found to miss the intersection of the centers of the section unless it is curved.

Section B

Section A

To demonstrate that a straight miter may be obtained between a straight section and a curved section only if the widths are unequal:

In the upper drawing xx = yy.
In the lower drawing xx is narrower than yy.

Straight miter line

FIG. 333 CURVED MITER LAYOUT

Curved miters are best cut oversized and then trimmed carefully to a pre-marked line with knife or chisel. Straight miters may be sawed, using a tablesaw or a miter box, but unless the moulding forms part of some carpentry construction that is to be painted, it is usually best to saw slightly oversize and then trim to perfection. This is not to accommodate inaccurate sawing but to produce a perfectly smooth joint.

Remember, when sawing with either handsaw or tablesaw, to make the cut so that any rag or fur-out occurs on the back side of the miter. With an external miter cut on the tablesaw, this properly requires the use of adequate holding devices for safety's sake.

If you use a sufficiently fine-toothed and sharp blade no trimming may be necessary on a joint made on a tablesaw, but miters cut in miter boxes with handsaws will invariably require a little handplaning. Do not attempt to do this freehand, but instead use a miter shooting-board or a donkey's ear shooting-board as appropriate.

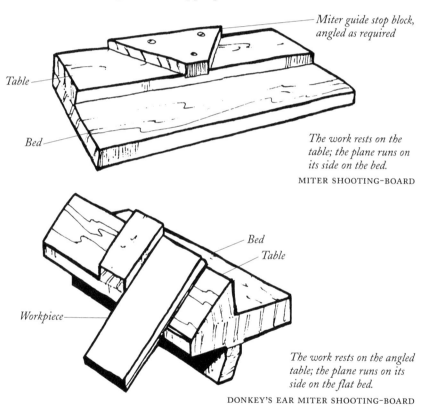

Miter guide stop block, angled as required

Table

Bed

The work rests on the table; the plane runs on its side on the bed.

MITER SHOOTING-BOARD

Bed
Table

Workpiece

The work rests on the angled table; the plane runs on its side on the flat bed.

DONKEY'S EAR MITER SHOOTING-BOARD

FIG. 334 MITER PLANING ACCESSORIES

A particularly confusing situation may arise when attempting to install moulding around irregular and short perimeters where the length of the perimeter to be moulded is shorter than the moulding is wide. When you

MOULDING

bisect each angle, the miters thus laid out will be found to overlap each other, and if you merely halve the difference in each case, and cut the miters from the two outer corners to meet at the single inner corner, as at *A* in FIG. 335, the profiles of the various pieces will not align. What must be done is to cut a third miter from the point at which the two miters overlap to the inside corner, so that all angles are truly bisected, which produces a smaller wedge-shaped piece of moulding.

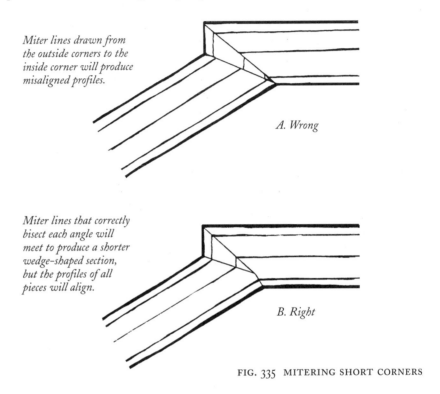

Miter lines drawn from the outside corners to the inside corner will produce misaligned profiles.

A. Wrong

Miter lines that correctly bisect each angle will meet to produce a shorter wedge-shaped section, but the profiles of all pieces will align.

B. Right

FIG. 335   MITERING SHORT CORNERS

Everything that has been said about mitering so far refers to joining moulding that is to be fixed flat against an interior surface. Much crown moulding, however, is often made of thin stuff designed to be fixed in a splayed fashion, for which purpose bevels designed to rest on vertical and horizontal surfaces are cut on the back. While it is possible, and indeed in some instances necessary, such as when making cabinet cornices, to make solid backing for such moulding (see FIG. 336), crown moulding used architecturally is often more conveniently left thin, and must be approached carefully if miters are to be cut correctly. Not only must the correct miter angle be obtained, but the angle of splay must be allowed for as well. If this is 45° it can be easily accommodated by fixing holding strips in a miter box sufficiently large to contain the moulding at this angle. Should the miter required also turn out of the horizontal — as at the end of a raking gable or an arched pediment — simply knock up a special miter box that will lead the saw down into the stuff to be mitered not at the normal 90° but at the angle of rake (see FIG. 337).

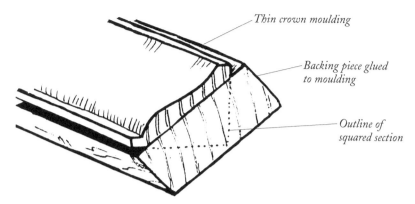

FIG. 336 SOLID-SECTION CROWN MOULDING

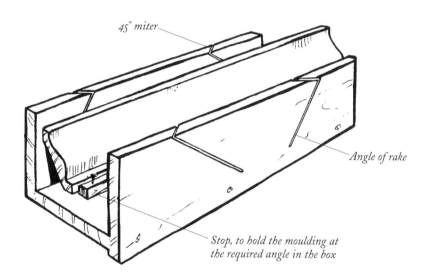

FIG. 337 PURPOSE-BUILT MITER BOX

A little effort spent mastering the techniques of coping and mitering will make doubly worthwhile your attempts at creating new moulding — which in turn will greatly enrich the design possibilities you can apply to furnituremaking.

MOULDING

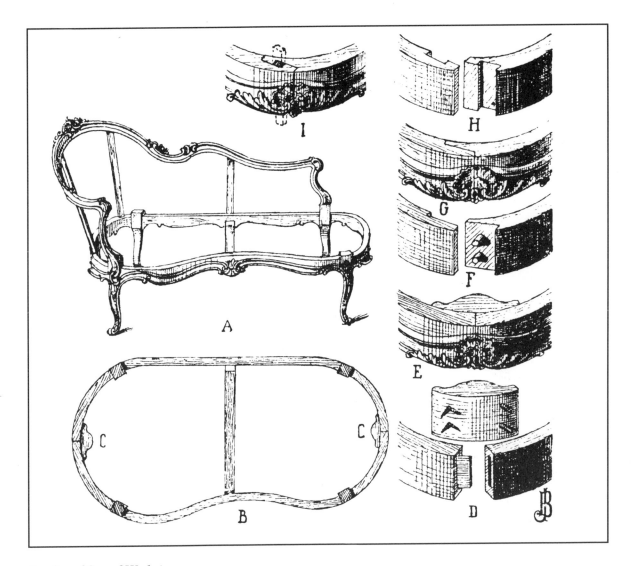

Scarfing of Curved Workpieces
from *Furnituremaking* by J. Boison, 1922

A. Louis xv chaise-longue.
B. Plan of the seat.
C. Curved pieces scarfed to avoid excessive short grain.
D. Disassembled loose-tenon scarf joint reinforced by an interior screwed corner block.
E. The assembled joint, disguised by a carved ornament.
F. Disassembled view of a scarf joint reinforced by dowels inserted from the interior.
G. The assembled joint hidden by the ornament.
H. Tabled scarf joint, disassembled.
I. Tabled scarf joint with wedge, assembled.

16

RUNNING CARVING

Tool Classification • A Basic Tool Selection • Sharpening •
Material • Mouldings • Setting Out • Basic Principles •
Sausage & Berry • Scalloped Moulding • Egg & Dart •
Channeled Mouldings • Leafage

THE TERM 'RUNNING CARVING' REFERS TO ANY CARVED SURFACE THAT RUNS ALONG OR AROUND AN EDGE, SUCH AS A PICTURE FRAME, A DOOR ARCHITRAVE, ARCHITECTURAL mouldings, or even the moulded edges of tabletops, desks, or cabinets. Especially favored in the Middle Ages, when it was part of an amazingly exuberant passion for carving which decorated virtually every inch of the woodwork of the great cathedrals and other important buildings throughout Europe, it has endured through many different styles and fashions, and although less common today is still alive and well in specialty areas such as picture framing and restoration work.

Masterpieces exist where every section is something new and where the designs are astonishingly intricate. Sometimes drawn from nature and sometimes completely abstract, sections may be as much as 9 in. wide and be carved with such an amount of undercutting and piercing that it is difficult to believe all this has been done in wood. Although such carving may only be possible after years of dedication and practice, in its simplest form, which often consists of nothing more than a basic pattern repeated over and over throughout the entire length, it can be usefully attempted by anyone with a basic familiarity with woodworking tools, and despite the underlying simplicity, to great effect.

Some of the simpler designs can look surprisingly good on even the severest of contemporary furniture and add an unexpected element of sophistication and craftsmanship. Even relatively pedestrian projects, such as simple bookcase units, small bedside tables, and utilitarian coffee tables, when finished with some form of running carving can be transformed into something special. At the other end of the scale, finishing a length of moulding, the inside of a framed section, or the edge of a surface with appropriately designed running carving can be the crowning achievement for that one-of-a-kind masterpiece.

What often strikes the uninitiated eye first is the apparent complexity. The immediate response is often: "That must have taken forever to do!" But in fact, with just a little practice, not only is it much easier than it looks but also it can be done very quickly. The trick is to design the repeated pattern so that it can be made with a minimum number of cuts, each of which is then made along the entire length to be carved before the next cut is made.

TOOL CLASSIFICATION

IT HAS BEEN ESTIMATED THAT AT THE HEIGHT OF THE GOTHIC era there may have been as many as three thousand different carving tools in use. The existence of many of these tools is suggested mainly by the complexity of the carving that was accomplished during this period. In more recent times, it has come to be accepted that a figure around three hundred more nearly represents the total armory of known and used tools, and of these the average trained carver counts perhaps no more than seventy or eighty in his or her kit, and of these uses only thirty or so on a regular basis. Specialized work can call for more tools than normal, of course, but on the other hand simple and yet very effective work can be done with as few as three or four tools.

It can be seen therefore that running carving occupies a place between chip carving on the one hand — a relatively simple technique which requires often only a single tool — and more involved and rigorous forms of carving on the other hand. At which end of the scale you prefer to work is entirely up to you, but the basic procedure remains the same no matter how sophisticated the carving becomes.

Selecting just a few appropriate tools from among the profusion of choices offered in almost any good tool catalog is not as hard as you might think, since there is an easily understood system used almost universally for describing carving tools, and if you match your design to the tools at hand, you can dispense with many sizes of the same tool. In practice, most woodcarvers refer to all their cutting tools as chisels. Strictly speaking, however, chisels are straight-sectioned tools, just like bench chisels such as paring chisels and firmer chisels. Tools with other sections, such as curves and V-shapes, are known variously as gouges, fluters, veiners, parting tools, and so on, according to their particular cross-section. These different families are referred to by numbers derived from a 19th century trade catalog known as the *Sheffield Illustrated List*.

Each section has a unique number, as does each longitudinal shape. Gouges, for example, are numbered from 3 to 10 according to 'sweep', the term used to describe the tightness of the curve. When combined with the width of a particular tool, this number provides an unambiguous way of describing any tool. It is not necessary to learn these numbers, since most catalogs list carving tools in easily read tables; what is important to realize is that a '¼ in, number 4' sold by one manufacturer will have the same size and shape as one made by any other manufacturer.

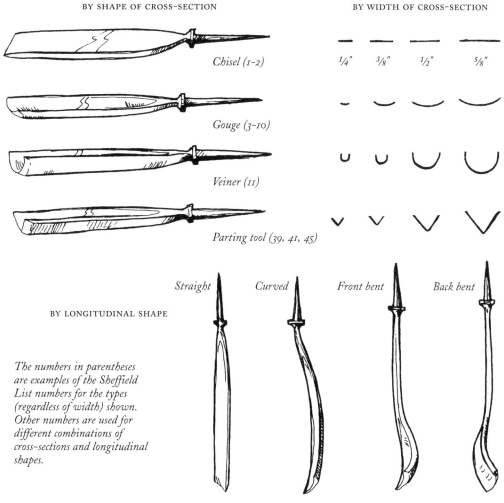

BY SHAPE OF CROSS-SECTION

BY WIDTH OF CROSS-SECTION

Chisel (1-2)

¼" ⅜" ½" ⅝"

Gouge (3-10)

Veiner (11)

Parting tool (39, 41, 45)

Straight Curved Front bent Back bent

BY LONGITUDINAL SHAPE

The numbers in parentheses are examples of the Sheffield List numbers for the types (regardless of width) shown. Other numbers are used for different combinations of cross-sections and longitudinal shapes.

FIG. 338 CARVING TOOL CLASSIFICATION

263

RUNNING CARVING

A BASIC TOOL SELECTION

THE FEWER TOOLS YOU HAVE AT YOUR DISPOSAL TO START WITH the better, since the fewer shapes you will be tempted to make. The following list may be taken as a starting point:
- Straight chisels (number 1): ½ in. and ⅞ in.
- Skew chisel (number 2): ¼ in.
- Gouges (numbers 7 or 8): ¼ in., ½ in., ⅝ in., and perhaps ¾ in.

You may find that even some of this small number become redundant, or you may end up insatiably adding to your collection for the rest of your life — it depends on your personality — but good results can be obtained with just these few tools.

If you buy all your tools from the same source they may already be handled, and the handles will undoubtedly all be of similar design. Unfortunately, especially for people who enjoy collecting things in sets, this is not a good idea, since it is infinitely easier to select the right tool from the whole collection when they are spread out before you on the bench if you are able to recognize a given shape and size by a unique handle. Professional carvers may well obtain many tools from the same source, but they are very likely to make their own handles for precisely this reason.

Carving chisels are invariably tanged, and it is easy to make handles for them. Using different woods and fashioning the handles in different shapes, ranging from plainly turned round handles to octagonal shapes, useful because they will not roll off the bench, helps a lot when it comes

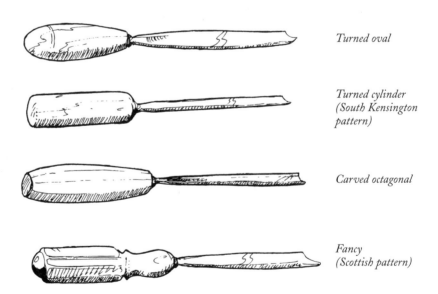

Turned oval

Turned cylinder (South Kensington pattern)

Carved octagonal

Fancy (Scottish pattern)

FIG. 339 HANDLE VARIETIES

to being efficient — and it is efficiency which is at the heart of the speed secret that makes running carving so attractive a technique.

There are numerous other items in a carver's toolkit, such as rasps, rifflers, frosting tools, and punches of various sorts, but so long as some form of bench equipped with the standard holding devices is available, the only other really essential piece of equipment is a mallet. Carver's mallets are made in various sizes. Bearing in mind that a large mallet can quickly became tiring to hold, you will probably find that a medium size is preferable for most running carving, even in a relatively hard wood such as oak. The advantage of a carver's mallet over the regular joiner's mallet is that since it is round you can use it from any direction without altering your grip and without having to stop and look to see which way the tool is pointed.

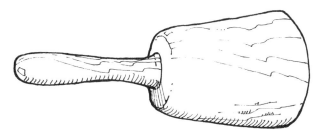

FIG. 340 CARVER'S MALLET

SHARPENING

UNDOUBTEDLY, THE HARDEST PART OF LEARNING TO CARVE IS learning to sharpen well. It is also the most important part, for without well-sharpened tools nothing of any value can be accomplished, and the process may even be dangerous into the bargain. Until a tool will cut cleanly across the grain of a relatively soft wood such as white pine you are wasting your time trying to carve with it.

This absolute need for well-sharpened tools is another reason for starting modestly. Tools may be bought or obtained ground to shape, but you will almost certainly have to sharpen and hone them yourself. If you begin with a dozen or more tools it will seem like it is taking forever before you have them all in good enough condition to use.

There is a lot that could be said about sharpening but the best way to learn is by example and experience. Provide yourself with a few stones of medium and fine grit in flat and shaped sections (see FIG. 341) so that gouges as well as chisels can be sharpened. Good results can be obtained using traditional Western oilstones such as Washita and Arkansas stones, although Japanese waterstones are preferred by many people. Placing some of the slurry that accumulates in the bottom of the buckets or the containers in which waterstones are soaked into grooves cut in a piece of

RUNNING CARVING

scrap wood will provide you with a sharpening hollow that will match perfectly the gouge used to cut it.

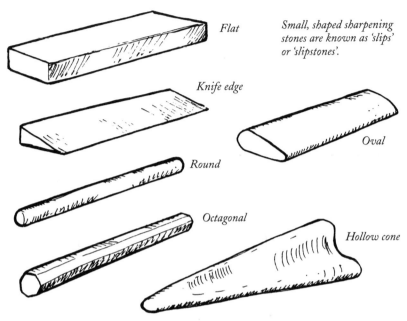

Flat

Small, shaped sharpening stones are known as 'slips' or 'slipstones'.

Knife edge

Oval

Round

Octagonal

Hollow cone

FIG. 341 SHARPENING STONES

Sharpening can become a discipline bordering on magic ritual. Much depends on the quality of the actual tool and the material it is being asked to carve. For example, a thin, long bevel may produce a very sharp edge, but at the same time it may not last as long when cutting in hardwood as would a shorter, thicker bevel. Furthermore, the steel of one tool may not take as fine an edge or as delicate a bevel as another tool's steel. Only repeated sharpenings of your individual tools will teach you what is most appropriate.

MATERIAL

WHEN RUNNING CARVING IS PLANNED AS A DECORATIVE ADDITION to any given piece, the wood to be carved will be predetermined by the wood the piece is made out of. But think twice before starting to work. Not only may stylistic considerations preclude the use of running carving on a particular piece, but in addition the particular species of wood may be so hard, so soft, or so figured that any form of carving would be impracticable. In some cases you may be able to carve more sympathetic material and fix this to the piece separately, especially if the whole is to be painted or heavily stained.

Other things to bear in mind about the relative carvability of wood are as follows: While it is true that softwood, such as pine, bass, and poplar requires less effort to cut, your tools must be that much sharper in order that the soft material can be cut cleanly. Harder woods, such as oak, will respond better to tools less than perfectly sharp, but this will require greater effort. Medium-density material, such as cherry, walnut, and mahogany, carves well and relatively easily without requiring as much work. At the same time, consider the grain structure of the wood. Fine, intricate detail is generally only possible in even, close-grained wood like lime; more coarsely grained material, like oak, should only be carved with broader strokes. Finicky details are liable to chip out of such material.

MOULDINGS

RUNNING CARVING IS ALMOST INVARIABLY USED ON THE EDGES of various pieces. These edges may be moulded before being carved. Sometimes the shape of the moulding is predetermined and the carving must be adapted to what is given, but sometimes the moulding may be made to accommodate a particular carving pattern.

Simple moulded edges suitable for running carving may be produced quite easily with a router or a shaper. Basic quarter-round shapes, ovolos, coves, and even ogees present little problem. It is also possible, however, to produce shapes more complicated than can be easily achieved with machine tools, as well as shapes that may be better suited to the design to be carved, by using various handtools or combinations of powertools and handtools.

When attempting to form a complex profile do not attempt to cut the entire profile all at once, but rather start by removing as much waste as possible, perhaps by taking rabbet-like passes through a tablesaw. Then refine the finished shape with the help of simple moulding planes, such as

Remove the large square first, then make smaller passes approaching the desired profile as closely as possible.

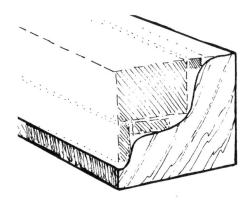

FIG. 342 ROUGHING OUT A PROFILE

RUNNING CARVING

hollows and rounds; if you have no moulding planes, a shop-made scratch stock can be a very effective profiler.

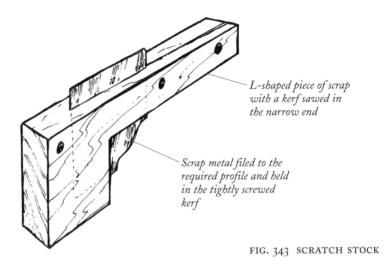

L-shaped piece of scrap with a kerf sawed in the narrow end

Scrap metal filed to the required profile and held in the tightly screwed kerf

FIG. 343 SCRATCH STOCK

SETTING OUT

WHATEVER THE PROFILE TO BE CARVED, CHOOSING A SIMPLE AND short pattern will prove to be most efficient because not only will this require fewer tools and fewer toolstrokes than a more complicated design, but it will also make it much easier to fit the design to the length to be carved. This is especially important if the carving is to go around corners or if there is a need to present a balanced and symmetrical appearance, such as along the front of a bureau.

In any event, it is usually a good idea to lay out, at least approximately, where the carving will go. The quickest and simplest way is to set a pair of dividers to the outside width of the repeat (the smallest complete section of the pattern) and then, marking the center of the length to be carved, step off first one side and then the other. This method works well if the pattern is relatively simple and short, because even should the ends of the piece to be carved not coincide exactly with the end of the repeat, the simplicity of the pattern will usually enable it to be adjusted easily enough to mask the discrepancy. Moreover, the shorter the repeat the greater are the chances that the repeat will indeed fit sufficiently closely into the given length.

If the pattern is so complicated that a simple dot marking its beginning and ending will not be sufficient to indicate its intricacies, then make a simple stencil of the pattern and use this instead of dividers. For the stencil to be useful it does not have to be a complete representation of all the details; the main outlines, sufficient to indicate the relative positions of the different elements, will do. You do not want to cut so much out that thin parts are left that can fall out with use. Make the stencil out of thin cardboard or even thin aluminum. Sheet metal is often better, since it can be bent to match the profile of the moulding and will then keep this shape. When using a stencil to determine how the pattern will fit into the length to be carved, mark with a pencil around the outlines or, even better, use some thick, almost dry watercolor paint with a big stencil brush. Providing you do not let the paint run under the edges of the stencil, this is the best method.

In the event that you cannot successfully fit the pattern to the length there are some other possibilities. Firstly, the pattern could be changed to something simpler or something shorter; perhaps removing just one small element will do the trick. Secondly, at the ends or corner of the carved piece the pattern might be altered, either so that it merges imperceptibly, or boldly so that the difference is used in its own right as a feature to mark the end or corner, as the case may be. Thirdly, the carving might be made to stop completely: either finish carving before the end in the manner of a stopped chamfer, or use a corner block, such as the square patera that is often found at the corners of old door architraves. This last method is frequently very useful when the mitering of a complicated profile would require excessive care.

BASIC PRINCIPLES

THE ESSENTIAL PRINCIPLE OF EFFICIENT RUNNING CARVING IS to make all corresponding cuts in each repeat of the pattern with the same tool along the entire length to be carved. Then proceed to the next cut, and so on. In practice, and certainly at the beginning, it is often wiser to proceed more cautiously. It helps to keep short lengths of every pattern you use for future reference, but even so, at the beginning of each session it can take a little while to get into the swing of things and establish a rhythm that will ensure a feeling of continuity along the entire length. It is all too easy to start so carefully that within a short distance, as you become more practised, the character of the carving changes, usually loosening up and acquiring a more comfortable, relaxed feeling. So always start on a practice length of the same material with the same profile.

Every pattern will dictate its own requirements and affect the way in which you work. It is best to start with something extremely simple in order to experience the rhythm and speed that is possible, and indeed necessary, if this form of carving is to be both efficient and effective, before becoming involved with more intricate ideas.

A good place to start is with the pattern traditionally known as 'sausage and berry'. This is very common and yet very effective. Following the steps in its formation will exemplify what has to be done for more advanced designs.

SAUSAGE & BERRY

THIS PATTERN CAN BE CARVED ON AN ARRIS (THE JUNCTURE OF two sides), or even in the center of a surface. What is needed is a bead formed either raised (an astragal) or sunk. The latter can have several forms defined by their position and number of quirks. No matter how the bead has been formed, whether by hand, moulding plane, router bit, or shaper, the first thing to do is to set out the pattern. Try a row of plain berries first. Even though this is an extremely simple pattern, it is still very important to be careful and exact in the setting out, for every small discrepancy will stand out glaringly.

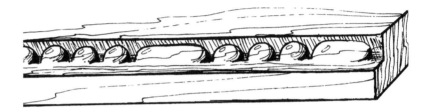

FIG. 344 SAUSAGE & BERRY

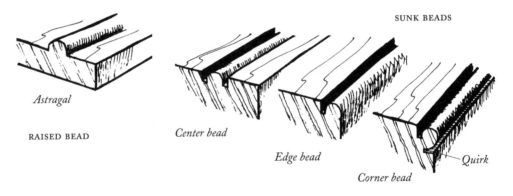

FIG. 345 BEADS

Open a pair of dividers to a little more than the diameter of the berries needed and step off this distance along the bead (or astragal), making dots *between* the berries, as in FIG. 346. If you make dots in the center of the berries these dots will remain to mar the finished carving.

The diameter of the berries should be the same as the width of the bead, which in turn should be closely matched by the width of the gouge to be used; the ¼ in. number 8 gouge recommended earlier is ideal. Having made a series of dots with the dividers, take a straight chisel and make a series of cuts at the dots across the grain of the bead. Do not use too large a chisel or you will cut into the future berries. If you are carving a softwood like pine do not cut so deeply that adjacent fibers are crushed.

Next, take the gouge and, holding it almost flat on the bead, center its edge in the middle of the berry. As you raise the tool upright, push down so that the edge enters the wood and ends up as shown at *B* in FIG. 347. When all the cuts in one direction have been made, turn the work around and make another series of cuts from the other direction.

Two points to remember are that softwood is easily crushed, so the tool must be sharp, and that taking two light cuts to complete the profile may be safer than making one heavy cut. Another way to avoid crushing is to use a shearing cut rather than a direct cut. Since most gouges are not complete semicircles, a certain amount of rotation will be necessary in any case to complete the cut from one side of the bead to the other, so rotate the tool slightly as you raise the tool and push down.

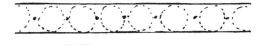

1. Step off the spaces between the berries with dividers.

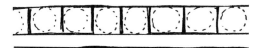

2. Make vertical chisel cuts between future berries.

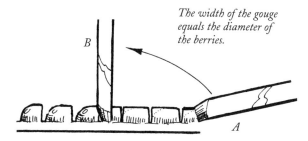

The width of the gouge equals the diameter of the berries.

3. Shape the sides of the berries with a gouge.

FIG. 346 SETTING OUT

FIG. 347 SHAPING THE FIRST SIDE

You will now have to clean out the corners of the berries. A carving chisel, sharpened on both sides unlike a regular bench chisel, is used to cut out the triangular waste bits. The ¼ in. number 2 (a skew chisel) is perfect for this. How carefully you do this will determine how well the berries look. Another trick that will improve things is to use a triangular-shaped punch that fits into the gap between the berries to clean up the bottom of the cut.

When carving a hardwood, like oak, use a mallet to help tap the gouge down, but be careful to continue the levering motion from the horizontal position to the vertical position as you cut, or you will end up making straight-sided pyramids instead of round-sided berries.

After having tried a row of berries, the complete sausage and berry pattern can be attempted simply by omitting every fourth (or fifth, or sixth, etc.) berry, leaving them to form sausages, or by introducing sausages of different lengths.

RUNNING CARVING

Further variations can be created by forming complete sausages but making the interposed berries a different shape, such as square, or giving them a centered punch.

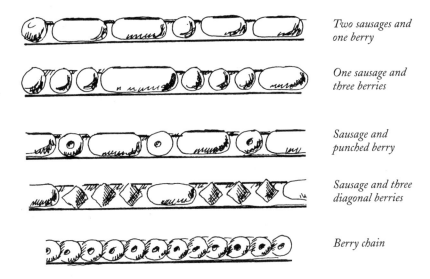

Two sausages and one berry

One sausage and three berries

Sausage and punched berry

Sausage and three diagonal berries

Berry chain

FIG. 348 SAUSAGE & BERRY VARIATIONS

SCALLOPED MOULDING

SCALLOPED MOULDING IS A PATTERN THAT CAN BE USED ON A variety of simple moulded edges such as tabletops or desktops. Such edges, if not left square, are often finished with very simple profiles such as a thumbnail, quarter-round, cove, or ogee, all of which may be made more interesting with this very simple scalloped pattern (FIG. 349).

As before, first mark a series of points. Then with the ⅝ in. number 7 gouge make the first series of cuts using a mallet, or by tapping the gouge with the heel of your hand. Next, connect these cuts with the second series. Both cuts are made with simple vertical blows that sink the corner of the gouge nearest the edge of the work deeper than the inner corner.

Finally, clean out the waste with a straight chisel, or by using the skewed chisel mentioned before, which is often easier since its pointed corner is better adapted for tight places. The only thing difficult about this pattern is to get the bottom points of the scallops cut and cleaned out to the same depth. In the moulding shown at *A* in FIG. 350 this is made easy by the actual profile, but if you are working on something with no such well-defined arris, use a penciled line to establish the required depth and edge of the scallops. The pattern illustrated at *B* in FIG. 350 is only a little more complicated, requiring six cuts to complete.

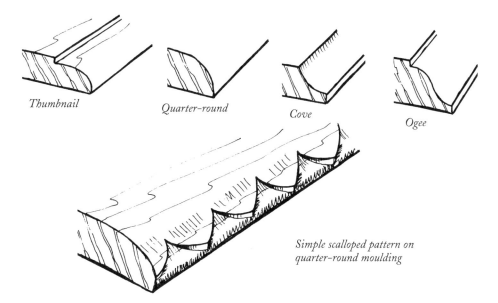

Thumbnail   Quarter-round   Cove   Ogee

Simple scalloped pattern on
quarter-round moulding

FIG. 349 SCALLOPED MOULDING

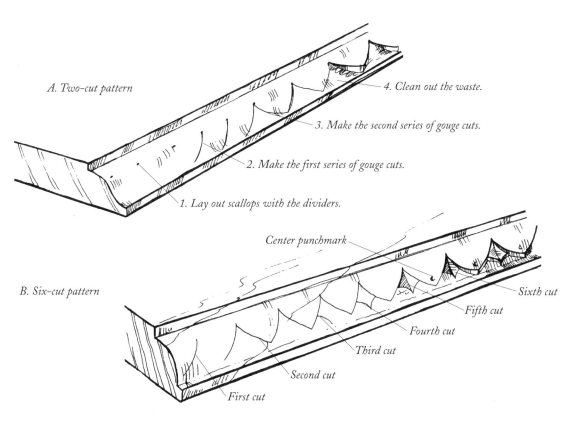

A. Two-cut pattern

4. Clean out the waste.

3. Make the second series of gouge cuts.

2. Make the first series of gouge cuts.

1. Lay out scallops with the dividers.

B. Six-cut pattern

Center punchmark

Sixth cut

Fifth cut

Fourth cut

Third cut

Second cut

First cut

FIG. 350 CUTTING SCALLOPED MOULDING

273   **RUNNING CARVING**

EGG & DART

USING SIMPLE GOUGE CUTS LIKE THOSE DESCRIBED ABOVE AND proceeding by the same method of setting out, making the preliminary strokes, and then shaping and cleaning the cuts, an almost endless variety of simple patterns can be produced. A slightly more advanced example of this class of running carving is that known as 'egg and dart'. The design is shown below. Note that the exact shape and proportions of the egg may be varied to accommodate the shapes of the various tools available.

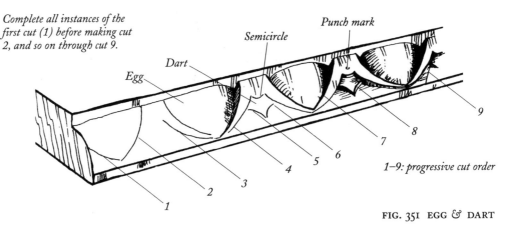

Complete all instances of the first cut (1) before making cut 2, and so on through cut 9.

1–9: progressive cut order

FIG. 351 EGG & DART

CHANNELED MOULDINGS

YET ANOTHER FORM OF RUNNING CARVING THAT IS SIMPLE BUT effective involves using a shaper or moulding planes to work a series of differently shaped grooves in the surface, and then carving the edges. This procedure is shown opposite.

LEAFAGE

AMONG THE MOST BEAUTIFUL AND MORE COMPLICATED PATTERNS used in running carving are many varieties of leaf pattern. Despite the apparent quantum difference in the complexity of their execution, they are made in precisely the same way as are the simpler designs. It is almost always easier if a simplified stencil of the repeat pattern is made first and then transferred to the work, the details being drawn in by pencil. The design should still be broken up into a series of cuts that can all be done one at a time, and then the design modeled out according to the principles described earlier. FIG. 353 shows a section set out and then finished to give some idea of this kind of work. Innumerable models may be found in furniture books as well as in books on period architecture.

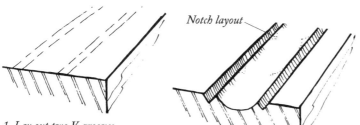

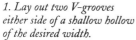

Notch layout

2. Cut the V-grooves with a parting tool (or appropriate router bit), and plane or rout the hollow.

1. Lay out two V-grooves either side of a shallow hollow of the desired width.

3. Step off the future gouge cuts with dividers.

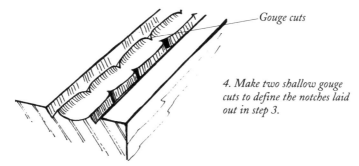

Gouge cuts

4. Make two shallow gouge cuts to define the notches laid out in step 3.

FIG. 352 CHANNELED MOULDING

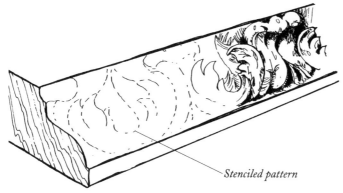

Stenciled pattern

FIG. 353 LEAFAGE

For designs that involve more complex features, such as partially freestanding elements with much undercutting, commensurately greater carving skill is required, as is a larger armory of carving tools. Tools with spade edges, as well as those with both front-bent and back-bent shanks, will be found indispensable for this kind of work, and greater use may be made of decorative stamps and punches, but if you have started with simpler designs you may well feel drawn into this immensely satisfying area of woodworking.

RUNNING CARVING

Panels & Wood Movement
from *Furnituremaking* by J. Boison, 1922

A. Paneled door, from a 16th century house in Rouen, now in the Cluny Museum. Some of the panels have been taken out to show the arrangement of muntins that make panels made of several boards unnecessary; this lends itself to a decorative arrangement and takes into account the needs of the wood.

B. Paneled door from the 18th century. Museum of Decoratve Arts. A part of every panel has been removed to show how the framing requires panels to be made of several boards whose joints interseƈt the carving. This situation should be avoided.

17

FRAME & PANELING

Structural Principles • Purposeful Design •
Framemaking • Panelmaking

FRAME-AND-PANELING, WHICH FIRST BECAME POPULAR IN THE MIDDLE AGES, CONTINUES TO THIS DAY AS ONE OF THE MORE IMPORTANT TECHNIQUES IN ALL WOODWORKING. Used in furniture construction for cabinetry and casework as well as architecturally for doors and as wall covering, its success is due to three facts: first, and most importantly, it is a way of creating a large area of woodwork that is dimensionally stable; second, it can be used modularly to accommodate an almost infinite variety of spatial requirements; and third, it is susceptible to an enormous variety of design alternatives, from both a proportional and an ornamental standpoint.

Since all wood will continue to change dimension in response to changes in ambient moisture conditions, the woodworker's first challenge is to design in such a way that this inexorable change can be accommodated while preserving an overall required form. If this is ignored the wood will still do what wood wants to do, with results as illustrated overleaf in FIG. 354. Framing, made typically from relatively narrow pieces in which shrinkage or expansion is relatively minor, can be designed to be dimensionally stable, while the paneling which constitutes the bulk of the area defined by the framing is by virtue of the construction free to shrink and expand without compromising the overall dimensions of the structure (FIG. 355). Additionally, framing, which by its construction of multiple opposing members remains flat, will also hold the larger panels flat, preventing them from warping or cupping.

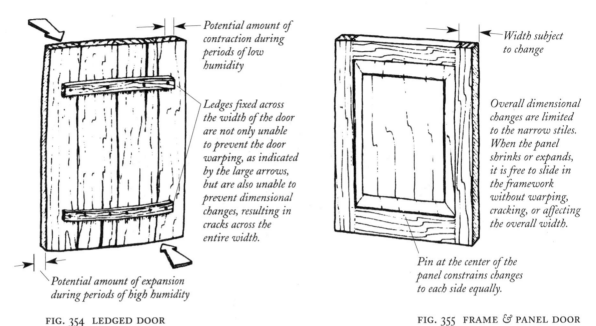

Potential amount of contraction during periods of low humidity

Ledges fixed across the width of the door are not only unable to prevent the door warping, as indicated by the large arrows, but are also unable to prevent dimensional changes, resulting in cracks across the entire width.

Potential amount of expansion during periods of high humidity

Width subject to change

Overall dimensional changes are limited to the narrow stiles. When the panel shrinks or expands, it is free to slide in the framework without warping, cracking, or affecting the overall width.

Pin at the center of the panel constrains changes to each side equally.

FIG. 354 LEDGED DOOR

FIG. 355 FRAME & PANEL DOOR

Panels may be used in framework that forms part of an integral carcase or case construction as well as in independent framing modules. These modules can be separate units — like doors or lids — or they can be used in combination to create a variety of enclosed structures such as chests, boxes, or cabinets, which may themselves form part of other units such as seating, or as covering structures as in the case of wall paneling. The great advantage is that however they are used, permanent dimensional stability is assured.

STRUCTURAL PRINCIPLES

THE CENTRAL ELEMENT IN THE SYSTEM IS THE PANEL, TO WHOSE support the design of the frame is dedicated. The panel may be large or small, plain or simple, made of one piece or several, and may either stand alone or be one of several or even many in any given section of frame-and-paneling (FIG. 356). But in all cases it must be free to move, so that it will neither split nor buckle with changes in ambient moisture content, and yet be securely held, so that it cannot warp out of perfect flatness.

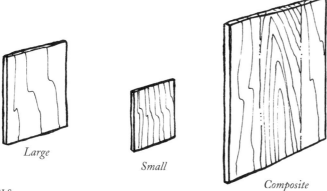

FIG. 356 PANELS

Most panels are typically held in grooves formed in the surrounding framing. Occasionally, the grooves are formed by adding one or two strips of moulding to a rabbeted or a square section, but most often the groove is integral.

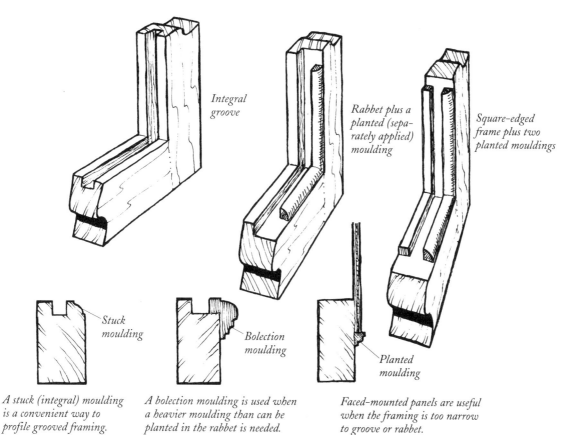

Integral groove

Rabbet plus a planted (separately applied) moulding

Square-edged frame plus two planted mouldings

Stuck moulding

Bolection moulding

Planted moulding

A stuck (integral) moulding is a convenient way to profile grooved framing.

A bolection moulding is used when a heavier moulding than can be planted in the rabbet is needed.

Faced-mounted panels are useful when the framing is too narrow to groove or rabbet.

FIG. 357 PANEL-HOLDING OPTIONS

The panels are rarely thin enough to fit directly in the grooves. Consequently, various methods of reducing their edges may be adopted consistent with the general style. These may range from ornately fielded raised panels to severely modern flush panels.

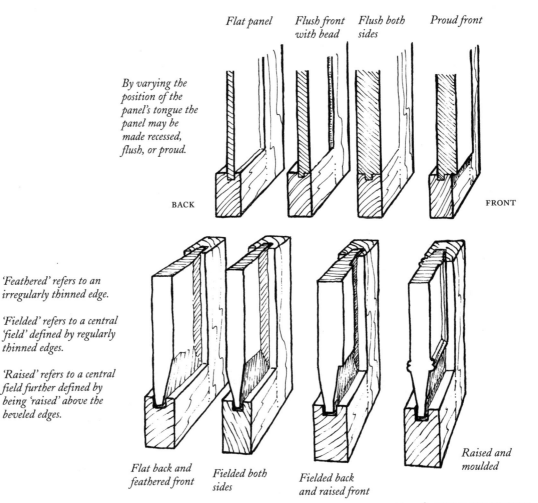

Flat panel *Flush front with bead* *Flush both sides* *Proud front*

By varying the position of the panel's tongue the panel may be made recessed, flush, or proud.

BACK FRONT

'Feathered' refers to an irregularly thinned edge.

'Fielded' refers to a central 'field' defined by regularly thinned edges.

'Raised' refers to a central field further defined by being 'raised' above the beveled edges.

Flat back and feathered front *Fielded both sides* *Fielded back and raised front* *Raised and moulded*

FIG. 358 PANEL VARIATIONS

The frame members, known variously as rail, stile, and muntin (FIG. 359), are most commonly mortised and tenoned together, although other methods, such as plate joinery, doweling, and even half-lap housed joints (FIG. 360), can be used if strength is not an issue.

The proportions of the joints may vary considerably depending on the size and function of the piece: frame-and-paneling intended for more substantial applications may be joined with tenons approximating one third of the thickness of the members involved; joints for lighter pieces may be no more than a quarter of the thickness (FIG. 361).

FIG. 359 FRAME MEMBERS

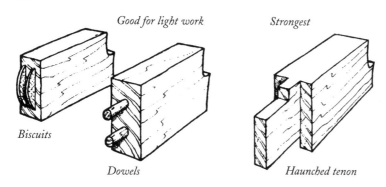

FIG. 360 FRAMING JOINTS

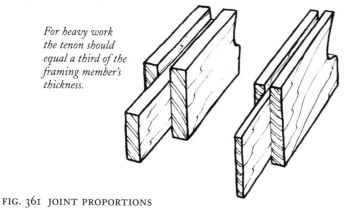

FIG. 361 JOINT PROPORTIONS

In either case, construction will be greatly facilitated by planning ahead so that tenon thickness and mortise location are both compatible with the width and location of the groove. It helps to design these details so they can be executed conveniently with whatever tools you have available, matching, for example, the width of the groove with the chisel or bit used to excavate the mortise. If the grooves and joints are all aligned, perhaps centered in the thickness of the workpiece, awkward situations will be avoided that might compromise the final appearance.

Since most panels are oriented vertically, the rails have the most work to do in preventing the panel from warping. Consequently, these usually form the widest parts of the frame. In order for the frame — whether it is a simple single-panel cabinet door or a multi-panel section of frame-and-panel work — not to appear top-heavy, the top rail may be made a little narrower than the bottom rail. The stiles may be a little narrower still. Central rails often fulfill the additional function of housing handles or locks, for which purpose they may be made wider than other members. Similarly, muntins may be made wider than would otherwise be necessary when they are called upon to balance the effect of two stiles coming together, as is the case with double doors.

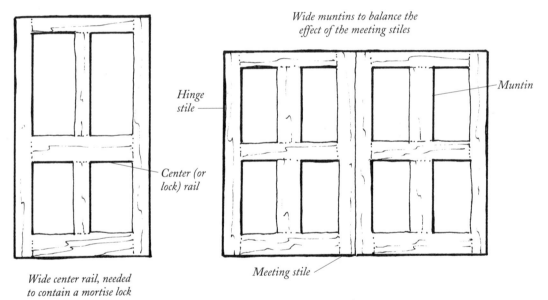

Wide muntins to balance the effect of the meeting stiles

Hinge stile

Muntin

Center (or lock) rail

Wide center rail, needed to contain a mortise lock

Meeting stile

FIG. 362 FRAMING MEMBER PROPORTIONS

Arranging the relative proportions of all these parts correctly from a structural standpoint will go a long way to producing a pleasing design. But without compromising structural integrity there remains much you can do to control the final appearance if you would build something that not only works well but that also looks well.

PURPOSEFUL DESIGN

IN ALMOST EVERY JOB THERE ARE CERTAIN CONSTRAINTS AND givens that have to be considered. These may be functional, structural, or esthetic, often in combination with each other, all of which can all affect the ultimate design.

The most important of these elements is function, which can dictate many proportions. For instance, a large exterior door will require more substantial framing — such as wider stiles to accommodate the larger joints necessary to support the extra weight, and a wide lock rail at a given height to house a mortise lock — than wall paneling. These facts being unavoidable, you might then feel it appropriate to make the rest of the framing members commensurately heavier.

Structural notes:

All framing members of the entry door are heavier than would be necessary for a cabinet door.

The door handle and lock determine the height of the lock rail .

Design notes:

1. Meeting stiles narrower than hinge stiles help preserve the horizontal balance.
2. Square top panels provide a lift to the cabinet and lessen horizontality.
3. Top rail plus cabinet top equals the width of the bottom rail.
4. Base plus bottom rail equals center rail plus top rail and cabinet top.
5. Muntins made narrower than the stiles create an added horizontal rhythm.

FIG. 363 ENTRY DOOR

FIG. 364 CREDENZA

But equally important for the ultimate success of a piece are esthetic considerations. For example, when designing a credenza with four doors, making the meeting stiles narrower than the lock stiles can avoid disproportionately thick verticals where doors meet. Furthermore, since the overall shape of the piece is horizontal, dividing the doors so that the top panels are smaller than the lower panels will give more lift to the piece and make it appear less squat and heavy. And so on with various elements, until a satisfying balance is achieved.

FRAME & PANELING

Location is yet another factor that may influence the design, perhaps by constraining the overall size, especially if the piece has to fit into a given space and not look too large or too small for its surroundings.

Beyond all this, material considerations such as wood species and your own equipment and ability may play a large part in the final design.

Essential though all these details are, the truly successful design will also require a clear understanding of the piece's character. One way to achieve this is to be clear about the focus of the piece and control it by emphasizing different elements of the design. Decide, for example, whether it is the frame or the panel that is the primary focus. A way to alter the focus is to change the apparent shape by adjusting elements such as the relative size, shape, and number of framing members, as well as controlling the grain pattern — make an extremely vertical door appear less tall and narrow, for example, by using multiple rails and orienting the panels horizontally rather than vertically or square.

Focus on the frame   *Focus on the panel*   *Vertical panels offset the basic squareness.*

Simplicity keeps the focus on the basic shape.   *Horizontal panels make the door appear wider.*   *Traditional balance, with slightly larger lower panels*

FIG. 365 VARIATIONS IN FOCUS

Whatever else is required, design in a style that is in harmony with the intended surroundings. A starkly modern piece can look out of place next to more traditional pieces. One way to do this is by following a particular style such as Art Nouveau, Arts and Crafts, 18th century, etc.

Art Nouveau *Arts and Crafts* *Gothic Revival*

FIG. 366 PERIOD VARIETIES

This should not be merely a matter of imitating various details, such as moulding profiles or particular shapes, but of using the same paradigms that informed the particular period. The Golden Mean, for example, is a sophisticated design paradigm that has been used for centuries as a basis for designing numerous styles of furniture and architecture.

The Golden Mean is a ratio that can be illustrated as a line divided so that the smaller part is to the longer part as the longer part is to the whole: AB : BC :: BC : AC

A *B* *C*

Also known as Ø (phi), for the Greek architect Phidias, it can be expressed as: $\frac{\sqrt{5}+1}{2}$, which produces an infinite value (1.618033998825751...).

BC can therefore be thought of as approximately 1.618 times longer than AB.

The door and its panels are all based on the Golden Mean ratio.

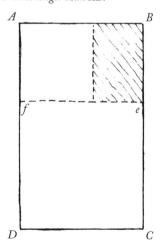

ABCD is a Golden Rectangle (the sides are 1.618 times longer than the ends).

Squaring a Golden Rectangle leaves a second, smaller Golden Rectangle (ABef); squaring this in turn leaves the smaller Golden Rectangle (shaded), which is used for the panels in the door opposite.

FIG. 367 GOLDEN MEAN

FRAME & PANELING

Another common design paradigm is that based on the *Five Orders of Architecture*, an analysis of classical Greek and Roman architecture which is often used for determining basic proportions, such as height to width and the number and relative sizes of panels and framing members.

Each Order uses a different ratio for determining all the dimensions and proportions of the building or piece of furniture in question.

The Tuscan column, which represents the first of the Five Orders, is built using a ratio of 1 : 7. The height of the column is seven times its width, the base and the capital each measure half the column width (a half unit), etc.

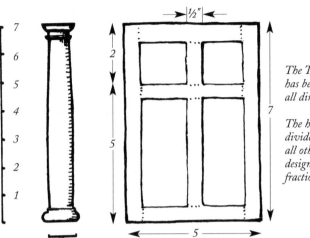

The Tuscan ratio (1 : 7) has been used to determine all dimensions of the door:

The height having been divided into seven units, all other dimensions are designed to be multiples or fractions of this basic unit.

FIG. 368 USE OF THE TUSCAN ORDER

Even simply dividing the piece into basic geometric shapes, such as squares, circles, rectangles, or other figures, is better than having no plan.

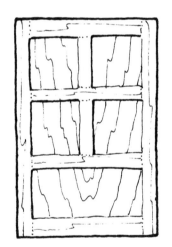

Cabinet frame-and-paneling based on squares

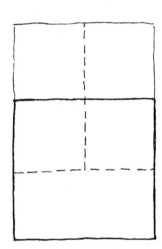

FIG. 369 GEOMETRIC PARADIGM

After all this, numerous decisions about sizes of various details may remain. Even very small differences in dimensions can affect the weight, balance, and symmetry of a piece. In particular, adjusting the relative sizes of individual members of a frame-and-panel piece can alter its character dramatically. Remember that balance is not just a question of symmetry; it can be achieved by adjusting the relative sizes of related areas.

Wide rails and horizontal top panels emphasize the width.

Vertical panels make the same door appear thinner.

Different sized panels can achieve a balanced asymmetry.

FIG. 370 DIRECTION, WEIGHT, & BALANCE

Finally, no matter what or how you are designing, pay attention to the actual material. Consider color as well as figure and the direction of the grain. Contrasting colors can play an important part in the overall balance of a piece, just as a grain pattern that curves the wrong way can make a piece appear to sag or bulge.

FRAMEMAKING

IN MOST CASES MAKING THE FRAMES IS THE FIRST PART OF ANY frame-and-paneling job, after which the panels are made to fit. Making frames by hand can entail a fair amount of ripsawing. There is no question that a bandsaw or a tablesaw will do this job faster, but ripping 4 ft. of three-quarter pine to width need not be particularly onerous if a properly sharpened and set handsaw is used.

When all the framing members, including the stiles, rails, and muntins, have been sawed to width, they should all be jointed true and square with a jointer plane, and then surface-planed with a smooth plane. After marking the faces of each piece so that all future work can be done referenced from the same surface, the next job is to cut the grooves to contain the panels. There are a great many ways to do this, using routers, shapers, tablesaws, as well as many planes. When powertools are unavailable or

FRAME & PANELING

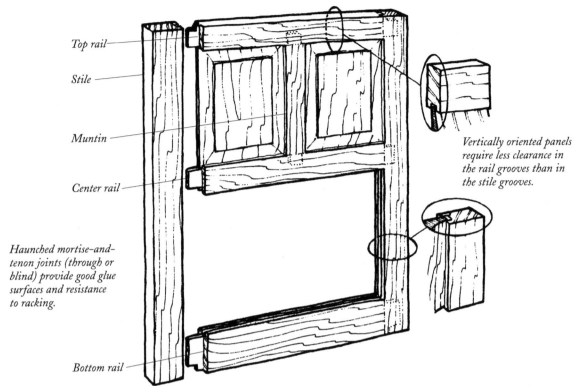

Top rail

Stile

Muntin

Center rail

Haunched mortise-and-tenon joints (through or blind) provide good glue surfaces and resistance to racking.

Vertically oriented panels require less clearance in the rail grooves than in the stile grooves.

Bottom rail

FIG. 371 BASIC FRAME & PANEL

their use is inconvenient, try to use handtools that are matched so that measuring at each step is unnecessary. This might be achieved by using one plane for ploughing, a mortise chisel of exactly the same width as the plane iron, and a regular marking gauge set to the same width as the previous two tools.

Any plane that is capable of ploughing and that has, or can be fitted with, a depth stop and a fence is fine. A combination plane, old or new, a wooden plough plane, the grooving member of a pair of wooden match planes, or any metal special-purpose plane all work equally well. The important thing is to work each board from the same side, using the same depth and fence settings, thereby ensuring consistency in depth and placement of the grooves. By placing the groove exactly in the center of ¾ in.-thick stock, and using panels of the same thickness but which are beveled from the front only, the panels may be made to stand proud of the surrounding framework (FIG. 372). This gives an extra depth to the whole work that you may find interesting. If you are aiming for a generally straightforward style, omit the stuck ovolo moulding frequently used around the inside of much framework, and go with a simple square edge. It is not much more complicated to stick a moulding, but it will require either setting the groove farther back from the front of the frame or using thicker stock, since the ovolo itself is usually at least ¼ in. thick.

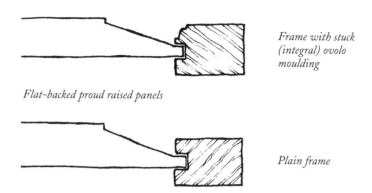

Frame with stuck (integral) ovolo moulding

Flat-backed proud raised panels

Plain frame

FIG. 372   PROUD PANELS

Cut as many framing members as will be required for the given section of frame-and-paneling, making each a little longer than will be necessary, and then groove all the inside edges before starting to cut any joints. The general principle to follow is to make the outside frame first and then, when this is assembled, measure directly to get the exact length of any intermediate members. It is usually easiest to cut the tenons in the rails first and then mark the mortises in the stiles directly from the tenons.

Always mark from the face side when laying out the tenons. Scribe the shoulders first and cut them with a fine dovetail saw. Next, using a tenon saw with a depth stop, cut the cheeks of the tenon. A depth stop can be easily improvised simply by clamping a strip of wood to the sawblade; if you have very many cheeks of the same depth to cut, such as a full-time framemaker in a millwork shop might have, you can save a lot of time and work more accurately if you bore through the blade and affix a permanent depth guide. After using a trysquare to mark the haunches wherever needed, and then cutting them, clean up the corners of the tenons where necessary with a chisel or a shoulder plane before presenting them to the adjoining framing member so that the mortise may be marked directly from the tenon rather than being measured independently.

When excavating mortises in softwood by hand, it is rarely necessary to do any pre-boring; the mortise chisel, if held straight, will quickly cut a clean mortise, the depth of which you should check frequently with the end of a wooden rule. But when working in hardwoods, removing as much of the waste as possible by boring with a bit whose diameter is a little smaller than the width of the mortise can be a great help. Whether working in hardwoods or softwoods it is always, however, an extremely good idea to put a clamp on the sides of the mortise while it is being

FRAME & PANELING

excavated, especially when the mortise is at the end of piece, in order to avoid splitting open the wood with a less than perfectly vertical thrust of the mortise chisel (see FIG. 283, chapter 12).

When all the joints have been cut, knock the whole frame together dry and check for winding and flushness, bringing all to truth with judicious paring and planing where necessary. Strictly speaking this should not be needed, but one of the advantages of frame-and-panel construction is that it is somewhat forgiving of a slightly imperfect joint by virtue of its inherent overall structural integrity.

PANELMAKING

TO MAKE PANELS, FIRST PREPARE BOARDS OF SUFFICIENT WIDTH, either by ripping wider boards if available or by joining narrower boards. What constitutes width and length is a function of which way the panels are to be oriented in the frame, longitudinally or vertically. This is a design consideration which should have been worked out beforehand.

Remember that the width of a panel equals the width of the opening in the frame plus the combined depth of the grooves either side of the panel in which the panel is to sit, less a certain amount necessary to allow for possible expansion of the panel. Obviously, you do not want to fit the panel in the grooves so loosely that should the panel contract it would fall out, but equally disastrous is a panel fitted so tightly that any expansion bursts the frame apart. The exact relation of panel width to grooved frame width is a function of the kind of wood being used, how it will be finished, the overall size of the panel, and how deep the grooves have been ploughed in the first place. Pine, for example, will expand and contract more than mahogany, and a painted panel will be more stable than an unfinished panel, so it is difficult to give any hard and fast rule, most especially since local humidity conditions may vary greatly. But try to bear all these factors in mind when planning the depth of the grooves and the finish fit of the panel.

Having got out your future panels to the right width, cut them to length, similarly allowing for the grooves in the framing, and at the same time taking care to end up with rectangles rather than rhomboids. Any out-of-squareness should be remedied by shooting the ends with a miter plane.

When making raised panels there are two lines to be scribed: one marking the width of the bevels and the other marking the thickness of the edges that will fit into the grooves of the frame. If your design calls for panels with equal-width bevels on every panel, set a cutting gauge to the width of this bevel and run it around all four sides of every panel.

This process is useful even if you use special panel-raising planes, since it ensures a crisp, clean edge to the central raised field. It is sometimes

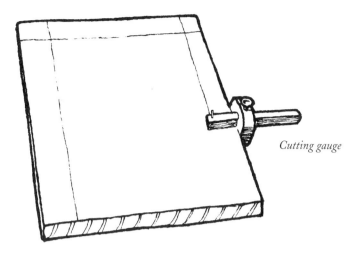

Cutting gauge

FIG. 373 MARKING THE FIELD

pointed out that authentic raised panels dating from the colonial period can be distinguished by the fact that the shallow sides of the central field do not form a perfect right angle to the surface of the field. This is because the shoulder angle of many raising planes was made considerably greater than 90° in order to accommodate panels with bevels of different degrees of steepness. Anything less would result in undercut fields, which would be weak. But while a raised panel with sides to its field at angles of more than 90° is not necessarily to be viewed as simply the best that colonial craftsmen could achieve, neither are panels with vertically sided fields to be viewed as spurious modern imitations, as a glance at much superior English and French paneling of the 18th and 19th centuries will prove. In any event, one of the virtues of frame-and-panel construction is the very variety possible in all its details of style. I like my fields to be crisply delineated, and first outlining them with a cutting gauge ensures this, whether they are subsequently made with period raising planes or by any other more modern method. Attention to this kind of detail may be mandatory if you are undertaking reproduction work of a particular period, but if an easy way to make things without powertools is the only consideration, then a common fillister or shoulder plane is often much easier to use than many antique fielding or raising planes.

Before beginning to work the bevel, however, it is necessary to use the last of the matched tools mentioned earlier. A regular marking gauge should be set to the same width as the groove in the framing, but used with one important difference: its fence should be held against the back side of the panels rather than being worked from the face side. This way the back surface of the panel will be recessed in the frame, and the face, when fielded, will stand proud of the surrounding framework giving an

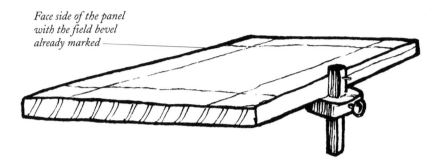

*Face side of the panel
with the field bevel
already marked*

FIG. 374 MARKING THE TONGUE

extra depth and feeling of solidness to the whole. Sometimes, of course, this is not convenient, and in order to ensure that the face of the framing and the panels lie in the same plane, the panels must either be made out of thinner stock or, as is more usual, be beveled on both sides — in effect centering the feathered edge or tongue that fits into the framing's groove. In the case of a fireplace surround, or any other form of wall paneling where the back of the work is never seen, it is irrelevant what form the back of the paneling takes, and since it is less work by half to work the bevels on one side of a panel only, it makes more sense to place the groove in the framing in the center to gain maximum strength, not only for the grooves themselves but for the mortise and tenons too, since these should be cut in the same plane as the grooves.

For maximum efficiency, design the system so that all components — grooves, panel edges, tenons, and mortises — line up and share common dimensions. But be aware that this is by no means the only way to proceed. There are many ornate examples of paneling where the use of planted or stuck mouldings, the necessity of finishing both sides, or the need to accommodate integral doors or glazed panels demands a more complicated and less regularly modular approach.

With the field and tongue laid out, the panel is ready to be fielded. Place a piece of scrap as thick as the panel at the side of the panel to prevent the end from splitting when planing across the grain. Secure these two pieces on the bench and begin to work on the ends of the panel first, cutting across the grain. By planing the ends first rather than the sides, the arris formed by the end and side bevels can be cut cleanly with no risk of splitting or tearout, since any such damage is easily cleaned up when planing along the grain of the sides.

Set the fence on a standard steel rabbet plane so that the inside of the blade just touches the cut made by the cutting gauge and, turning the plane's spur, if so equipped, out of the way, since although you are cutting across the grain, the fibers have already been severed by the cutting gauge, plane straight down — not at the angle you will want the bevel to lie in — until you reach the depth by which the fielded part of the panel is to be raised, which in the case of a simple raising not designed to be further carved or moulded is usually about ³⁄₁₆ in. to ¼ in.

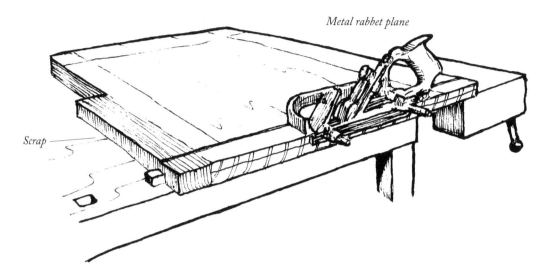

Metal rabbet plane

Scrap

FIG. 375 PANEL RAISING

For the woodworker who would use no powertools I have suggested the use of a metal rabbet plane, since this is the tool most readily available; both the Stanley™ model and the Record™ model can be bought quite cheaply. There are, of course, many alternatives that work equally well. Universal planes, or their modern successors, the combi-planes, can be used, as can plain wooden rabbet planes (FIG. 376, overleaf), many of which can be found with skewed blades and even spurs — a distinct advantage when cutting across the grain. And for the true enthusiast, although at greater cost, it is possible to use an antique panel-raising plane (FIG. 377, overleaf).

Using a genuine panel-raising plane has the advantage of saving the next step, and at the same time of producing a somewhat more sophisticated bevel, as explained below, but it is not a tool commonly found in the average shop or tool chest.

In any event, once you have planed down to the depth of the raised panel, set the fence a little further in, if necessary, so that the whole width of the bevel may be surfaced. If the bevel is narrower than the width of the plane iron this will not be needed, and you can proceed to step two, which is to hold the plane now at such an angle that the slope of the bevel begins to be worked. If you work evenly with a sharp iron, you can use the light to watch the angled facets increase in width until you achieve one

FRAME & PANELING

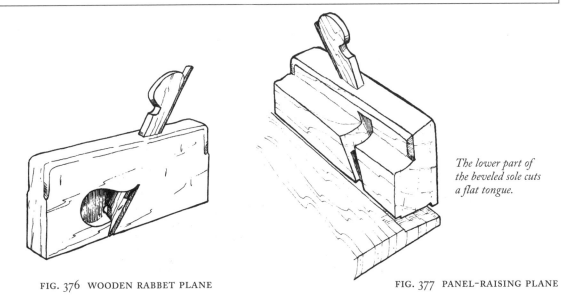

The lower part of the beveled sole cuts a flat tongue.

FIG. 376 WOODEN RABBET PLANE

FIG. 377 PANEL-RAISING PLANE

broad uninterrupted plane from the shoulder of the field to the gauged and penciled line along the edge of the panel. When this point is reached, turn the panel end-for-end and similarly work the other end-grain bevel. When both ends have been cut you may work the sides, this time without the necessity of using a scrap piece to prevent splitting.

When all four sides have been beveled it is time for the last job — which a panel-raising plane might have rendered unnecessary — namely, the final trimming and fitting. Since the framing members were grooved before being cut to length, you should have at least one short piece of grooved framing stock which can now be used as a mullet. It needs to be only a couple of inches long, as it is used to slide along the feathered edge of the panel to test whether it will fit in the framing's groove.

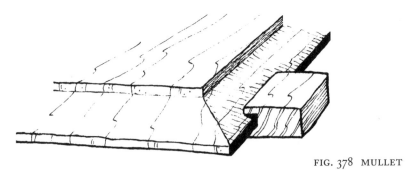

FIG. 378 MULLET

Proceeding in the same order as before, and using a metal rabbet plane with its iron set very fine, a skewed rabbet plane, either wooden or metal, or even a shoulder plane, preferably an older one with a skewed blades, work the bevel down, taking care to keep it in one plane, until the mullet will fit over the edge and slide comfortably the whole length of every beveled side.

As you plane, take care not to damage the clean line of the field's shoulder as cut by the cutting gauge. If you do, this will have to be cleaned up with a shoulder plane or a bullnose plane, with obvious detriment to the size of the field, and such cleaning up, if not done with extreme care, can in turn necessitate recutting of the adjacent bevels, and so on and so forth. At the same time pay attention to the arris formed by adjacent bevels. This should proceed in a straight line from the very corner of the field to the very corner of the panel. It is all too easy to end up with a curved line because the bevels themselves consist of more than one plane, or to get one bevel lower than the next. And lastly, while maintaining as flat a bevel as is possible, form the edge of the panel to fit evenly into the mullet.

It is this last point where the use of a well-tuned panel-raising plane has an advantage. Since the essence of frame-and-paneling is to allow unfixed panels to expand and contract in the framing's grooves, a panel edge that is of even width, like a regular tongue, will show any such expansion and contraction less than will a panel's edge that is wedge-shaped. Some, but not all, panel-raising planes have their irons and soles made in such a way that the fielding bevel consists of two planes: one sloping, with reference to the field, and the other flat, so as to form the flat tongue just mentioned. Since you are cutting an essentially wedge-shaped bevel, you must allow for the panel's expansion and contraction. If you fit the mullet so that the panel's edge touches the bottom of the mullet's groove, then any contraction will cause the panel to rattle around in its frame. Conversely, if the panel wedges into the groove before touching the bottom, any expansion will split the sides of the framing. To what degree this is likely depends both on the steepness of the bevel and the expected change of size of the panel. It will therefore be helpful either to have designed a panel with bevels sloping as shallowly as possible, or to have allowed the edge of the panel to be somewhat flatter than the main part of the bevel.

The final operation is to fit the panel into the framing, being careful to allow for expansion and contraction. When fitting very large panels, such as the central panel in an overmantel, secure the panel at the very center of each end so that any dimensional changes occur equally on both sides of the panel. Elsewhere the panel should be perfectly free in its frame, and care should be taken that any glue from the corner joints of the framing does not seep into the grooves and set fast to the edges of the panel, for these, being the thinnest parts, are most susceptible to any splitting.

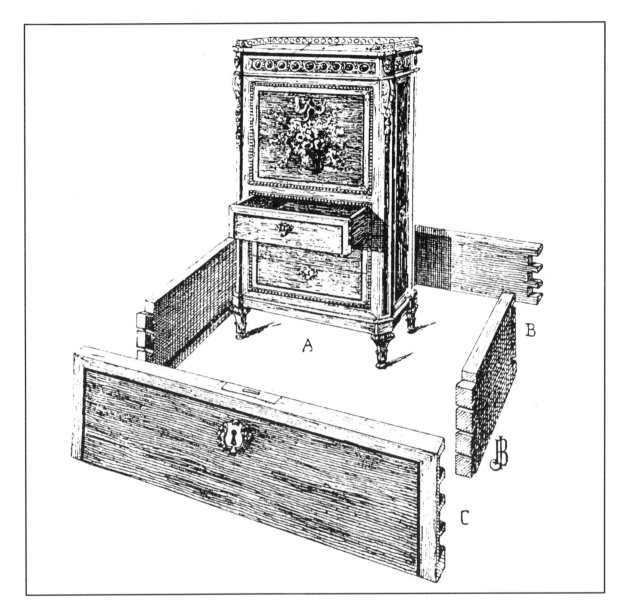

Dovetails
from *Furnituremaking* by J. Boison, 1922

A. Chiffonier-secretary, of cabinetmaking wood with gilt bronzes, after Riesener, 18th century. Museum of Decorative Arts.
B. Through dovetails joining the side of the drawer to the back.
C. Lapped dovetails joining the side of the drawer to the front.

18

DRAWER MAKING

Drawermaking in the Age of Oak • Cabinet-made Drawers •
The First Factory Drawers • Balance & Kickers • Center
Runners • Side-hung Drawers • Metal Runners & Slides

MAKING DRAWERS REPRESENTS AN ADVANCED LEVEL OF WOODWORKING, SINCE IT REQUIRES THE ABILITY TO FULFILL WELL SEVERAL REQUIREMENTS SIMULTANEOUSLY. Measurements are invariably critical since drawers must fit snugly into other parts; construction needs to be strong, since drawers must be able to resist a lot of pulling and pushing and at the same time hold often considerable weight; and their arrangement and individual form need to be sensitive, since they frequently constitute one of the most visible design elements of a piece.

Thoughtful design, strong construction, and accurate execution — if you can accomplish all this you can call yourself a woodworker. Making anything that actually moves and interacts with other parts is always demanding; making your first functioning drawer can be an especial thrill — unless it all goes wrong, when it can become a terminally frustrating experience. One reason why disappointment may overwhelm you is the large number of alternatives facing the drawermaker. Not only are there many different ways to join the front, back, and sides, but there are also many different ways to make and fit bottoms, different methods of installing the drawers in their cases, and many ways of fitting to ensure the correct opening and closing parameters.

This chapter concentrates on the last two aspects: installation and the mechanical design, by which is meant the system adopted to achieve removable drawers, how they are slid in and out, how and where they hang, and what arrangements are made to ensure that the requisite motion is within desired bounds and they neither open too far nor close at any point other than the required position in relation to their case. If you are able to assess which method is appropriate for any given situation, you will be better able to make intelligent design choices and concentrate most of your attention on the actual execution, such as how neatly you cut your dovetails, and how well fitting are the bottoms in their grooves. This will give you the best chance of achieving a drawer that looks right and works well.

It is difficult, if not impossible, to separate installation from mechanical design and adjustment; the one thing affects and often determines the other. Moreover, many techniques are interchangeable from one style to another, so although an historical approach has been adopted for the purposes of describing some of the different ways to make drawers, bear in mind that many of these details can be recombined as the occasion demands. Unless the job or project in hand calls for stylistic accuracy for the sake of historical purity, there is no reason why a newer, and perhaps better, technique may not be combined with something older.

DRAWERMAKING IN THE AGE OF OAK

OLDER PIECES OF FURNITURE THAT UTILIZE OTHERWISE EMPTY interior spaces by fitting them with drawers typically have drawers with

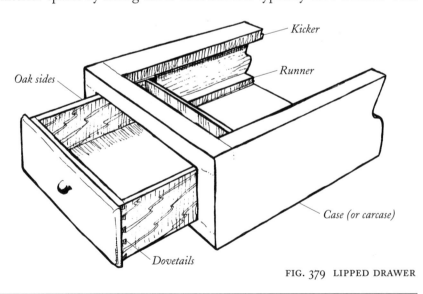

FIG. 379 LIPPED DRAWER

fronts made larger than the drawer openings. The side and top edges of these fronts, and sometimes the bottom edges as well, are rabbeted, so that in the best work the sides may be lap-dovetailed into the front piece. Cheaper construction may permit drawer sides that are more simply butt-jointed or nailed to the front's rabbet. This has the double advantage of providing a built-in stop for the drawer when being closed, as well as completely hiding the drawer opening, which makes it unnecessary to strive for as perfect a fit as an exposed joint might require. This is not just a way to accommodate sloppy workmanship but rather serves the purpose of allowing for dimensional changes caused by changing ambient moisture content, since a drawer that fits in its opening with extremely close tolerances is subject to seizing in damp weather, when everything swells to the point that the original clearance is eliminated.

The bottom edges of the sides of this kind of drawer rest and run on horizontal pieces called runners, which are fixed to the inside of the case of the piece in question. Very old drawers dating from the 15th and 16th centuries were often made to run directly on the bottoms of the drawers (FIG. 380). This was never a very good idea, since it is both wasteful of material and makes a less secure bottom — the weight of whatever is kept in the drawer is all concentrated on the vertical nails that are typically used to hold the bottom to the bottom of the sides. In order to withstand better the heavy wear that this can entail, it was common to make the drawer sides of oak, even during the Age of Walnut which followed the many centuries when most furniture was built entirely of oak.

HISTORICAL PROGRESSION

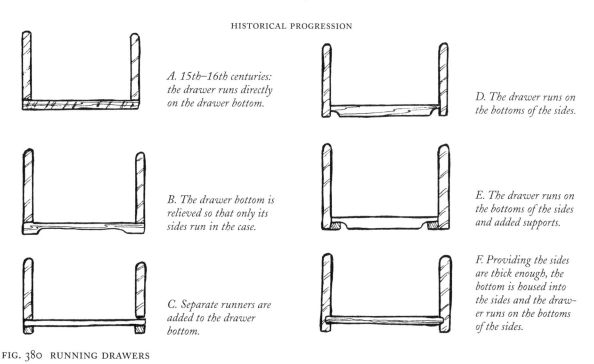

A. 15th–16th centuries: the drawer runs directly on the drawer bottom.

B. The drawer bottom is relieved so that only its sides run in the case.

C. Separate runners are added to the drawer bottom.

D. The drawer runs on the bottoms of the sides.

E. The drawer runs on the bottoms of the sides and added supports.

F. Providing the sides are thick enough, the bottom is housed into the sides and the drawer runs on the bottoms of the sides.

FIG. 380 RUNNING DRAWERS

DRAWERMAKING

When bottoms started to be installed in the sides of the drawer sides rather than being simply nailed to the bottom edge, other problems developed which are well to bear in mind, lest in designing something new you reinvent an old problem. If you use plywood, such as ¼ in. finish-grade luan mahogany, the choice of which way to have the showing grain run is one of esthetics. But if you use solid wood for the drawer bottoms, bear in mind that installing the bottom so that the grain runs front to back, as was commonly done up to the end of the 18th century, is a risky proposition. Any shrinkage in the bottom leaves it susceptible to falling out of the grooves in the drawer sides in which it is fitted. Trying to avoid this difficulty by fixing the bottom with nails is to court a different disaster: you will still not be able to prevent any shrinking that might occur, and as a result either the nails will pop, the bottom be wrenched free, possibly splitting the sides, or the drawer will be radically distorted, causing problems with its niceness of fit, possibly to the extent that it may become balky and even jam. The moral of all this, as was at last commonly recognized around 1790, is that the grain of solid-wood drawer bottoms should run from side to side. If the back of the drawer must be fixed by nailing to the bottom of the back piece, let this be with one brad only, so that should the bottom shrink from front to back and a gap appear at the very front of the drawer, where the bottom is free to slide in and out of its receiving groove in the drawer front, it will be relatively easy to remove and reposition it.

As important as grain direction is the way in which the bottoms may be fixed to the sides. Mention has been made of a simple groove, but all too often the sides not thick enough to permit grooving, and in any case additional support may be necessary. In these instances separate pieces known as slips are used, glued to the inside of the sides. Several designs are shown below. The rounded slip has the advantage of preventing dusty corners. A square slip and a beaded bottom, or a beaded slip and a square-edged bottom will make any side-to-side shrinkage and gapping along the edge of the bottom less noticeable by virtue of the quirk that defines the bead. And of course, any kind of slip can, if glued in the right position, provide an additional wear surface to the bottom of the sides where they contact the drawer runners.

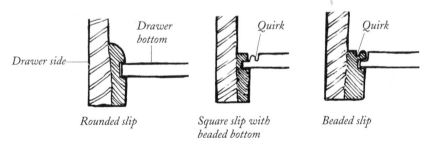

Rounded slip   *Square slip with beaded bottom*   *Beaded slip*

FIG. 381 SLIPS

CABINET-MADE DRAWERS

AROUND THE BEGINNING OF THE THIRTEENTH CENTURY THE joiner first made his appearance in Europe as a representative of a trade quite distinct from that of the carpenter. Up until this time it had been the carpenter who had been responsible, along with his house-framing duties, for the manufacture of such furniture as was then in use. This was admittedly not much, just a few benches, the box-chair, and the basic chest. But there was a problem with carpenter-made furniture: it weighed a lot and had a great tendency to shrink and warp, since it was generally made out of large, thick planks joined together with iron nails that inevitably rusted out in the acidic oak that was the principal material.

The solution was a new technique that joined much thinner boards in such a way as to allow the wood to shrink or expand with very little change in overall dimensions, and, most importantly, without having to rely on nails. This technique was made possible by the use of the mortise-and-tenon joint, held together by wooden pins known as trenails, with which a framework could be constructed, in which variously sized free-floating panels could be held.

By 1570, carpenters in Britain had become limited to rough house-framing. All finer work, necessary for things like windows, stairs, doors, and especially wall paneling, was from this point on subcontracted out to joiners. In 1632, in addition to the mortise-and-tenon joint, joiners were further allowed to use dovetail joints. It was this advance that made it possible for them to make the first 'drawing-boxes', as drawers, which up till then had been known as 'tills', were now called, fitting them into the chests, cupboards, and presses of the time, and in the process become responsible for practically all furniture production, with the exception of chairmaking, which remained a separate trade.

Although joiners used dovetails to make drawers, they were not much interested in using this particular technique for making anything larger, preferring instead to stick with frame-and-panel construction for most articles. It was immigrant Flemish chestmakers who popularized the use of large, dovetailed boards to make bigger case furniture, and from whom the 18th century English cabinetmakers developed as representatives of a trade distinct from that of the joiner. The distinction survives to this day, especially in Britain. Carpenters are responsible for house framing, joiners are responsible for the better grade of purpose-built millwork, while furniture is the domain of cabinetmakers. In America, 'cabinet-maker' has become a somewhat altered term, and refers now to the maker of kitchen cabinets, requiring the maker of fine furniture to be called a furnituremaker. Nevertheless, even the kitchen cabinetmaker depends on large sheets of material rather than on a frame-and-panel construction.

With the increasing use of exotic imported veneers in the 18th century, traditional frame-and-panel construction became largely unnecessary. At the same time the greater dimensional stability produced by the use of veneered parts made possible closer tolerances between moving parts such as drawers and their cases. Cabinet-made drawers as opposed to joiner-made drawers are therefore often made with fronts designed to fit flush with the surface of the piece that contains them. As a result, greater care is needed to ensure a closer fit so that unsightly gaps do not appear around the drawer when it is closed.

A common way to deal with such gaps is to draw attention away from them by introducing some other feature such as a moulding. In the case of drawers this is often achieved by the use of cock beading. Standing somewhat proud of the surface of the drawer front and its case, the cock bead obscures the exact relationship of the possibly unequal planes of these two surfaces.

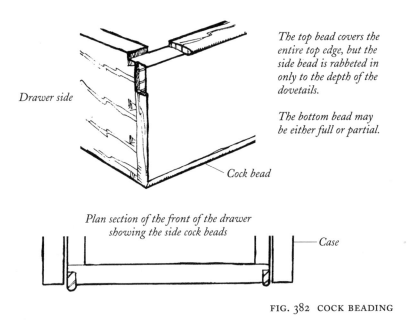

Drawer side

The top bead covers the entire top edge, but the side bead is rabbeted in only to the depth of the dovetails.

The bottom bead may be either full or partial.

Cock bead

Plan section of the front of the drawer showing the side cock beads

Case

FIG. 382 COCK BEADING

A further result of flush-fitted drawers was the need to provide a new way of regulating how far in the drawer could be pushed. This is often done quite simply by fixing a small block of wood known as a 'stop' to the top of the runner at the back of the case. Another method, somewhat easier to install but which is not to be recommended since it can pose a very real danger to the integrity of the drawer front if it should suffer hard-handed use, is to pin or glue thin pieces to the front rail, so that the inside bottom of the drawer front closes against them. When using either method consider placing the stops so that the drawer closes slightly inside the surrounding case. This can often look better than having supposedly flush drawers which in fact are somewhat proud.

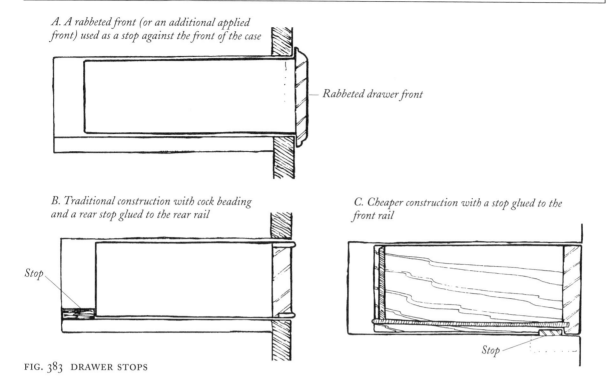

A. A rabbeted front (or an additional applied front) used as a stop against the front of the case

— *Rabbeted drawer front*

B. Traditional construction with cock beading and a rear stop glued to the rear rail

Stop

C. Cheaper construction with a stop glued to the front rail

Stop

FIG. 383 DRAWER STOPS

Incidentally, simply making the depth of the drawer equal to the depth of the case might seem the most straightforward way of automatically achieving correct closure, but not only would this call for greater care and exactness when making the drawer, but such a procedure would also be doomed to failure because of the limited compressibility of air. If a drawer is made to fit almost exactly in an enclosed space, when it is closed the air trapped behind it will be forced to look for other escape routes. In a unit with multiple drawers this can have the effect of pushing some of the other drawers open; as fast as you shut one, another pops open. For this reason, closely fitting drawers should always be made an inch or two shorter than their case is deep. This need to make drawers somewhat shorter than their case can, however, often provide an opportunity to make interesting secret compartments or hidden storage areas.

Another trick to ensure easy action when constructing drawers with close tolerances is to make the drawer slightly narrower at the back than at the front. This will allow the drawer to be pushed in easily, no matter how damp the weather, without sacrificing a close fit at the front. If the front binds, a little wax or even soap rubbed on the tight areas works well as a lubricant. But make sure that you do not make the drawer so narrow at the back that it falls off its runners when pulled out to the front; all that is necessary is perhaps no more than ⅛ in. reduction in width at the back for a 12 in.-deep drawer.

DRAWERMAKING

THE FIRST FACTORY DRAWERS

WHEN FACTORY-MADE PIECES WERE INTRODUCED EARLY IN THE 19th century, much cheap furniture, such as the commodes, dressers, kitchen tables, chests of drawers, and other examples now sold as French Provincial or English country-pine furniture, became common. Drawers in such pieces are often made of soft secondary woods such as pine, which quickly becomes so worn that their proper action is soon compromised. with the inevitable result that they become sloppy and difficult to open. This in turn leads to worse problems such as wrenched-off handles, loose joints, and even broken sides.

Late 19th century books on woodwork and household repair are full of tips on how to repair the bottoms of such worn drawers by adding strips of harder material, such as oak. Repairing the runners themselves, also usually made of some inappropriate softwood, is somewhat more difficult, and only serves to underline the fact that drawers built to run on runners integral with the carcase should have all rubbing parts constructed out of long-wearing hardwood.

BALANCE & KICKERS

WHEN DRAWERS ARE MADE AS DESCRIBED ABOVE, HUNG FREELY within a case and running on the bottoms of their sides, attention must be paid to their overall balance. This is a question of the drawer's total weight in proportion to its front. If the front is very heavy, like many Age of Oak types, which were often carved and embellished with applied moulding, the rest of the drawer must be constructed out of material heavy enough to prevent the drawer from tilting down excessively before it is even halfway open. There are two ways to deal with this problem.

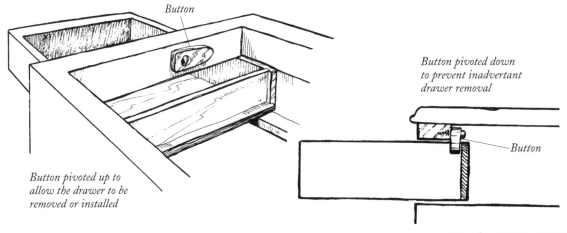

Button

Button pivoted down to prevent inadvertant drawer removal

Button

Button pivoted up to allow the drawer to be removed or installed

FIG. 384 PIVOT BUTTON

The first is to provide a way of preventing the drawer from being opened past the point at which it becomes front-heavy. Two methods are common: one entails a stop, fixed to the case, that engages the back of the drawer when it is pulled a certain distance forward, and the other consists of a button or peg, inserted through the side of the drawer, that engages part of the case when the drawer reaches the desired limit. Related to these techniques is the use of a pivoting button fixed inside the bottom of the drawer opening's top rail. Once the drawer has been installed, this button is turned so that it will engage the back of the drawer when the drawer is opened to a certain point, thus preventing it from being pulled completely out of its case. To remove the drawer, the button is simply turned around (FIG. 384).

The second method of dealing with drawer-tipping is to install kickers (see FIG. 379) in the casework. Kickers are extra pieces fitted to the framework, often to the inside of the front top rail and from side to side at different points, which prevent the drawer sides from 'kicking' up as the drawer is pulled out. If the case containing the drawer is solid, kickers are unnecessary, but in open construction, such as a typical chest of drawers, they are indispensable, and are usually an integral part of the framing.

CENTER RUNNERS

A METHOD OF INSTALLING DRAWERS THAT LIES HALFWAY BETWEEN the oldest free-running method described above and the contemporary use of drawer slides and extensions is that often used by corner drawers.

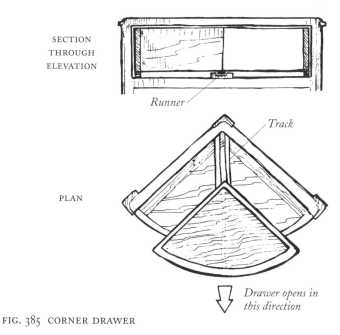

SECTION
THROUGH
ELEVATION

Runner

Track

PLAN

*Drawer opens in
this direction*

FIG. 385 CORNER DRAWER

DRAWERMAKING

A single strip, often no more than 1 in. by 1 in., is fixed to the underside of the drawer in its center, running from front to back. It rides in a track, formed by either a single ploughed member or two separate pieces placed parallel, fixed in the case. Although it was originally designed to accommodate non-rectangular drawers without parallel sides, such as corner or curved drawers (FIG. 385), there is little reason why it cannot be applied to other situations where it is inconvenient to use the sides as runners, always providing, of course, that the sides of the drawers are full height and can bear against the front opening so that the drawer is prevented from tipping down as it is opened.

Hinging the drawer at one of its front corners is an even simpler way to install this kind of drawer in pieces where it is not important to maintain a consistant relationship of the front of the drawer with the front of the case during opening.

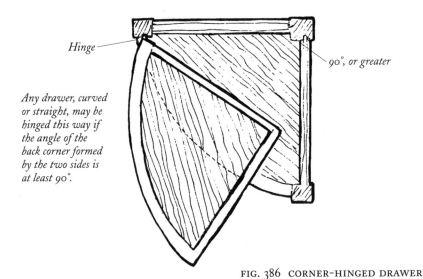

Hinge

90°, or greater

Any drawer, curved or straight, may be hinged this way if the angle of the back corner formed by the two sides is at least 90°.

FIG. 386 CORNER-HINGED DRAWER

SIDE-HUNG DRAWERS

INSTALLING DRAWERS SO THAT THEY RUN ON TRACKS ENGAGING grooves cut in their sides can be exacting work, but it has the advantage of making a lot of traditional casemaking unnecessary. There is no need for a system of runners, kickers, or stops, and it is a very efficient way to make a case that contains a lot of relatively small drawers where the use of dustboards (horizontal partitions between drawers) is not needed. Since intermediate rails are not required, side-hanging also makes a very clean design possible where drawer fronts are made flush or recessed in the case. It is also a very useful method for installing drawers with reduced fronts or sides, such as are common in wardrobes or closets where a series of drawers are often needed that partially display their contents even when closed.

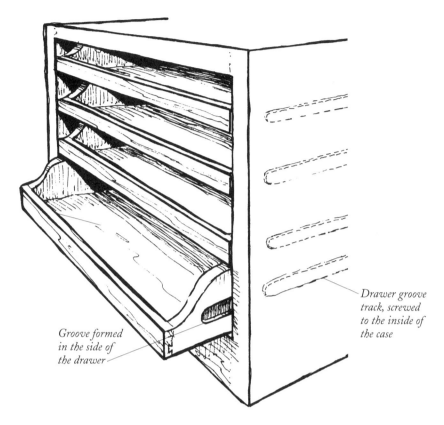

Drawer groove track, screwed to the inside of the case

Groove formed in the side of the drawer

FIG. 387 SIDE-HUNG LOW-FRONT DRAWERS

Several methods are shown overleaf in FIG. 388. When ploughing the grooves in the drawer sides to receive the track, try to position the grooves so that they run out between the dovetails at the end of the sides; this avoids having to make stopped grooves and, assuming you cut the grooves with a router, avoids having to round the ends of the track.

The track should be made of the hardest wood you can find, since although this kind of drawer initially runs more easily than one which rests on the bottoms of its sides — because the total rubbing area is less — it is, for the same reason, subject to greater wear, and furthermore depends on the tracks to keep it from tipping down when pulled out. Fit is therefore crucial. Although the interior parts of much furniture or cabinetry are not often finished, this is one case where it will pay to do so. Sealing the slides and the sides of the drawers to prevent as much moisture content change as possible will help avoid sticky drawers in damp weather. Tried and true remedies for sticky drawers such as rubbing

DRAWERMAKING

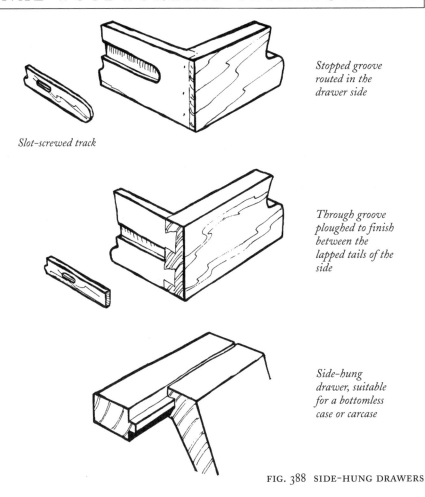

Slot-screwed track

Stopped groove routed in the drawer side

Through groove ploughed to finish between the lapped tails of the side

Side-hung drawer, suitable for a bottomless case or carcase

FIG. 388 SIDE-HUNG DRAWERS

with soap, paraffin candles, or regular wax also work but are no real substitute for a carefully designed and executed construction. The sides to which the tracks are attached must also be strong enough to bear the weight, and should the grain of the sides run perpendicularly to that of the tracks, the track must be slot-screwed in place or the sides may crack or cause the tracks to become misaligned. Slot-screwing also makes it much easier to position the track exactly.

There are many advantages to side-hung drawers, but after you have wrestled with some of their difficulties for a while, you may come to appreciate the wisdom inherent in the simpler designs of the Age of Oak.

METAL RUNNERS & SLIDES

THE FORERUNNERS OF MODERN METAL EXTENSION SLIDES WERE variously designed metal runners suspended between the case's front rail and the back of the unit. These runners are often found fitted with small wheels designed to engage matching tracks fixed underneath the drawer.

Nowadays, one of the more common ways of hanging kitchen-cabinet drawers is to use easily installed extension slides. Curiously, this technique requires a return to the earliest form of drawermaking in so far as fronts wider than the sides are needed — not to provide a method of stopping the drawer but to hide the fronts of the slides. Construction, which is quick and easy but rather wasteful, usually consists of making the base drawer to which the slides are attached, and then applying a second wider piece to the front. This second front may be made to close flush with the enclosing cabinet or, more commonly, to close on it. The advantages of this method include substantial weight-carrying ability — many slide extensions can carry differing weights at a given length, for which reason the weight rating should always be checked — and easy action regardless of the size or load of the drawer made possible by wheels or rollers. Many slides are also designed to be self-closing and, if installed properly, will close accurately, guaranteeing the required alignment of drawer front and cabinet.

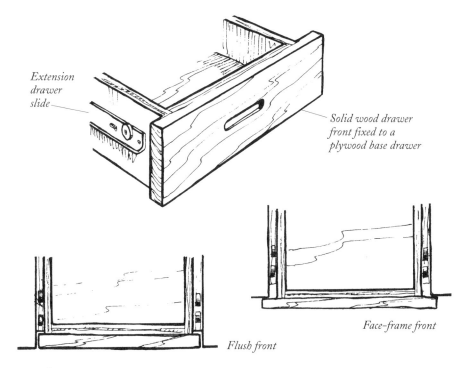

Extension drawer slide

Solid wood drawer front fixed to a plywood base drawer

Flush front

Face-frame front

FIG. 389 EXTENSION DRAWERS

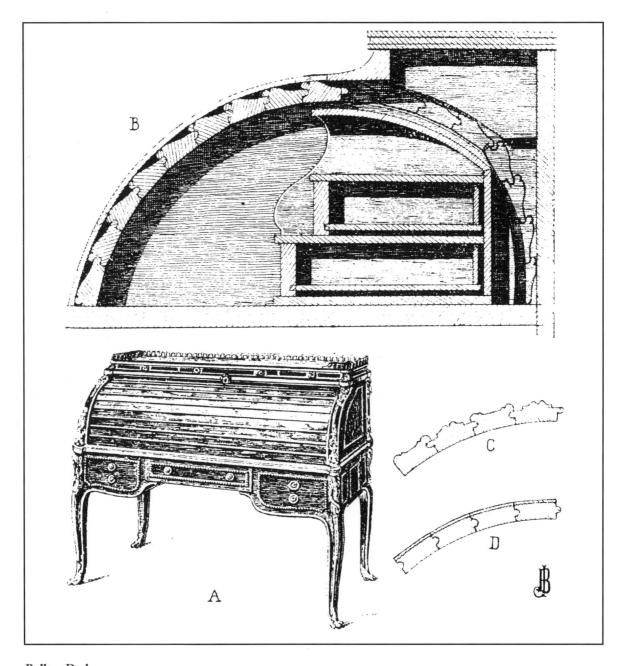

Rolltop Desks
from *Furnituremaking* by J. Boison, 1922

A. Desk: rolltop with moving slats; mahogany and gilt bronzes, by Riesener, 18th century (Louvre Museum).
B. Section through desk showing: the interior compartments; the groove in the side in which the rolltop slats slide; the position of the slats behind the inner compartments when the desk is open; the franking of the slats (modern method).
C. Another slat profile, after Roubo.
D. Slats, exterior surfaces, leveled for marquetry (desk belonging to King Louis xv, Louvre).

19

FURNITURE STYLES

The Pilgrim Century • The Mahogany Period • Federal •
The Nineteenth Century • Shaker • Arts & Crafts •
The Twentieth Century

KNOWING WHAT JOINERY TECHNIQUES ARE APPROPRIATE FOR ANY GIVEN PROJECT IS ESSENTIAL, BUT IF ANYTHING IS TO LOOK RIGHT AS WELL AS FUNCTION WELL, SO IS A basic familiarity with various esthetic principles, a number of elements of which were mentioned in chapter 17. Of ultimate importance in this regard is how well a piece fits in with its surroundings. This implies an understanding of what these surroundings might be, and in particular what informs and constitutes a particular style. This chapter provides a concise overview of American furniture over the last four hundred years, putting the various styles into an historical perspective based on their defining characteristics and the changing techniques that wrought them.

The progress of style is continual, and so all attempts to categorize definitively the products of a given period are necessarily inexact. The following divisions are therefore suggestions only, concentrating on the most characteristic and salient aspects of the better-known periods. There is always much overlap, and it is in the very nature of furniture design to evolve, often haphazardly, taking a little from here and a little from there, sometimes making a large leap with the invention of a new technique or a new material, but most often developing into something recognizably new by a process of gradual assimilation from much that has gone before.

While British furniture is most often described in terms of the various monarchs during whose reigns it was made, a more general division of furniture styles can be made using the following categories, at least for American readers. Nevertheless, it remains true that most American furniture is very similar to the contemporaneous British styles. Much from the first four periods was imported, and much that was made in America was made by craftsmen either trained in Britain or who used British pattern books. By the 20th century, however, the world had become a smaller place, and nowadays differences often have more to do with individual makers than national styles.

THE PILGRIM CENTURY: 1620–1750

DURING THE EARLY COLONIAL PERIOD OF AMERICA MUCH FURNITURE arrived with the first immigrants, including most famously the Pilgrims. They brought with them, and then made, pieces typical of the Jacobean, William and Mary, and Carolean periods in Britain; pieces that were still largely representative of the so-called Age of Oak. These were in general sturdy pieces heavily carved, many with cup-turned legs and bun feet, but pieces often representative of a straightforward and utilitarian life.

Oak,
frame-and-panel
construction,
by Nicholas Disbrowe,
ca. 1660

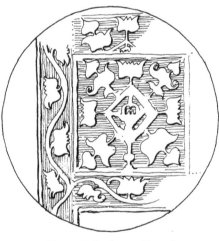

Low-relief tulip-motif carving
covering the entire front

Uncompromisingly rectangular, this chest by the first known American maker, who was actually born in England, is very similar to earlier English Age of Oak styles, but is already recognizable as a distinct American style, known as a Hadley style chest, from the Connecticut River valley.

FIG. 390 THE NICHOLAS DISBROWE CHEST

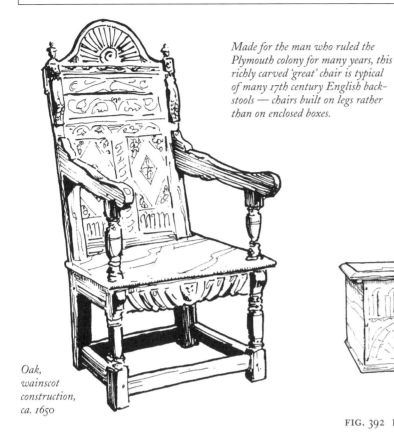

Made for the man who ruled the
Plymouth colony for many years, this
richly carved 'great' chair is typical
of many 17th century English back-
stools — chairs built on legs rather
than on enclosed boxes.

Most small boxes were simply
nailed but frequently carved.
Known as 'Bible Boxes', they were
designed for secure storage, even
though pine was sometimes used,
at least for the tops and bottoms.

Oak,
wainscot
construction,
ca. 1650

Oak, nailed construction, 1670

FIG. 392 BIBLE BOX

FIG. 391 THE ELDER BREWSTER CHAIR

Although used as a communion table (the endless pattern carving on the front apron symbolizes
eternity), this table is typical of 17th century domestic dining tables, whose framed bases had
gradually supplanted the earlier trestle type common since the Middle Ages.

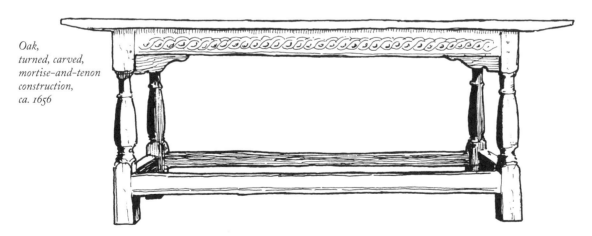

Oak,
turned, carved,
mortise-and-tenon
construction,
ca. 1656

FIG. 393 LONG TABLE

FURNITURE STYLES

Other influences were also present during the Pilgrim Century, most notably Dutch and French in the Northeast and Spanish in the Southwest. Although recognizably different from their British-inspired counterparts, Dutch pieces are essentially in the same tradition, whereas the different climate and different species of lumber available to Spanish colonists produced — and continue to produce — a distinct style known as Mission or Southwestern.

Walnut, leather covered, mortise-and-tenon, 17th century

The very practical and durable style of furniture that derives from pieces made by the early Spanish colonizers and missionaries is often cruder and heavier than this Spanish example, itself less sophisticated than other European forms.

FIG. 394 SPANISH CHAIR

THE MAHOGANY PERIOD: 1702–1760

THE LATER COLONIAL PERIOD, COVERING THE FIRST HALF OF THE 18th century, roughly parallels those periods known as Queen Anne and Georgian in Britain. Walnut, which had gradually supplanted oak as the most popular wood for fine furniture, gave way to mahogany as the predominant wood, and the beginning of the period saw a sudden simplification of style into a less ornamented and more severely elegant esthetic. Perhaps the most typical element of this whole period is the cabriole leg, at first plain and finished with a simple turned pad foot, and later developed into a much carved element complete with ball-and-claw, hairy paw, or lion's feet. Furniture was now made by cabinetmakers rather than joiners, and the list of American Chippendales (Thomas Chippendale being the most famous English cabinetmaker of the period, and by whose name furniture of the middle of the period is often known) is long. It includes the Goddards and Townsends of Newport, Rhode

Island, and many notable Philadelphia makers, such as William Savery, Thomas Affleck, and Benjamin Randolph. New York and Boston were also important centers of furniture production, and many pieces can be identified by characteristics peculiar to particular cities.

The Mahogany Period began as a reaction to the stylistic excess of the preceding era. The emphasis is on simple flowing lines — of which the cabriole leg is the quintessential characteristic — rather than inlay, veneer, or copious carving. This armchair, made by a Philadelphia cabinetmaker, has a plain profiled splat, simple feet, and three minimal shell carvings.

*Mahogany,
by William Savery,
ca. 1750*

FIG. 395   ARMCHAIR

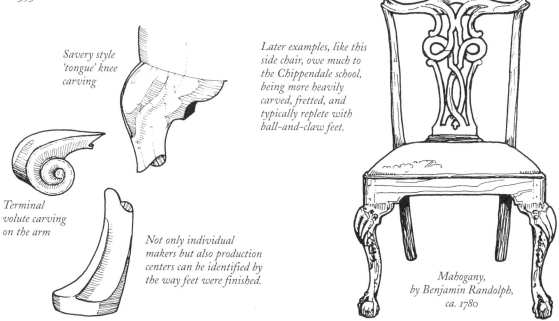

Savery style 'tongue' knee carving

Later examples, like this side chair, owe much to the Chippendale school, being more heavily carved, fretted, and typically replete with ball-and-claw feet.

Terminal volute carving on the arm

Not only individual makers but also production centers can be identified by the way feet were finished.

*Mahogany,
by Benjamin Randolph,
ca. 1780*

FIG. 396   CHAIR DETAILS

FIG. 397   CHIPPENDALE STYLE SIDE CHAIR

FURNITURE STYLES

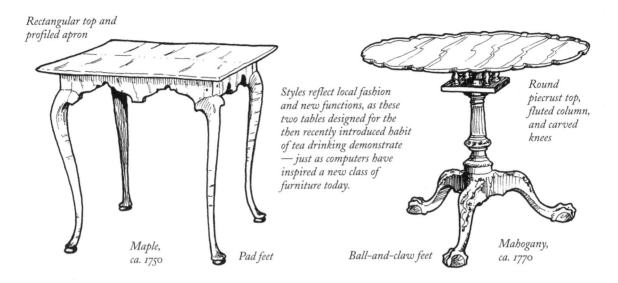

Rectangular top and profiled apron

Styles reflect local fashion and new functions, as these two tables designed for the then recently introduced habit of tea drinking demonstrate — just as computers have inspired a new class of furniture today.

Round piecrust top, fluted column, and carved knees

Maple, ca. 1750

Pad feet

Ball-and-claw feet

Mahogany, ca. 1770

FIG. 398 NEW ENGLAND STYLE TEA TABLE

FIG. 399 PHILADELPHIA STYLE TEA TABLE

Bureaus, highboys, chests-on-chest, and secretaries represent the apotheosis of the 18th century cabinetmaker's craft. Rich veneers, masterful carving, and designs based on classical paradigms such as the Golden Mean (see page 285) define this style.

Mahogany, poplar, and pine, cabinetmaker construction, ca. 1770

Mahogany, chestnut, pine, and poplar, cabinetmaker construction, by John Townsend, ca. 1765

FIG. 400 HIGH CHEST OF DRAWERS

FIG. 401 BUREAU TABLE

FEDERAL: 1760–1840

AFTER THE REVOLUTION, AMERICAN TASTES AND SYMPATHIES were in many things transferred from Britain to France, especially with regard to furniture styles. The French 'Empire' style planned and fostered by Napoleon was adopted with distinctive modifications by American cabinetmakers, and is typically known as 'Federal'.

In comparison to the light and well-proportioned furniture typified by the Hepplewhite and Sheraton style pieces of the end of the Mahogany Period that preceded it, much Federal-period furniture is dark, heavy, and vulgar. The finest, however, is often superb, and owes much to one of the most famous of all American cabinetmakers, Duncan Phyfe, a New York cabinetmaker possessed of great taste and a wonderful eye for proportion.

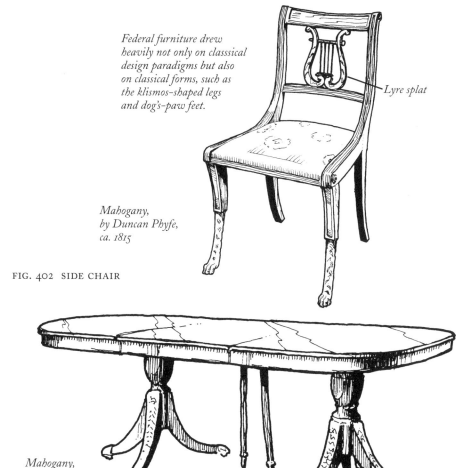

Federal furniture drew heavily not only on classical design paradigms but also on classical forms, such as the klismos-shaped legs and dog's-paw feet.

Lyre splat

Mahogany, by Duncan Phyfe, ca. 1815

FIG. 402 SIDE CHAIR

Mahogany, by Duncan Phyfe, ca. 1815

This two-part dining table with Federal style tripod legs retains elements, such as the reeded support legs, that hark back to the two English masters who succeeded Chippendale, Hepplewhite and Sheraton, as well as details, such as the feet, that are derived from French cabinetmakers of the Directory and Consulate styles.

FIG. 403 DINING TABLE

FURNITURE STYLES

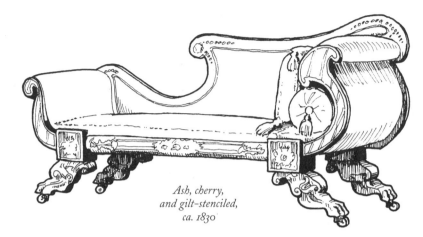

Federal furniture might be massive and extremely ornamented like this couch, or more restrained like the pier table below, which nevertheless is much painted and decorated with classical motifs.

Ash, cherry, and gilt-stenciled, ca. 1830

FIG. 404 CURVED DAY COUCH

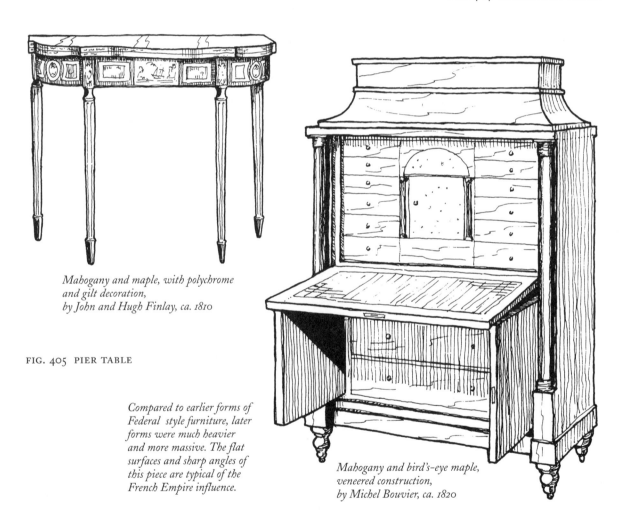

Mahogany and maple, with polychrome and gilt decoration, by John and Hugh Finlay, ca. 1810

FIG. 405 PIER TABLE

Compared to earlier forms of Federal style furniture, later forms were much heavier and more massive. The flat surfaces and sharp angles of this piece are typical of the French Empire influence.

Mahogany and bird's-eye maple, veneered construction, by Michel Bouvier, ca. 1820

FIG. 406 SECRETARY

THE NINETEENTH CENTURY: 1840–1910

THE MID–NINETEENTH CENTURY SAW MASS-PRODUCTION BECOME the norm in many areas of American life, from farming to high-end furnituremaking. Some furniture historians refer to this as the era of the 'degraded styles', and while commercialism certainly resulted in much cheap, shoddy, and undistinguished work produced for its novelty value and designed to take advantage of the current fad, such as the endless stream of various revival styles — Rococo, Egyptian, Gothic, Italian, Beaux Arts, etc. — there was also a remarkable burgeoning of vigorous new styles, which produced clearly defined forms such as Art Nouveau and Arts and Crafts.

Nineteenth century furniture, often referred to as Victorian, after the reigning British monarch, tends to be thought of as extremely ornamented, overstuffed, and often in terrible taste, but there is, in fact, no one common characteristic of the period other than that of diversity, as the following pages show.

Not only mass-production but also new technology gave rise to new furniture forms. John Henry Belter, a leading figure of the Rococo Revival, is also famous for having patented a method of laminating many thin layers of wood and shaping them in a steam mould.

*Carved and laminated
rosewood,
by John Henry Belter,
ca. 1860*

FIG. 407   BED

FURNITURE STYLES

Like many successful 19th century firms, such as Cottier & Co., Pottier & Stymus, and Herter Brothers, the partnership of Anthony Kimbel and Joseph Cabus produced furniture in the so-called Modern Gothic Style as well as in the Renaissance Revival style illustrated here.

Ceramic plaques, marquetry panels, gilt ornaments, rich veneer, and abundant carving are all typical of much late 19th century manufactured furniture.

*Rosewood with marquetry panels,
by Kimbel & Cabus,
ca. 1876*

FIG. 408 CABINET

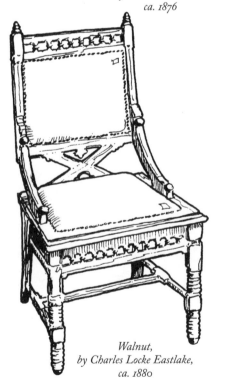

*Walnut,
by Charles Locke Eastlake,
ca. 1880*

The beginnings of a simpler, more modern design sensibility can be traced to Charles Locke Eastlake, an English architect who wrote an enormously popular book called 'Hints on Household Taste' that influenced the popular demand for so-called Reform furniture in America.

Together with artists, architects, and designers such as Pugin, Ruskin, and William Morris, Eastlake played an important part in the development of styles based on rigorous esthetic principles, such as Arts and Crafts, that occurred towards the end of the 19th century.

FIG. 409 SIDE CHAIR

SHAKER: 1800–1900

THROUGHOUT THE ENTIRE NINETEENTH CENTURY, THE RELIGIOUS communities known popularly as the Shakers were producing furniture so different from everything else that was being made that it has come to be recognized as a distinct and major American style. Its essential quality is simplicity. Eschewing ornamentation, the Shakers produced furniture that was not only eminently practical and honest but which was also possessed of a restrained elegance. Often giving the appearance of great delicacy, Shaker pieces are nonetheless constructed on sound and sturdy principles, and have frequently been the original inspiration for many beginning woodworkers attracted by their apparent simplicity and straightforwardness.

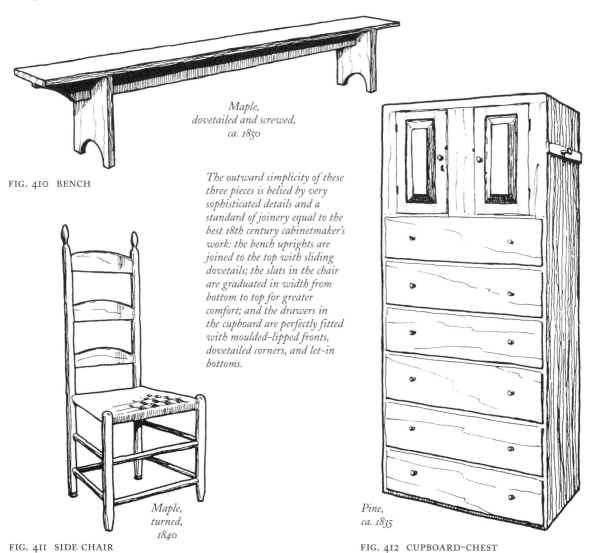

*Maple,
dovetailed and screwed,
ca. 1850*

FIG. 410 BENCH

The outward simplicity of these three pieces is belied by very sophisticated details and a standard of joinery equal to the best 18th century cabinetmaker's work: the bench uprights are joined to the top with sliding dovetails; the slats in the chair are graduated in width from bottom to top for greater comfort; and the drawers in the cupboard are perfectly fitted with moulded-lipped fronts, dovetailed corners, and let-in bottoms.

*Maple,
turned,
1840*

*Pine,
ca. 1835*

FIG. 411 SIDE CHAIR

FIG. 412 CUPBOARD-CHEST

FURNITURE STYLES

ARTS & CRAFTS: 1890–1920

FURNITURE KNOWN VARIOUSLY AS 'MISSION' FURNITURE, 'ARTS and Crafts' furniture, and 'Craftsman' furniture was largely the result of a reaction inspired by critics and designers such as John Ruskin and William Morris against shoddy mass-production. Their writing produced several generations of furniture designers dedicated to honesty, utility, and above all good-quality workmanship. Designers and craftsmen such as Elbert Hubbard and Gustav Stickley produced a body of furniture which has remained popular and distinct to the present day, taking its place as a legitimate major American style. Compared to most of what had gone before — with the exception of Shaker furniture — the style stands out as relatively rectilinear, largely unencumbered by ornament and carving, and primarily made of oak with exposed joinery.

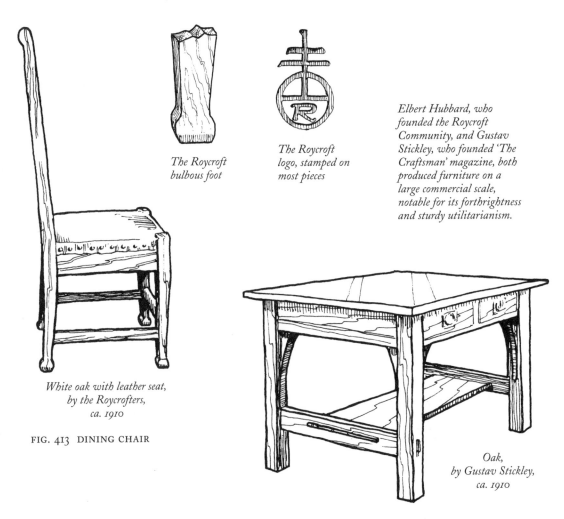

The Roycroft bulbous foot

The Roycroft logo, stamped on most pieces

Elbert Hubbard, who founded the Roycroft Community, and Gustav Stickley, who founded 'The Craftsman' magazine, both produced furniture on a large commercial scale, notable for its forthrightness and sturdy utilitarianism.

White oak with leather seat, by the Roycrofters, ca. 1910

FIG. 413 DINING CHAIR

Oak, by Gustav Stickley, ca. 1910

FIG. 414 LIBRARY TABLE

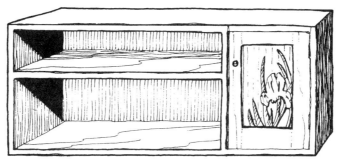

Extreme simplicity of design informs this version of the Arts and Crafts style made in the utopian community founded by Ralph Whitehead in 1903.

Poplar, stained and polychromed, by the Byrdcliffe Workshops, 1904

FIG. 415 WALL CABINET

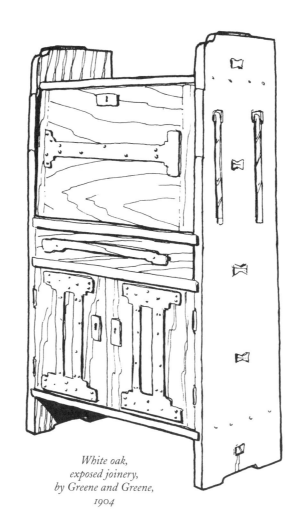

At the top end of the market, the Arts and Crafts style was also adopted by prestigious architects and designers such as Frank Lloyd Wright and Charles and Henry Greene. Their output, while considerably more expensive than pieces by Stickley or the Roycrofters, and in many ways more sophisticated, remained true to the fundamental ideals of the movement and as such is instantly recognizable as belonging to this quintessential American style.

White oak, exposed joinery, by Greene and Greene, 1904

FIG. 416 DESK

THE TWENTIETH CENTURY: 1900–2000

WHILE MASS-PRODUCTION REMAINED THE DOMINANT FORCE IN furniture production throughout the 20th century, it also developed some extremely high quality reproduction companies specializing in many of the most distinctive styles of the past, most notably of the later Colonial period. At the same time, various new 'modern' styles appeared, ranging from Art Nouveau and Art Deco to Bauhaus and Post-modernism.

By the middle of the century, responding in part to current modern design movements and in part to a resurgent interest in craftsmanship, a whole generation of individual furnituremakers appeared, including widely different designers such as Wendell Castle, George Nakashima, Sam Maloof, and James Krenov. Because of a greater availability of a wider array of materials, and an expanding awareness of historical and cross-cultural esthetics, the history of 20th century design may be regarded as more diverse than the entire three centuries that preceded it.

While Nakashima's Conoid chair represents a new form of construction compared to the more traditional techniques used in Krenov's cabinet, both share the individual craftsman's concern for the inherent beauty of the material in a way rarely considered in mass-produced furniture.

Walnut and hickory, cantilever construction, by George Nakashima, 1980

FIG. 417 CONOID CHAIR

Cherry and hornbeam, by James Krenov, ca. 1970

FIG. 418 CABINET

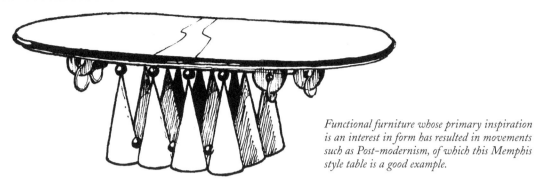

Functional furniture whose primary inspiration is an interest in form has resulted in movements such as Post-modernism, of which this Memphis style table is a good example.

Purpleheart veneer, leather, and copper, by Wendell Castle, 1985

FIG. 419 'NEVER COMPLAIN' TABLE

The contemporary furnituremaker thus has more choices than ever, not only with regard to materials and techniques, but also with regard to style, motivation, and economy. Whether the primary motive is a love of the material, which can result in pieces constructed around the intrinsic beauty of a particular piece of wood, or a concern with form above all else, the methods for achieving these goals are now more varied than ever. At the same time, success and ultimate satisfaction still depend on the level of craftsmanship involved. There is a world of difference between a Gustav Stickley piece and a Jacques-Émile Ruhlmann piece; the one is built to be affordable by all, the other avowedly only for the very rich, but both are made with consumate craftsmanship. The development of a firm foundation for this essential craftsmanship is what this book has tried to make possible.

SELECT BIBLIOGRAPHY

THE ILLUSTRATED ENCYCLOPEDIA OF WOODWORKING HANDTOOLS, INSTRUMENTS, & DEVICES, TOGETHER WITH TRADITIONAL WOODWORKING HANDTOOLS, — which may be read as essential companions to this book — contain in their Select Bibliographies many titles both interesting and pertinent to the aspiring furnituremaker. Rather than duplicate those lists, I have included here titles not previously mentioned, many of which pursue in greater detail more specialized aspects of the craft.

Note that many books have been reprinted by different publishers. I have listed where possible the original edition, but an Internet search may turn up more easily obtained editions.

Blackburn, Graham. *The Illustrated Encyclopedia of Woodworking Handtools, Instruments, & Devices.* 1974. 3rd ed. Bearsville, New York: Blackburn Books, 2000.

Blackburn, Graham. *Traditional Woodworking Handtools.* Bearsville, New York: Blackburn Books, 1998.

Boison, J. *Industrie du Meuble: Principes de Construction, Éléments Généraux.* Paris: Dunod, Éditeur, 1922.

— *A trade school text based on traditional techniques that deals with fundamental wood science, furnituremaking wood conversion, and a host of construction and joinery techniques illustrated by high-style French furniture.*

Frank, George. *88 Rue de Charonne: Adventures in Wood Finishing.* Newtown, Connecticut: The Taunton Press, 1981.

— *One of the very best books on one of the least understood areas of furnituremaking; history, anecdotes, and techniques.*

Grauber, Wolfram. *Encyclopedia of Wood Joints.* Newtown, Connecticut: The Taunton Press, 1992. (Originally published as *Holzverbindungen: Gegenüberstellungen japanischer und europäischer Lösungen.* Stuttgart: Deutsche Verlags-Anstalt GmbH, 1986.)

— *A comparison of two major schools of joinery, profusely illustrated with photographs and line drawings.*

Hasluck, Paul N. *Manual of Traditional Wood Carving.* 1911. Reprint. New York: Dover Publications, Inc., 1977.

— *A wonderfully thorough introduction to traditional carving tools and a variety of practical carving techniques, with hundreds of examples from all periods.*

Hayward, Charles H. *Antique Furniture Design.* New York: Charles Scribner's Sons, 1979.

— *A close look at the structure and construction techniques of various examples of furniture from the 17th and 18th centuries.*

Hayward, Charles H. *Woodwork Joints.* ca. 1960. Reprint. New York: Drake Publishers Inc., 1970.

— *The basic primer for traditional joinery techniques, illustrating many examples from the major families of woodworking joints.*

Hoadley, R. Bruce. *Understanding Wood: A Craftsman's Guide to Wood Technology.* Newtown, Connecticut: The Taunton Press, Inc., 2000.

— *The book that explains exactly what it is that wood wants to do and how and why it does it; an essential book for all those who would build furniture to last.*

Hodgson, Frederick T. *Modern Carpentry: A Practical Manual.* 1902. 2nd ed. Chicago: Frederick J. Drake & Co., 1902.

— *As well as containing much useful information for drafting and setting out, and although originally written for end-of-the-19th-century joiners and carpenters, this book has an excellent section on casemaking.*

SELECT BIBLIOGRAPHY

Kassay, John. *The Book of Shaker Furniture*. Amherst, Massachusetts: The University of Massachusetts Press, 1980.

— *A comprehensive study of Shaker furniture with many measured drawings and photographs.*

Mehler, Kelly. *The Table Saw Book*. Newtown, Connecticut: The Taunton Press, Inc., 2003.

— *Inasmuch as the tablesaw has become a basic feature of many contemporary woodshops, this should be considered an essential text for a complete and safe understanding of a potentially dangerous machine.*

Pain, F. *The Practical Wood Turner*. 1956. Reprint. New York: Sterling Publishing Company, Inc., 1979.

— *Almost as good as being there in person at the side of a master who minces no words about one of the more popular branches of woodworking.*

Palladio, Andrea. *The Four Books of Architecture*. 1570. Reprint of the Isaac Ware edition of 1738. New York: Dover Publications, Inc, 1980.

— *The influential Renaissance treatise on Roman architecture.*

Popular Mechanics Company. *Mission Furniture: How to Make It (Parts I, II, and III, Complete)*. 1909, 1910, 1912. Reprint. New York: Dover Publications, Inc, 1980.

— *A comprehensive study of Shaker furniture with many measured drawings and photographs.*

Villiard, Paul. *A Manual of Veneering*. Princeton, New Jersey: D. Van Nostrand Company, Inc., 1968.

— *An excellent introduction to an important furnituremaking technique, complete with instructions on pressmaking.*

Watson, Aldren A. *Country Furniture*. New York: T. Y. Crowell Company, 1974.

— *A handsomely illustrated book describing the history and daily life of the pre-mechanized furnituremaker, his shop, tools, and techniques.*

Wearing, Robert. *Woodwork Aids & Devices*. London: Bell & Hyman, Ltd., 1981.

— *A properly tuned tool is only half the battle; knowing how to use it with ease and accuracy requires a knowledge of innumerable jigs and fixtures illustrated here.*

INDEX

Numbers in boldface (e.g., **312**) indicate pages with illustrations.
References to ranges greater than two pages (e.g., 106–109) may
also include illustrations.

ABOUT THE AUTHOR

Graham Blackburn was born and educated in London, England before moving to New York City to continue his studies at the Juilliard School. While pursuing a career as a professional musician, he built his first house in Woodstock, NY. Since then, he has published more than twenty books, including both novels and books on all aspects of house building, interior carpentry, traditional woodworking, cabinetmaking, furniture making, handtools, and design.

While running his own custom furniture-making shop, he also became a regular contributor to leading woodworking publications, including *Fine Woodworking, Popular Woodworking,* and *Woodwork*—of which he was also the Editor-in-Chief for a number of years.

In addition to being a writer and illustrator, he has been the subject of several books on crafts and design. He was featured in Maxine Rosenberg's *Artists of Handcrafted Furniture at Work* (Lothrop, Lee & Shepard) and Jane Smiley's *Catskill Crafts: Artisans of the Catskill Mountains* (Crown Publishers) and has made numerous television appearances, including serving as the national spokesperson for Boyle-Midway's media campaign: *Secrets of the Master Craftsmen.* He was a featured speaker at the nationwide Woodworking Shows for over a decade and a frequent lecturer at woodworking schools, guilds, and colleges across the country.

Visit Graham at BlackburnBooks.com or, better yet, take a class with him at the Graham Blackburn School of Traditional Woodworking in Woodstock, NY.

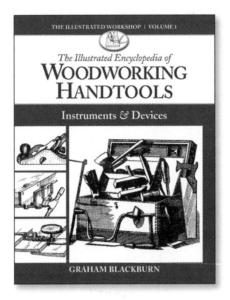

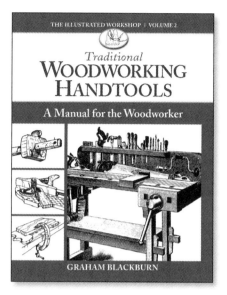

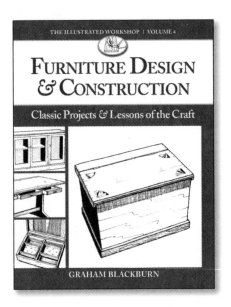